COORDINATION IN COOPERATIVE VOCATIONAL EDUCATION

**THE MERRILL SERIES
IN CAREER PROGRAMS**

Editorial Board: Director, Robert Taylor, The Ohio State University; Theodore Cote, Temple University; Aleene Cross, University of Georgia; Louise Keller, University of Northern Colorado; Mary Klaurens, University of Minnesota; Wilbur Miller, University of Missouri; Carl Schaefer, Rutgers—The State University of New Jersey; Robert Warmbrod, The Ohio State University.

COORDINATION IN COOPERATIVE VOCATIONAL EDUCATION

WARREN G. MEYER
University of Minnesota

LUCY C. CRAWFORD
Virginia Polytechnic Institute
and State University

MARY K. KLAURENS
University of Minnesota

CHARLES E. MERRILL PUBLISHING COMPANY
A Bell & Howell Company
Columbus, Ohio

Published by
Charles E. Merrill Publishing Company
A Bell & Howell Company
Columbus, Ohio 43216

Copyright © 1975 by Bell & Howell Company. All rights reserved. No part of this book may be reproduced in any form, electronic or mechanical, including photocopy, recording, or any information storage and retrieval system, without permission in writing from the publisher.

Library of Congress Catalog Card Number: 74-21347

ISBN: 0-675-08736-8

1 2 3 4 5 6 7 8 / 79 78 77 76 75

Printed in the United States of America

CONTENTS

Preface xi

Chapter

1 **Purposes of Cooperative Vocational Education** 1

Definition of Cooperative Vocational Education, 2; Search for Viable Vocational Education Programs, 5; Background of Cooperative Vocational Education, 7; Expectations from Cooperative Vocational Education, 11; Local Program Purposes and Objectives, 13; Advantages of Cooperative Vocational Education, 17; Concluding Statement, 24; References, 24.

2 **Roles of a Teacher-Coordinator** 27

The Teaching Role, 28; The Coordination Role, 30; The Curriculum Specialist Role, 37; The Counseling Role,

41; The Placement Role, 43; The Supervisory Role, 45; The Public Relations Role, 47; The Administrative Role, 49; The Recording and Research Role, 51; Role as a Professional Educator, 53; Concluding Statement, 55; References, 56.

3 Tasks of a Teacher-Coordinator 59

The Teacher-Coordinator as a Program Manager, 60; Task Analysis of the Teacher-Coordinator's Job, 68; The Teaching-Learning Tasks, 72; Concluding Statement, 77; References, 78.

4 Facilitating Career Development 80

The Career Development Process, 81; Outcomes of Career Education, 89; Facilitating Career Development, 91; Concluding Statement, 95; References, 96.

5 Teaching Work Adjustment Competencies 98

Current Interest in Work Adjustment, 99; The Relevance of Work Adjustment, 100; A Theory of Work Adjustment, 105; Measures of Work Adjustment Factors, 108; Some Basic Problems in Work Adjustment, 115; Concluding Statement, 121; References, 122.

6 Recruiting and Guiding Student-Trainees 124

Overview of the Task, 125; Publicizing Program Goals and Objectives, 126; Providing Realistic Occupational Information, 129; Gathering Information about Students, 133; Admission Policies and Procedures, 144; Concluding Statement, 147; References, 147.

Contents

7   **Placing Student-Trainees**   150

Importance of Excellence in Placement, 151; Career Development and Placement, 153; Placement Surveys, 155; Planning Placement of Student-Trainees, 159; Selection of Training Agencies, 163; Aligning Students with Training Agencies and Positions, 168; Preparing Students for the Interview, 173; A Perspective on Placement, 177; Concluding Statement, 179; References, 179.

8   **Developing the Occupational Experience Laboratory**   181

Purpose and Nature of the Occupational Experience Laboratory, 182; The Training Sponsor, 185; The Training Plan, 191; Concluding Statement, 199; References, 205.

9   **Organizing and Articulating Instruction**   206

Concern for Relevant Content and Instruction, 207; An Instructional Planning System, 208; Vocational Competency Areas, 213; Articulation of Instruction, 221; Facilities and Equipment, 223; Concluding Statement, 230; References, 230.

10   **Following Up Student-Trainees at Work**   232

Purposes of Follow-Up Calls, 233; Planning a Coordination Schedule, 239; Scheduling Calls on Training Agencies, 245; Preparing for a Follow-Up Call, 247; Executing the Follow-Up Call, 249; Detecting the Need for a Follow-Up Call, 251; Evaluating Occupational Experience Laboratory Achievement, 256; Performance Rating Forms, 260; Concluding Statement, 264; References, 265.

| 11 | Evaluating the Program | 267 |

Systematic Evaluation of Outcomes, 268; Cost-Benefit Analysis, 279; Evaluation of Program Characteristics, 280; Concluding Statement, 286; References, 286.

Appendix A	Vocational Education Amendments of 1968	289
Appendix B	Teaching Career Analysis	292
Appendix C	Performance Requirements for Teacher-Coordinators	293
Appendix D	Application for Certificate to Employ Student Learner	310
Index		313

THE MERRILL SERIES IN CAREER PROGRAMS

In recent years our nation has literally rediscovered education. Concurrently, many nations are considering educational programs in revolutionary terms. They now realize that education is the responsible link between social needs and social improvement. While traditionally Americans have been committed to the ideal of the optimal development of each individual, there is increased public appreciation and support of the values and benefits of education in general, and vocational and technical education in particular. With occupational education's demonstrated capacity to contribute to economic growth and national well being, it is only natural that it has been given increased prominence and importance in this educational climate.

With the increased recognition that the true resources of a nation are its human resources, occupational education programs are considered a form of investment in human capital—an investment which provides comparatively high returns to both the individual and society.

The Merrill Series in Career Programs is designed to provide a broad range of educational materials to assist members of the profession in providing effective and efficient programs of occupational education which contribute to an individual's becoming both a contributing economic producer and a responsible member of society.

The series and its sub-series do not have a singular position or philosophy concerning the problems and alternatives in providing the broad range of offerings needed to prepare the nation's work force. Rather, authors are encouraged to develop and support independent positions and alternative strategies. A wide range of educational and occupational experiences and perspectives have been brought to bear through the Merrill Series in Career Programs National Editorial Board. These experiences, coupled with those of the authors, assure useful publications. I believe that this title, along with others in the series, will provide major assistance in further developing and extending viable educational programs to assist youth and adults in preparing for and furthering their careers.

Robert E. Taylor
Editorial Director
Series in Career Programs

PREFACE

In this book the authors aim to help readers develop insight into the relatively wide variety of purposes and goals of cooperative vocational education. They attempt to place cooperative vocational education in perspective among the several approaches to helping students learn vocational competencies and capabilities that are appropriate for their needs. The definition of cooperative vocational education stated in the Vocational Education Amendments of 1968 was selected to delimit the scope of the subject matter except when otherwise noted.

Primacy of the Student

The authors have attempted to stress student needs within the confines of the existing manpower supply and demand situation and of the policies and practices of the local school system. This means that the *primary* factor in making judgments and decisions about policies and procedures is the effect an action might have on a student or on a number of students. Of course, the effect on persons other than the student (primarily employers, co-workers and other students) is always considered carefully in any cooperative venture, but it should not be the central factor. Teacher-coordinators soon learn that occasionally they must think in terms of what is best for the entire class or for the students in future classes. Nevertheless, the policy of giving the student first consideration is a time-tested axiom. In a similar vein, another aim of this textbook is to examine procedures and practices of the past, as well as the viewpoints of those who discredit anything associated with the pre-1963 period in vocational education, and to select content in terms of what is known about the behavior of contemporary youth in a vocational learning environment.

Focus on Behavior as a Future Worker and Learner

Further, this book stresses the type of student learning activities and behaviors that hopefully young people will practice after they have completed their cooperative vocational education venture. Why not teach them to use properly the sources of knowledge at their disposal in a regular work environment not associated with school, so that they will continue their learning habits after they leave the teacher-coordinator's supervision? Why not stress the development of personal responsibility for one's own occupational and vocational growth? During the time that they are enrolled in a cooperative education program, why not teach them the techniques of learning a new job effectively and efficiently? In the authors' minds, this is largely what is meant by "bridging the gap" between school and job, but this is not all of it.

The authors also hope to accustom the reader to thinking of coordination duties as being directed primarily toward the improvement of instruction. Whether they are performed in or out of the classroom, the point of view taken is that the purpose of coordination duties is to bring into harmony the efforts of all parties concerned with helping the student develop beneficial vocational behaviors.

Focus on Managerial Role

Teacher-coordinators' role concepts in the instructional program are critical factors in the productivity of the several sources of learning used by student-trainees; namely the school, the job, the community, and the youth group organization. When they see their jobs as primarily that of teachers whose students work part-time, the inputs from sources outside the classroom usually are sporadic and inadequate for the production of well-balanced workers. On the other hand, when they envision themselves as managers of instructional service enterprises operated by the schools and accept responsibility for the productivity of the other learning resources, the likelihood of well-articulated programs and an increased flow of inputs will be much greater. Primarily for this reason, the authors have stressed the teacher-coordinator's managerial role.

Whether or not an organized theory of vocational education exists is debatable. Through the years a number of eminent vocational educators have recorded general beliefs about vocational education which provide a viable philosophical foundation, but a theoretical base has not been established via research. The authors make no attempt to establish a theory of vocational education or of cooperative vocational education; however, they have tried to relate the principles and procedures that are discussed to the tenets of career development and the theory of work adjustment which are based on creditable research.

It appears as though these two facets of vocational education development, career development and work adjustment, have much to contribute to a theoretical base for cooperative vocational education—one on which teacher-coordinators can rely when choosing courses of action that are not prescribed in regular operating policies and procedures. Therefore, chapters 4 and 5 have been written and placed early in the sequence of chapters so that the procedures and practices of cooperative education that follow may be related to this evolving theory.

Identification of Coordination Principles

The authors tried to establish the realization that in all cooperative vocational education the principles are essentially the same, but frequently applications of those principles should differ because of the variations inherent in the occupational fields for which students are being prepared and in the students' vocational needs. Thus, the intention here is to describe the cooperative education approach to developing vocational competencies across the board and to provide illustrations from several vocational services regarding the application of these principles.

The Cooperative Vocational Education Image

It is not the purpose of this book to extol cooperative vocational education as the epitome of vocational education, to set it up as the best method of vocational instruction, or to claim that it is superior to other vocational education plans in all respects. Hopefully, the reader will be led to identify the unique role of the cooperative plan among the various instructional plans that combine education and work and to identify its limitations as well as its strengths. This strategy seemed cogent in light of the fact that numerous educational innovations have been repressed because they did not live up to the exaggerated claims of their proponents and "promoters." To the best of our knowledge, nothing will defeat an educational movement as quickly as overestimated and overstated claims that arouse the indignation of colleagues, educational administrators and community supporters.

There is no single educational plan that meets all student needs well, so let us not go overboard on cooperative vocational education, thereby retarding its long-range development, even though it has received some very strong support at high levels and in various circles. Let us instead strive to develop cooperative vocational education programs that will measure up to the goals that are set for them.

Warren G. Meyer
Lucy C. Crawford
Mary K. Klaurens

**ADDITIONAL PUBLICATIONS
IN THE
CAREER PROGRAMS SERIES**

Adult Education in Agriculture
Ralph E. Bender, et al.

Career Behavior of Special Groups
Campbell/Picou

Career Guidance: A Handbook of Methods
Campbell/Walz/Miller/Kriger

Organization and Administration of Distributive Education
Crawford/Meyer

Home Economics Evaluation
Aleene Cross

Elementary School Careers Education
Frank Cross

Agricultural Education: Approaches to Learning and Teaching
Drawbaugh/Hull

Foundations of Vocational Education
Rupert N. Evans

Career Development in the Elementary School
Robert L. Gibson

Principles of Post-Secondary Vocational Education
Angelo Gillie

Career Education: Perspective and Promise
Goldhammer/Taylor

Developing Careers in the Elementary School
Gysbers/Miller/Moore

Teaching Related Subjects in Trade and Industrial and Technical Education
Milton E. Larson

Principles and Techniques of Vocational Guidance
H. H. London

Curriculum Development for Trade and Industrial and Technical Education
Gordon G. McMahon

Planning Facilities for Occupational Education Programs
Richard F. Meckley

Emerging Woman: Career Analysis and Outlooks
Samuel H. Osipow

Teaching Shop and Laboratory Methods
Albert J. Pautler

Individualizing Vocational and Technical Instruction
Pucel/Knaak

Vocational Education and Guidance—A System for the Seventies
James A. Rhodes

Career Guidance: An Individual Developmental Approach
K. Norman Severinsen

Introduction to Trade, Industrial and Technical Education
Strong/Schaefer

Leadership in Administration of Vocational and Technical Education
Wenrich/Wenrich

Chapter 1 PURPOSES OF COOPERATIVE VOCATIONAL EDUCATION

This textbook was written for all persons who may be involved in cooperative education, but it was intended primarily for teacher-coordinators of local school programs. It describes and discusses what a teacher-coordinator does when building and maintaining a viable cooperative education operation within the total vocational education program of his school. It was meant to serve both teacher-coordinators in service and those who are preparing for such positions.

During this period of emphasis on *relevancy,* which to the authors means relevance to a learner's needs and wants, it is customary to inform the learner about the objectives of the material to be treated during the instruction. This custom is usually acceptable to teacher-coordinators because they are by nature service-minded and like to know what will be expected of them. They appreciate being informed about the purpose of the instruction at hand. For this reason, each of the chapters in this book begins with a set of objectives which is based on the competencies associated with the content area. The objectives are behavioral in nature, but they do not meet the precise standards of performance objectives. We hope that you will find them useful in doing previews and postviews of the chapters.

Careful study of this chapter should help the reader develop the following competencies:

1. Define cooperative vocational education and recall the criteria used in identifying it;
2. Explain the ways in which cooperative vocational education satisfies educational administrators and lawmakers who seek more viable forms of vocational education;
3. Characterize the two major periods in the history of cooperative vocational education in the United States;
4. Describe the variety of expectations from cooperative vocational education held by various groups of interested people.
5. Explain how students' career goals, vocational needs, and attitudes toward work and school are considered in arriving at local program purposes and objectives;
6. Give illustrations of each of the six categories of advantages of cooperative vocational education discussed in this textbook.

Definition of Cooperative Vocational Education

Cooperative education has become an umbrella term which means many different things to individuals. Therefore, in order to communicate effectively with fellow educators, employers, and laymen, a teacher-coordinator must be aware of the various concepts that the term may call to mind. Likewise, the authors of this book must define the term so that readers will understand their meaning of it.

The exact title of the program that is the subject of this book is Cooperative Vocational Education. The word "vocational" (4, Sec. 108) is important because it conveys the idea that the purpose of the program is to prepare students for gainful employment in one or more of the occupational clusters; usually in such vocational areas as agriculture, business and office, distributive, health, home economics related, technical, or trade and industrial education. When programs combining work and education for other reasons are discussed, they will be clearly identified.

Since the philosophical concepts and basic principles of cooperative vocational education are the same regardless of the occupation or occupational field for which the student is preparing, the purpose of this book is to introduce these concepts and principles so that those responsible for the various types of cooperative education programs may design procedures and practices to meet the needs of the students they serve.

WORKING DEFINITION

Although the legal definition of cooperative vocational education given in the Vocational Education Amendments of 1968 is found only in Part G of the Act (4), the part which describes cooperative programs for those with special needs, that definition is one that adequately treats cooperative education for all types of students. It is defined as follows:

> Sec. 175. . . . a program of vocational education for persons who, through a cooperative arrangement between the school and employers, receive instruction, including required academic courses and related vocational instruction by alternation of study in school with a job in any occupational field, but these two experiences must be planned and supervised by the school and employers so that each contributes to the student's education and to his employability. Work periods and school attendance may be on alternate half-days, full-days, weeks, or other periods of time in fulfilling the cooperative work-study program.*

PURPOSES OF COOPERATIVE VOCATIONAL EDUCATION

The Congress was explicit in describing the nature of the type of cooperative vocational education it wished to stimulate in a section titled "Findings and Purpose."

> Sec. 171. The Congress finds that cooperative . . . programs offer many advantages in preparing young people for employment. Through such programs, a meaningful work experience is combined with formal education enabling students to acquire knowledge, skills and appropriate attitudes. Such programs remove the artificial barriers which separate work and education and, by involving educators with employers, create interaction whereby the needs and problems of both are made known. Such interaction makes it possible for occupational curricula to be revised to reflect current needs in various occupations.

The Ninetieth Congress apparently thought so highly of the record of cooperative vocational education in preparing the types of students usu-

---

*There is an inconsistency in the terminology of the Act in Part G which is titled "Cooperative Vocational Education Programs" and the definition in Section 175 which refers to "cooperative work-study programs." It was decided by the task forces of the National Conference on Cooperative Vocational Education, conducted by the University of Minnesota under contract with the U. S. Office of Education in Minneapolis on February 26-28, 1969, that the term "cooperative work-study" should be dropped and the term "cooperative vocational education" be used in order to avoid confusion between vocational instruction programs in Parts B and G of the Act and the work-study program treated in Part H.

ally enrolled in such programs that it earmarked an authorization of funds so that more students could participate, particularly those in areas with high rates of school dropouts and youth unemployment. The obvious underlying assumption, reinforced by the definition, is that the same type of plan, policies and procedures would be equally effective with all kinds of students—an assumption that remains to be tested.

JOB-RELATED INSTRUCTION

The reader's attention is directed to the section of the definition which calls for instruction as a part of the plan, including required "academic" courses and "related vocational instruction" that is planned and supervised both *in school* and *on the job* and contributes to the student's employability. It is this element of planned vocational experiences both in school and on the job that points out the main difference between cooperative vocational education and other educational plans that combine education and work. In this textbook the term will only be used when this element is present and in addition when student-trainees are paid for their work at the prevailing rate for the type of work done or at the rate prescribed in a student-learner certificate to be described later in this book.

RELATIONSHIP TO WORK-STUDY PROGRAM

Although this book does not deal with the work-study program per se, it is necessary to mention this type of program at this point so that readers will be able to differentiate between cooperative vocational education and work-study programs (1, Secs. 102.96-.113). Both types, which have very different purposes, are included in the 1968 Amendments. The mission of cooperative vocational education is to provide viable vocational instruction; the purpose of the work-study program (Part H) is to provide financial assistance for individuals in order to enable them to commence or continue vocational education programs. Such assistance is achieved through providing employment in public, nonprofit agencies. The jobs held by work-study students are not necessarily related to the student's career goal. Job-related classroom instruction is not required of work-study students. Appendix A, page 289, consists of a helpful chart which lists the essential characteristics of the work-study program in the right-hand column.*

---

*The reader will note that the regular cooperative vocational education expenditures will be partially reimbursed under Part B of the Act, State Vocational Education Programs. Thus each state may formulate its own requirements for federally assisted programs within the language of Parts B and G of the Act, which may also be found in the regulations for state plan programs (6).

Search for Viable Vocational Education Programs

At no time in history has there been as much interest in vocational education on the part of so many people, and at no time has so much been expected of it. During the 1960s and early 1970s vocational education has been under the microscope.

CURRENT INTEREST

Each of the traditional vocational education services has been examined; instructional methods and systems have been scrutinized; substantial amounts of funds have been invested in research analyzing the problems of vocational education and in exploring new approaches; attention has been focused on the post-secondary level, the junior high school, the elementary school, senior citizens, the home, the inner city, rural areas, career development, exploratory programs and other facets of vocational education—hardly a stone has been left unturned. A sincere attempt has been made to look into the possibilities of vocational education for "all of the people" mandated in the purposes of the two most recent vocational education acts. The statement of purpose of the Vocational Education Act of 1963 (3) and that of the Vocational Amendments of 1968 are identical. The declaration of purpose is as follows:

> It is the purpose of this title to authorize Federal grants to States to assist them to maintain, extend, and improve existing programs of vocational education, to develop new programs of vocational education, and to provide part-time employment for youths who need the earnings from such employment to continue their vocational training on a full-time basis, so that persons of all ages in all communities of the State—those in high school, those who have completed or discontinued their formal education and are preparing to enter the labor market, those who have already entered the labor market but need to upgrade their skills or learn new ones, those with special educational handicaps, and those in post-secondary schools—will have ready access to vocational training or re-training which is of high quality, which is realistic in the light of actual or anticipated opportunities for gainful employment, and which is suited to their needs, interests, and ability to benefit from such training.

REDISCOVERY OF COOPERATIVE VOCATIONAL EDUCATION

During the interval between the two recent acts, cooperative vocational education was "rediscovered." It had been in existence since the turn of the century, but it never seemed to have been accepted very widely at any educational level. It had been the only educational plan under which high school and post-secondary distributive education programs could be reimbursed with federal funds, and it accounted for the bulk of the secondary school enrollment in that field; but it was infrequently used in the established trade and industrial education or in education for the office occupations. A relatively small number of students representing a cross-section of occupations had been enrolled in cooperative diversified occupations programs, particularly in the southern states. A number of colleges and universities offered cooperative education programs and at least one, Antioch College, used the cooperative plan exclusively, but the program's prestige was limited. All this information leads one to wonder what caused Congress to single out cooperative vocational education for earmarked funding in the Vocational Education Amendments of 1968. For the answer to this question one may turn to the notes and working papers of the congressional committee of the United States Senate (2, p. 41). The section on "Part-Time Cooperative Education and Work-Study" states that ideal vocational education combines formal instruction with learning on the job and that cooperative vocational education should be made available to all who desire it. It makes the following claims for cooperative vocational education:

1. It yields high placement records.
2. It yields high employment stability.
3. It yields high job satisfaction.
4. It develops leaders.
5. Students cannot be trained faster than they can be placed. The availability of training agencies with employers is limited by the needs of the employer.
6. The program is popular with the students. Pay, real-life instruction, and prestige contribute to its popularity.

It also states that the cooperative plan is "undoubtedly the best program" we have in vocational education. In describing cooperative vocational education the following characteristics are cited:

1. While at work the student is supervised by a school-employed coordinator.
2. The coordinator makes certain that the student receives worthwhile instruction while at work.
3. The student spends one hour* studying his occupation while in school.

---

*See 2, pp. 6-11 for information about the number of hours students spent studying their occupations in school.

4. The coordinator who teaches the class makes certain that what the student learns in class is related to his work.
5. The student takes other academic subjects.

Background of Cooperative Vocational Education

A brief sketch of the background of cooperative vocational education may help the reader to understand why there is such interest in cooperative vocational education today.

EARLY HISTORY

Accounts of the early history of cooperative vocational education are controversial. Some of the disparities found in books and bulletins may emanate from geographical loyalties, some from occupational pride, and some from poor records. Thus, it is quite possible to get several versions of the origin of the cooperative approach to developing vocational competencies. There is good reason to believe, however, that the first educator to implement the plan was Dr. Herman Schneider, who started a cooperative education program for engineers at the University of Cincinnati in the school year 1905-6. This program is still active. At the secondary school level of instruction, the available information is confusing. Claims for the first program are made for the Boston Public Schools and by the Cincinnati school system. The Boston venture involved retailing as well as industrial education. Which of these should receive the credit has little relevance to the purpose of this book. The fact that the cooperative plan began at the college and secondary school levels at about the same time has some bearing on the movement.

FUNDING OF VOCATIONAL EDUCATION FIELDS, 1917-1963

Federal vocational education beginning with the Smith-Hughes Act of 1917 through the George-Barden Act of 1946 was defensive and protective in nature. Congress had been disillusioned by educational legislation of the nineteenth century, namely by the Morrill Acts and the Hatch Act, in that it did not result in the production of skilled or trained practitioners, an essential element to national welfare in time of war or peace. Hence Congress provided earmarked funds by vocational fields—agriculture, home economics, and trades and industry—for the states to distribute to the public schools for training at the secondary, post-secondary, and adult education levels. Collegiate training, except for vocational teachers, was excluded from vocational funding at the collegiate upper-division and graduate-level programs. Each succeeding act added money, and some of them added vocational fields, but the basis of funding remained fundamentally the same.

The era of nearly a half-century of federal funding by vocational fields may be divided into four time-intervals: (a) a period of exploration lasting until approximately 1930, (b) early expansion of cooperative education, (c) the George-Deen decade, (d) and the post-war period. Cooperative vocational education was condoned by various trade associations and by the U.S. Office of Education throughout this period, but growth was slow largely because of the time required for educators to adjust to a "new" plan of education.

Exploration—1917-1930. Following World War I, several eastern universities adopted the cooperative education plan. Included were Simmons College of Boston, Carnegie Institute of Technology, and New York University. Also during that period, a number of high schools in large cities from coast to coast established cooperative vocational education programs that prepared students for specific vocational fields. For example, by the end of this period there were at least forty high school cooperative distributive education programs, nearly all of which were in large cities.

Expansion—Early 1930s. The great depression of the early and mid-1930s retarded the growth of the movement, but strong programs survived and gained strength as a result of the experience. Up to this time, one receives the impression that most of the classes were made up of students with relatively homogeneous occupational goals. However, in the mid-1930s numerous diversified occupations programs were organized in the southern states under the leadership of C.E. Rakestraw, a U.S. Office of Education regional agent. Diversified occupations programs enrolled students with "diverse" occupational training goals in the same class.

The George-Deen Decade—1937-1947. Near the end of the great depression (1936), Congress passed the George-Deen Act, which for the first time earmarked funds for the training of people *employed* in distribution. Since there was no provision for financial reimbursement of pre-employment training, school systems were forced to use the cooperative vocational education plan for secondary school students in this occupational area if the school wanted to receive federal funds. Thus, in order to meet the legal requirements of employment, a student had to be employed at least as many hours as he spent in the classroom. This requirement led to some of the policies and regulations concerning hours of work and wages which persist to this day.

Purposes Of Cooperative Vocational Education

Up to the time of World War II, enrollments and programs in cooperative vocational education grew at a very modest rate. School administrators in comprehensive secondary schools and junior colleges gradually became accustomed to the "questionable" practice in which a student spends a part of his school day in the community. The National Youth Administration (NYA) and Civilian Conservation Corps (CCC) posed a mild threat to the traditional school procedure in that they demonstrated that good educational results can be obtained when education is combined with work. During this period, the teacher education for cooperative vocational education that existed was provided in summer school or during the time that the teacher-coordinator was practicing his profession with the few skills he possessed. Although the major thrust during World War II was on defense training at the adult level, enrollment in secondary school cooperative vocational education held steady.

The Post-World War II Period—1947-1962. The George-Barden Act of 1946 relaxed some of the curriculum restrictions of the earlier legislation. Prior to this time there were two curriculum arrangements: students received one period of related vocational instruction daily and worked at their training stations over a two-year period (known as Plan A), or they spent two periods per day in related vocational instruction and worked at their training positions during a one-year period (known as Plan B). A new arrangement under the George-Barden Act (Plan C) permitted one period of related instruction and daily work over a one-year period, provided the student received two Carnegie units of credit in vocational instruction prior to entering his senior year of cooperative education.

The high economic productivity following World War II, with the accompanying shortage of labor, augmented the interest of employers in starting cooperative programs. Chain store managers and branch plant managers in particular were responsible for stimulating local interest in the cooperative system.

During the 1950s there seemed to be a maturation period in which organizational and operating procedures and practices were tested. The large city school systems which had been operating diversified occupations programs gradually divided their large classes into groups of students with relatively homogeneous occupational goals. Small towns retained the diversified type of program.

Like the other systems of vocational education, cooperative education was affected by Sputnik, but there was no noticeable retrenchment. Individual study materials were produced for both types of programs.

THE PROGRAM PLANNING PERIOD

The program planning period really began with the 1963 Act (5, pp. 206-45). Although this act retained the Smith-Hughes and George-Barden monies and categorical funding by vocational fields, the new funds that were authorized were not designated by vocational fields, and for the first time states could transfer funds from one vocational field to another. The new Advisory Council, periodic program evaluations, and authorization of earmarked funds for research, set the stage for the systematic planning that characterized the 1968 Amendments.

The Vocational Education Act of 1963. The Vocational Education Act of 1963 played into the hands of cooperative vocational education supporters. The cardinal purpose of the act was to reduce unemployment. The act itself was part of the educational component of a total manpower program which transcended a number of government agencies. Previously, unemployment was to have been counteracted solely by accelerating the economy. This was to be an era of manpower planning. Education suddenly became a factor in economics, so the economists built into the legislation an accountability system based on costs and benefits with training inputs and outputs. Fortunately, cooperative vocational education fared very well on the criteria used in this evaluation compared to other forms of vocational education. The act also stimulated interest in research and innovative programs which brought about some worthwhile information for program developers.

The 1968 Amendments. Many people feel that the term "amendment" is a misnomer for the 1968 Act and that vocational educators are now in an entirely "new ball game." This act eliminated completely categorical funding by occupational field, such as agricultural education and distributive education, and replaced it with categorical funding by programs, one of which is cooperative vocational education. The purpose was to force vocational educators to provide training for "all of the people," not only those in occupations served by the traditional vocational fields.

Perhaps an even greater impact of vocational education was the implementation of a planning system which started with manpower and population needs. This system involves projecting and planning on a long-range and annual basis. It legally involves the employment service and other government agencies in the planning procedure.

Reference was made earlier to Part G of the Vocational Education Amendments of 1968 which provides funds for cooperative vocational education in geographic areas of high rates of school dropouts and youth unemployment. Since the type of persons to be served in such areas may cause costs to employers over and above the usual costs of training cooperative students in the more fortunate economic areas, provision can be made for certain types of reimbursement to equalize training costs. Also, it is possible to use federal funds to provide for certain unusual student expenses in such areas. Both types of funding will be explained in more detail later in this book. One of the problems now facing vocational educators is how to extend cooperative vocational education to the areas eligible for this special funding.

Expectations from Cooperative Vocational Education

Up to this point you have learned what cooperative vocational education is, you know something about its history, and by reading the preface you have a preview of the basic philosophy of the authors. You are now ready to examine the wide variation in expectations of various groups of individuals regarding cooperative vocational education.

All of education is confronted with a variety of problems. High on the list of those in vocational education is the matter of adapting the program to meet the needs of people and the needs of society at the same time, not only at the present time but for years to come. Another challenge is that of providing vocational instruction that is meaningful and attractive to students who have not been motivated by school in the past. The mandate of Congress to serve "persons of all ages in all communities of the State" has stimulated much imagination and has caused some people to search for an educational "sinecure." To some people, cooperative vocational education seems to fit this role.

CHANGE—A PERPETUAL PROBLEM

Change has been described as an unavoidable, coercive, challenging, and sometimes a discomforting and perplexing phenomenon —like the horizon, one never seems to be able to keep abreast of it. Change is a constant, potent factor in the vocational education process. No other type of education, not even the professions, is affected as much by fluctuations in economic and social conditions. The market for vocational graduates is a dynamic one in which fluctuations in the demand for skills impose rigorous constraints on the program.

Through the years vocational educators have been particularly mindful of the need to adjust their curricula and their instruction to accommodate changing requirements of the employers who hire their graduates, and they have been concerned with maintaining a balance between the number of persons trained for an occupation and the number that the market can accommodate. Occupational survey, manpower inventories, graduate follow-up studies, advisory committees and job analyses have been the common tools used for gathering information that is useful when planning and operating a viable vocational education program.

This persistent concern for keeping abreast of technical changes affecting occupations has been intensified in recent years because of the rapid expansion of technology. Manpower and educational planners have been so imbued with the problem of producing the desired quantity and quality of trained personnel that they have been examining the feasibility of using educational media outside of the public schools. A variety of innovative programs are being studied in hope of finding a more effective and efficient way of regulating the flow of trained personnel into the labor pool. Thus, in the minds of educational policy makers the best answers to the manpower training problem are still on the horizon. Lawmakers now are fascinated by the curriculum flexibility of cooperative vocational education and its adaptability to changes in manpower needs.

REACHING DISSATISFIED YOUTH

Concurrently with the interest in changing vocational education to improve the manpower training situation, there exists a growing concern for the welfare of the recipients of vocational training and for those who should participate in vocational education but do not do so. In recent years there has been grave concern about changes in the attitudes of workers, particularly about young people just entering the labor market. Increased attention is being given to employers' needs for workers who can adjust readily to a work environment. Particularly since 1963 there has been a growing effort to provide vocational training for unemployed youth and adults, for school dropouts, and for the socially and economically handicapped. To some extent, employers have modified their attitudes toward young workers; however, a wide gap still exists between the motives of the two. Thus, educators, social workers, congressmen and the general public by and large have been searching for a type of education which will appeal to a large segment of youth who have rejected, either wholly or in part, the traditional school program and who may question much of the "establishment."

The purpose of the brief description of the current educational setting in the paragraphs above was to give the reader some idea of the expectations of several influential population and political groups who look to vocational education to make a major contribution to some vexing economic and social problems during these changing times. Bear in mind that these expectations of vocational education change with the times and may be quite different in the years ahead. If vocational education is to design a program of instruction which will meet social and economic needs over a long period of time, provision for change must be built into the system proper.

Local Program Purposes and Objectives

Selection of local program purposes and determination of program objectives are the most crucial steps in cooperative vocational education planning. Decisions about purposes and objectives determine the destiny of the program; therefore, great care must be taken in formulating them. Excitement about the potential benefits of the cooperative plan to students, employers, and the community may lure program planners into trying to do too much for too many people within the limits of the available economic and human resources. Each program purpose and objective should be carefully appraised in terms of its feasibility under *existing* conditions. Tenure of cooperative vocational education depends on continuous program support by all cooperating parties; therefore, *reasonable* purposes and goals are imperative.

Cooperative vocational education has an outstanding record of helping young people bridge the gap between school life and work world. There are numerous illustrations of how young people made successful transitions from school to jobs with the help of cooperative vocational education. Some of the more spectacular stories relate to students whom the schools had previously failed to challenge. Research shows that cooperative vocational education program graduates have the lowest youth unemployment rate. Facts like these have stimulated great interest in the potential contributions that cooperative education can make in solving the problems of assimilating youth into the mainstream of adult society.

CONVENTIONAL SELECTION OF LOCAL PROGRAM PURPOSES

Unfortunately, no one has been able to design a plan of vocational education that simultaneously will satisfy the needs of all youth; their needs are too diverse for this ever to happen. Yet school after school continues to offer identical sections of cooperative vocational education through which student-trainees are routed with little regard for their individual needs. One may wonder why this blunder is so prevalent. The most probable cause is faulty establishment program purposes and objectives. On account of the long-range importance of this aspect of planning, it seems prudent to relate a common procedure here.

Usually schools make a reasonable effort to determine whether the community employers are willing and able to support cooperative vocational education, and there are some general estimates on the part of school administration and/or faculty about the number of students who would enroll in the program. Frequently the program is described in capsule form to the student body and a questionnaire measuring student interest is distributed. If enough employers and students respond favorably, the program is installed. If the purpose and objectives of the program are recorded at all, more than likely they will have been selected by an individual or small group using available literature or a list of objectives from a neighboring school.

EXPECTATIONS AND PURPOSES

As was stated earlier, there are many widely heralded expectations of cooperative vocational education, particularly by adult groups. Also, there are many expectations of the program on the part of students that are not well communicated to teacher-coordinators and counselors. Some of the expectations of the two groups conflict. Certainly those of the latter group are more important to the long-run success of cooperative vocational education. If a local community wishes to avoid future dissatisfactions with the program it must make at the very outset of program planning some selections from many potential program purposes.

After the feasible purposes have been selected, it is important that they are well understood by all of the parties involved in the program—students, the teacher-coordinator, parents, participating employers, school administrators, faculty and counselors—because the behavior of these groups will depend on their concepts of what the program is to achieve.

Since the needs and expectations of students are so important in the selection of program purposes, it is obligatory that program planners examine these needs in detail as a means of determining which types of students can be served best. There are a number of characteristics of potential students which should be considered carefully when selecting student groups to be served. The three which will be described briefly here are students' career goals, students' vocational maturity, and students' attitudes toward work and school.

Students' Career Goals. Specification of the scope of student career goals to be served is a crucial element in planning the program's purposes. Since placement of students on jobs that enable them to progress in their career development is mandatory, the scope of occupational goals that can be accommodated by a program depends on the availability of training agencies (information about which is obtained through occupational surveys). Assume, for discussion purposes, that appropriate training agencies are available; then program planners must agree on the occupations for which training will be offered.

When making decisions regarding the occupational scope of a training program, program planners should take into account the educational level of prospective students, availability of training agencies that can provide meaningful occupational experience, and the occupational competency of the teacher-coordinator to be assigned to the group. Lower-level educational programs usually are broader in occupational scope than are those at the higher levels. Regardless of educational level of students, the more homogeneous the occupational goals of the students are, the more effective the instruction is likely to be, provided, of course, that the teacher-coordinator is highly competent in his occupational content field. Therefore, program planners should select homogeneous occupational training purposes whenever possible.

Students' Vocational Needs. Students may be classified according to their vocational maturity (8, pp. 14-15), which is one index in forming relatively homogeneous classes. The categories of needs shown below range from economic needs, to personal-social needs, to vocational guidance needs, to occupational preparation needs. The categories are not mutually exclusive.

1. To earn money in order to remain in school (nonvocational);
2. To develop the necessary social skills and work attitudes and habits necessary for job tenure or entry into other vocational training programs;
3. To develop a viable career plan based on realistic self-appraisal and accurate occupational information;
4. To develop a well-balanced combination of vocational capabilities that enables graduates to advance more rapidly in a satisfying career.

When economic resources and human resources (teachers trained to cope with specific types of students) exist, independent classes for each group should be organized. When this is not possible, decision makers must determine how much diversity in student vocational needs the assigned teacher can manage and still provide optimal learning for all class members.

Students' Attitudes toward Work and School. There is a range of student attitudes toward work and school that is a counterpart of the vocational needs categories. It ranges from dedicated, socially sensitive, career-oriented students to educable youth and adults who have antisocial characteristics and may be alienated from school and/or work. Persons who may benefit from cooperative vocational education may be found in one of the following clusters:

1. Regularly enrolled students at all educational levels who have well chosen career plans;
2. Regularly enrolled students at all educational levels who are conscious of the need for career plans and are pursuing understandings which will lead to satisfying careers;
3. School dropouts and potential dropouts who are willing to work and to develop the social and vocational capabilities necessary for job tenure but have unrealistic or poorly selected career goals;
4. School dropouts and potential dropouts who realize the need for earning a living but who lack the understanding of social vocational capabilities necessary for job tenure;
5. School dropouts and potential dropouts who are not concerned with the rewards of earning a living.

It can be readily understood why an individual who has not been trained as a special needs teacher-coordinator might have difficulty with students in groups four and five above. He may be able to cope with one student of this type, probably at the expense of reduced attention to the needs of other class members. Usually it is prudent to exclude some types of students from a program until their needs can be met satisfactorily through the cooperative vocational education plan.

OTHER FACTORS AFFECTING PROGRAM PURPOSES

In addition to students' career goals, their vocational needs, and their attitudes toward work and school, there are a number of other factors which may be considered by program planners when selecting program purposes. Some of these are: (a) students' plans for further education, (b) students' cultural background, (c) ethnic group membership, (d) physical handicaps, and (e) emotional control. Whether or not any of these factors affect the selection of program purposes, persons who are involved in a program's operation should know the status of individuals possessing these affiliations or characteristics.

Criteria for admission of individuals to ongoing programs are discussed in chapter 6.

Advantages of Cooperative Vocational Education

Program planners and operators will benefit from a brief treatment of the values inherent in effective cooperative vocational education (8, pp. 2-3) because of the need for this type of information in preparing program objectives and in formulating desired student behavioral outcomes. Functional knowledge of these values also aids a practitioner in daily decision making.

GREATER RELEVANCE OF CURRICULUM AND INSTRUCTION

Without doubt, the greatest contemporary concern about education in general is the relevance of curriculum and instruction to the needs and interests of present-day youth. Cooperative vocational education has some built-in features that almost ensure relevant instruction. A few of the more salient points relating to the relevance of cooperative education are given below. In relating these claims, the assumption is made that the definition of cooperative vocational education found in the 1968 Act applies.

1. Students are placed on jobs that are in harmony with their abilities and interests.
2. Each student follows a plan of on-the-job experiences which is based on occupational requirements and individual student needs.
3. Students have the opportunity to learn skills on real jobs under actual working conditions.
4. Classroom instruction, on-the-job training, and student club activities are articulated in the development of clearly identified competencies.
5. Students have an active role in the choice of content and methods because of their unique experiences which incite them to seek education for their developing personal needs.
6. The teacher is not the sole authority. His teachings are supplemented with the practices and ideas of employers and employees of the occupational envir. ment.
7. Students can better evaluate the contribution of general and vocational education in terms of their own needs and aspirations.

8. Students are able to identify with the world of work in a meaningful way.
9. Students encounter daily situations in an adult environment which cause them to examine their values and reappraise their potential in occupational and social situations.
10. Students receive the guidance of trained teacher-coordinators who have had wide experience in the occupational field when making vital vocational decisions.
11. Students make the transition from school to work gradually under the skilled guidance of a teacher-coordinator, giving them time to comprehend the significance of the learning situation and the world of work.
12. Students receive direct on-the-job contact with professionals whose responsibility it is to keep up-to-date in their profession.
13. Curriculum revision is more rapidly reflective of current occupational requirements.
14. Cooperative vocational education enables the student to relate education to his occupational interests at a period in life when it is natural for him to look outside the school for learning and earning.
15. Cooperative education may provide the most influential means of coordinating the home, the school, and the world of work in behalf of the student.

BETTER APPLICATION OF LEARNING

One of the most apparent values of cooperative vocational education is the opportunity it affords for almost immediate application of classroom learning to a real-life test. This value is particularly important in the development of the capabilities needed for good occupational adjustment. Simulated occupational environments rarely provide a laboratory of real-life employers and employees and seldom one with actual customers or clients. Occupations vary widely in the extent to which genuine job experience is required in order to learn the technical competencies. Evidence concerning the better application of learning in cooperative vocational education follows:

1. Students are able almost immediately to test their occupational learning voluntarily and independently in a real-life situation.
2. The job usually functions as a learning laboratory in which structured assignments that do not interfere with production

are carried out on the job. When they do interfere, arrangements may be made for special instruction outside of working hours.
3. Students apply their learning in a variety of job situations and return to the classroom for analysis and group discussions. Thus, they understand better and appreciate the difference in practices among employing organizations. Such variances in applications would not be possible in almost any simulated environment.
4. Students acquire a better understanding of problem solving and the scientific method. Problems arise on the job or in school; they are identified; they are investigated. Alternatives are explored and some are chosen. They are tried out on the job and observations are made. The action succeeds or fails and the cycle is dropped or repeated.
5. Well-chosen training agencies become rich learning resources and usually furnish more valid information than is available to learners through other means. Carefully prepared on-the-job training sponsors take a personal interest in the student's development and function as excellent laboratory instructors.
6. Under guided experiences on their jobs, and sometimes in unplanned situations, students are led to appreciate the values of general education.
7. The total physical and psychological job environment adds materially to the laboratory and teaching facilities available.
8. Frequent periodic applications of classroom learning to an employment situation remove artificial barriers to learning.

IMPROVED BALANCE IN VOCATIONAL COMPETENCIES

Vocational education has done a commendable job of developing technical skills and knowledge in the traditional vocational fields. The same cannot be said of occupational adjustment and career development, yet studies show that most people lose their jobs for reasons other than incompetency in the technical skills and also that occupational tenure among vocational education graduates leaves much to be desired. Many vocational educators attribute this phenomenon to an inadequate training environment in the traditional vocational education setting. A few cogent points regarding balanced vocational competencies follow:

1. Properly designed occupational experience provides opportunities for exploration of the three major vocational

competency areas: (1) technical, (2) occupational adjustment, and (3) career development, through the employing organization's physical facilities and its human environment.
2. First-hand guidance information is available at the job training site. Chances are that, when properly solicited, such information will be more complete and accurate than could normally be communicated because of the bond between the student and the employing firm or organization.
3. Teacher-coordinators are likely to be more sensitive to the need for balanced instructional content than other vocational teachers because of the continuous feedback from training sponsors and other employees on the behavior of the student.
4. Continuous dialogue among the coordinator, the employer, and the student provides ample opportunities for a balanced viewpoint in formulating the student's individual curriculum.
5. The coordinator's regular contacts with employers, employees, and the student facilitate helping the student personally bridge the generation gap as well as master the technical competencies.
6. As wage-earners, students develop an appreciation and respect for work and are aided in obtaining worthwhile jobs.
7. Students are able to observe and assess the importance of personal traits so necessary for employment: punctuality, dress, regular attendance, and responsibility for completing assigned tasks.
8. Cooperative vocational education provides many students with their most useful contacts with society outside of the home.
9. Cooperative vocational education helps students clarify relationships between education and employment and earnings.
10. Cooperative vocational education adds breadth and depth of meaning to the student's studies.
11. Work periods offer opportunities for independent exploration of environment providing for new knowledge, practices, and experiences.

EXTENSION OF TRAINING TO ADDITIONAL OCCUPATIONS AND STUDENTS

Even with programmed instruction and computerized practices, the schools cannot provide adequately in the school alone for the multitude of occupations which compose our labor force. Even if the technical

Purposes Of Cooperative Vocational Education 21

training could be automated, it would not be possible to provide training in the personal and social capabilities needed in large numbers of behavioral-science-based occupations. In many occupations, however, cooperative vocational education can furnish the essential elements that complement classroom work and provide a reasonable training program. Some of the most prevalent points relating to this value of cooperative education are as follows:

1. Cooperative education is well-equipped to prepare students for new and emerging careers with some assurance that they will be gainfully employed.
2. Cooperative vocational education is relatively well-equipped to accommodate students of a wide range of ability as compared to vocational education offered without occupational experience.
3. Cooperative vocational education is better equipped to provide for the needs of occupations which draw on more than one discipline than is vocational education which is limited to classroom instruction.
4. In these times of rising costs, educational institutions can utilize their staff and facilities much more effectively by shifting part of the costs of education to the employing community. This enables the school to provide for the expansion of the occupational training.
5. Cooperative vocational education is a significant means of aiding low-income students.
6. Cooperative vocational education enables some students to stay in school who otherwise would drop out to seek employment.

BUILT-IN MANPOWER TRAINING CONTROL

Congress has great concern for balancing the demand and supply of manpower. Reducing unemployment has been one of its major goals for the past decade. Though the record is favorable in recent years, congressional concern remains. Hence, the manpower control feature inherent in cooperative vocational education appealed to Congress and will appeal to other groups dealing with manpower problems. Some of these features may be described as follows:

1. The number of persons training for an occupational field is limited to the number of available training agencies (employing firms) unless an alternating plan is used in which two students hold one job.

2. Advisory committees representing employers and employees are an essential feature of cooperative vocational education. These committees counsel the school on the manpower supply and demand problems.
3. Cooperative vocational education should be started only after adequate employment, demographic, and other essential data have been collected, analyzed, and a favorable report is made.
4. Cooperative vocational education promises to have a stabilizing effect on the labor market because of its occupational tryout and guidance features.
5. Cooperative vocational education is equipped to help disadvantaged and handicapped youth become well-adjusted members of the labor force in quantities that can be absorbed.
6. Cooperative vocational education consistently yields high placement records, high employment stability, and high job satisfaction.

CLOSER RELATIONSHIP WITH THE COMMUNITY

Part G of the 1968 Amendments stresses the use of the employment service, employers, labor, and other community agencies and groups in identifying training opportunities. Extension of cooperative vocational education into new occupational areas, and including disadvantaged and handicapped students, both in and outside of school, thrusts new responsibilities on the community, and calls for new relationships between the school and community groups. These ties serve to strengthen the program. Major contributions are as follows:

1. A closer partnership between the schools and the occupational world is necessary in order to maintain the proper relevance of training and the basic subjects to support the occupational training.
2. In cooperative vocational education the schools and the employing community are brought together on mutual educational problems that are within their power to understand and handle.
3. When employers engage in vocational education in their stores, shops, and offices, an appreciation of the school's problems is inevitable. This phenomenon holds for the school's understanding of employers' problems as well.
4. As the program expands to accommodate new groups of students, the need for wider community support grows and new groups are involved which introduce fresh perspectives on established policies and procedures.

5. Student achievement is accelerated when academic and employment environments are combined. The environmental experience in one supports and influences the experiences provided in the other.
6. Business and industry spokesmen, who participate with youth in cooperative education, may provide the community with vital understandings about education when they speak to civic clubs or in other ways participate in community activities.
7. An excellent source of future employees may be developed through involvement of business, industry, and government with educators who help to develop young people via cooperative education.
8. Employers and students have a chance for a trial acquaintance before full-time employment.
9. The two-way working relationship with the wider community adds quality and distinctiveness to the school as a whole.

IMPROVED VOCATIONAL GUIDANCE

Opportunities for improved vocational guidance abound during the period of cooperative employment when students can engage in occupational tryouts to see whether or not they are suited for the type of career in which they are gaining experience. Opportunities to investigate the way of life of persons engaged in an occupational field are much more favorable to a cooperative student than to students not in the program. Among the vocational guidance advantages and opportunities of cooperative vocational education are the following:

1. Cooperative vocational education provides career guidance in making suitable choices of a field of work. Students may receive the help of teacher-coordinators who have had successful occupational experience in addition to teaching, of regular vocational counselors, of employers, and of co-workers at their training agencies.
2. Students who have the opportunities afforded by cooperative education are provided early occupational experiences which are vital in making immediate and long-range career decisions.
3. Cooperative vocational education encourages students to finish high school and to enter employment or continue into higher education.
4. Students may try a variety of work situations under trained teacher-coordinators as cooperative education students before they leave school.

5. The ability to get and hold a job helps the young person bridge the gap between school and work. Alternated periods of school and work under guidance allow for gradual induction into the work world.
6. Cooperative vocational education provides the student with a wider range of possibilities for employment after graduation.

Concluding Statement

In order to derive full benefit from a study of coordination in cooperative vocational education one must first have a clear understanding of the nature of the cooperative education plan, the philosophy and principles on which it is based, and an accurate knowledge of its parameters. Cooperative vocational education is successful in the long run only when it is organized around carefully planned purposes derived from (a) the vocational education needs of youth which have been gleaned from accurate factual information about the students to be served, and (b) from opportunities for meaningful employment. One also must be thoroughly familiar with the advantages of the program and be fully aware of its limitations in order to select cogently a program's purposes from the multitude of possibilities.

A quotation from the 1972 Manpower Report of the President furnishes the reason for the relatively slow growth of cooperative education prior to 1970, but more importantly it capsulizes the nature of the cooperative vocational education plan and implies the need for careful planning:

> Although the advantages of cooperative education are widely recognized, enrollments in the program totaled less than 300,000 in 1970. Cooperative education has grown slowly because it requires special, time-consuming attention to each individual student by the teaching staff and because the concept must be sold to prospective employers over a period of time. The continuous increase in funding of vocational education and the Office of Education's recent emphasis on the cooperative education approach may provide the necessary impetus for expansion of this system of vocational training. (7, p. 93)

REFERENCES

1. "State Vocational Education Programs," *Federal Register* 35, no. 91, Part II (May 9, 1970): Sec. 102. 96-113.

2. Senate Subcommittee on Education of the Committee on Labor and Public Welfare. *Notes and Working Papers Concerning the Administration of Programs Authorized under Vocational Education Act of 1963, Public Law 88-210, As Amended.* Washington, D.C.: U.S. Government Printing Office, 1968, 430pp., p. 41.
3. U.S. Congress. Public Law 88-210, 88th Congress, December 18, 1963.
4. U.S. Congress. Public Law 90-576, 90th Congress, October 16, 1968.
5. U.S. Department of Health, Education, and Welfare. *Education for a Changing World of Work,* Report of the Panel of Consultants of Vocational Education, Prepared at the Request of the President of the United States, Bul. OE-80021. Washington, D.C.: U.S. Government Printing Office, 1963, 296pp., pp. 206-45.
6. U.S. Department of Health, Education, and Welfare. *Vocational Education Amendments of 1968 for State Plan Programs,* Bureau of Adult, Vocational and Library Programs. Washington, D.C.: U.S. Government Printing Office, April, 1969.
7. U.S. Department of Labor. *Manpower Report of the President, Including a Report on Manpower Requirements, Resources, Utilization, and Training,* transmitted to Congress March, 1972. Washington, D.C.: Government Printing Office, 1972, p. 93.
8. University of Minnesota College of Education, Division of Vocational and Technical Education. *A Guide for Cooperative Vocational Education.* Minneapolis: Nicholson Hall Bookstore, 1969, 126pp., pp. 14-15.

ADDITIONAL REFERENCES

Crawford, Lucy C., and Warren G. Meyer. "Legislation Affecting Distributive Education." *Organization and Administration of Distributive Education,* Chapter 11. Columbus, Ohio: Charles E. Merrill 1973, pp. 255-88.

Evans, Rupert N. "Cooperative Programs." *Foundations of Vocational Education,* Chapter 12. Columbus, Ohio: Charles E. Merrill, 1971, 292pp., pp. 193-203.

Koeninger, Jimmy G., and Kendrick L. Spooner. *The Glen Oaks Simulation.* Columbus, Ohio: The Center for Vocational and Technical Education, The Ohio State University, 1974.

National Association of Secondary School Principals Curriculum Committee. "School-Supervised Work Education Programs." *Curriculum Report* 3, No. 2 (December 1973): 12pp.

Swanson, Gordon I., Howard F. Nelson, and Warren G. Meyer. "Vocational Curriculum: A Conceptual Framework." *American Vocational Journal* 44 (March 1969): 22-24.

Venn, Grant. *Man, Education, and Work: Post-secondary Vocational Education.* Washington, D.C.: American Council on Education, 1962, 185pp.

Wallace, Harold R. *Review and Synthesis of Research on Cooperative Vocational Education.* Research Series No. 60, VT 010-859. Columbus, Ohio: ERIC Clearinghouse on Vocational and Technical Education, The Ohio State University, 1970, pp. 1-10.

SUGGESTED ACTIVITIES

1. Ask at least three vocational educators and three general educators to define cooperative vocational education. How are the definitions different?
2. Ask any high school principal to describe what he or she expects out of a viable vocational program. Compare the response to the claims made in the text.
3. Prepare a list of statements supporting the need for studying the history of vocational education.
4. Ask representatives of business, labor, and school administration to list their expectations of cooperative vocational education. How do their expectations compare to those listed in the text?
5. Interview at least two teacher-coordinators to determine to what extent student career goals and student vocational needs and attitudes toward work and school are considered in arriving at local program purposes and objectives. How do their responses compare to those discussed in the text?
6. Give an example from operating vocational programs for each of the six categories of advantages of cooperative vocational education discussed in this textbook.

Chapter 2 ROLES OF A TEACHER-COORDINATOR

A teacher-coordinator wears many hats. He is a teacher, a coordinator, a curriculum specialist, a guidance counselor, a placement director, a supervisor, a public relations person, an administrator, a researcher and a professional education leader. Readers may wonder why a person accepts a position in which there are so many tasks to perform and responsibilities to assume. There are many reasons, but the main one usually is that the satisfactions received from the favorable feedback of students and employers more than compensate for the great amount of work involved in contrast to the usual straight classroom teaching assignment. In this chapter the teacher-coordinator's role is described briefly under ten categories of duties and responsibilities. Its purpose is to assist the reader in acquiring the following capabilities:

1. Name and describe briefly the ten major roles of a teacher-coordinator;
2. Explain the teacher-coordinator's role in articulating classroom activities, occupational experience, and youth organization practices in helping student-trainees acquire vocational competencies;
3. Name the usual agencies, organizations, and community groups that should be contacted by a trained teacher-coordinator;

4. Explain why the curriculum specialist role of the teacher-coordinator is his most challenging assignment;
5. Describe the basic functions of the training agency in cooperative vocational education;
6. Compare the teacher-coordinator's counseling role with that of a classroom teacher;
7. Explain the importance of careful selection of training agencies;
8. Contrast the teacher-coordinator's supervisory responsibilities with those of a classroom teacher;
9. Justify the teacher-coordinator's role in public relations;
10. Explain why a successful teacher-coordinator must be a good record keeper and researcher;
11. Illustrate the importance of proper time management in achieving the objectives of cooperative vocational education;
12. Describe the teacher-coordinator's division of loyalties to education and to his occupational field(s).

The Teaching Role

The primary role of a cooperative vocational education teacher-coordinator is teaching, but not teaching classes or subject matter in the traditional sense of the word; rather, it is one of directing a learning program which will permit student-trainees to master the skills, knowledge, and attitudes necessary to become a well-adjusted citizen-worker. Briefly, well-adjusted citizen-worker refers to a worker who is satisfied with his occupation and with the way of life in his occupational field. Also, it means that his job performance is satisfactory to employers and that he is qualified to perform jobs for which there is a demand for workers.

The focal point of instruction in cooperative vocational education is the classroom. It is here that learning experiences on the job and in the community are placed in perspective and focused on the development of occupational competencies—not just the technical skills and knowledge needed for specific occupations, but those competencies included in making occupational adjustments and career development, terms which will be explained in chapters 4 and 5.

When performing his teaching role, a teacher-coordinator should use his classroom and individual conference facility to (1) teach certain skills, knowledge, and attitudes that are prerequisite to performance on a real-life job; (2) help student-trainees plan their job and community experiences; (3) assist students in forming concepts and principles from their learning experiences outside of the classroom, and (4) guide students in developing rational-thinking and problem-solving skills. If he is to carry out these responsibilities he must use democratic procedures.

TEACHER-COORDINATOR AND RELATIONSHIP WITH STUDENTS

The teaching style of a successful teacher-coordinator is democratic, almost by necessity. The reason is simple, namely that he is not recognized as the sole authority to the same extent as are his colleagues who teach mathematics, foreign languages, or other relatively concrete subjects. His students are constantly comparing or contrasting what their teacher says with the opinions of the people they associate with on their jobs, some of whom may not agree with the teacher-coordinator. Thus the position of a teacher-coordinator may not always be glorious, but it is one in which he learns and grows in knowledge about occupations and careers along with his students. The challenges he encounters usually make his job interesting.

DIRECTING TRY-OUT ACTIVITIES

The classroom is a place for student-trainees to try out many skills, procedures, and ideas before they are used on their jobs. It may be too costly or too threatening for beginners to practice new skills in the real job situation. Therefore, the learning of many tasks must be initiated in the classroom, and a minimum standard of performance must be reached before it is advisable for the student to put them into practice on a job. Obviously, this holds true for many manipulative and clerical skills, but it is also a valuable procedure for teaching many occupational adjustment and career development competencies. Frequently it is necessary to use role playing and other classroom learning activities to teach human relations skills. Appropriate facilities and equipment are often needed for proper execution of the activity and optimum learning.

HELPING PLAN JOB LEARNINGS

A very important duty of the teacher-coordinator is to help his students plan their experiences outside of school in such a way that each individual may judiciously integrate what he learns into his pattern of living. Thus a teacher-coordinator is like a coach, a guide, or a consultant who helps student-trainees plan the learning of their jobs and solve their problems. He also helps student-trainees plan how they will obtain information about the way of life of those with whom they work and what to do about their individual strengths and weaknesses. These experiences in total usually result in the launching of a satisfying career.

TEACHING THE PRINCIPLES INDUCTIVELY

The classroom provides opportunities for student-trainees to gain insight into the why-and-wherefore of what happens or has happened on the job and to arrive at transferable behavioral principles. Usually things happen too fast on the job for most student-trainees to reflect on their experiences or to derive full benefit from them.

TEACHING PROBLEM-SOLVING SKILLS

The school is frequently the place for students to work out solutions to common or individual problems that arise during their employment at their training agencies. Common problems may be taken up with the class as a whole. Rather than furnish a student with the solution to a problem or provide an answer to a question, the teacher-coordinator may discretely elect to engage the group in a problem-solving session or to help an individual arrive at a feasible solution. Thus he may be able to teach present student-trainees and future workers problem-solving methods in preparation for the time when they will be on their own, so to speak. This type of transferable cognitive skills may be very difficult to learn on the job alone.

The Coordination Role

Webster defined the verb "coordinate" as "to place in harmonious or reciprocal relation." In order to convey the complexity of the coordination role in cooperative vocational education, an early definition of "coordination" used in California employed the word "orchestration."

There are many types of educational positions that include the word "coordinator" in the title, so one should be certain to include a qualifying adjective when he wishes to communicate accurately. In this book the term "teacher-coordinator" will be used. Hence a teacher-coordinator is defined as:

> A member of a local school staff who teaches occupational and related subject matter to students preparing for employment and coordinates the efforts of all helpful agencies which can assist in a training

program designed to meet the needs of learners in a cooperative vocational education program. He may have varying degrees of responsibility in adult vocational education. (1)

Readers will observe that in the above definition, coordination is an educational activity directed toward the *improvement of instruction* via combining the efforts of all who influence the learner. Instruction is the ultimate purpose of this part of the teacher-coordinator's responsibilities; all other purposes are subservient to it. Therefore, when "placing" a student in a training agency, the objective is to obtain the best on-the-job instruction possible to meet that student's needs. When engaging in public relations work, again the ultimate goal is to enlist the cooperation of the recipients of that effort in facilitating the learning for the present or future students in cooperative vocational education. When a teacher-coordinator appeals to the school administration for facilities, equipment, or supplies, the ultimate purpose concerns instruction. With this thought in mind, we shall look briefly at individuals and groups of people whom the teacher-coordinator usually contacts in fulfilling his role as a coordinator.

STUDENT GROUPS

Without doubt, the most important cluster of constituent groups with whom a teacher-coordinator must work is the one composed of students, his student-trainees in particular. Although other student groups are equally as important in the mind of a well-educated teacher-coordinator, his efforts are directed primarily toward the student-trainees. Next, in order of the amount of effort expended, are the prospective cooperative vocational education students. A progressive teacher-coordinator plans several years ahead; hence he engages in guidance and promotional efforts in junior high school or middle schools, both public and private, as well as in the senior high school. Many teacher-coordinators teach pre-employment classes as prerequisite courses for cooperative vocational education. A truly student-oriented teacher-coordinator is also interested in bringing school leavers back into school and in preventing students from dropping out of school.

In these days of teenage concern for emancipation and self-direction, youth organizations are very important. National youth organizations composed of state associations, which in turn are made up of local chapters, have a profound effect on local cooperative vocational education objectives and activities. Coordination of efforts is required to maintain harmonious relationships among the youth group organization, the training agencies, and school personnel. Usually there are opportunities for cooperation among youth organizations, and occasionally there are conflicts of interest. Then the teacher-coordinator or a delegated chapter member of the youth organization communicates with other vocational or general education groups. This may require skillful coordination efforts.

PARENTS AND PARENT GROUPS

Until recently, communication with parents of students and with parent groups such as the Parent-Teachers Association (PTA) at the high school level was woefully neglected. Among school personnel only home economics and agriculture teachers bothered to visit a home of a student unless the youngster was in serious trouble. Today, nearly all teacher-coordinators maintain close ties with the parents of their student-trainees. They make a point of meeting the parents of prospective trainees and of calling on them in their homes if possible. They cultivate good relations with these parents so that they will have their cooperation in bringing about habits of living that affect work behavior.

EMPLOYERS AND EMPLOYER GROUPS

Good relations with employers and employer groups are the life-blood of cooperative vocational education because the effectiveness of the occupational experience laboratory, usually called the training agency, depends on their cooperation. That is largely what this book is about.

Employer groups are numerous because employers usually are great organizers. For this reason the way employers communicate among themselves is surprising to a neophyte teacher-coordinator. Many employers think that teacher-coordinators should participate in some of their trade association meetings in order to keep abreast of the rapidly changing employment environment. Therefore, they frequently invite a new person to join the local Junior Chamber of Commerce and/or one of the local service clubs. Frequently a teacher-coordinator is appointed to the Education Committee soon after becoming a member of the organization. Because the teacher-coordinator's role in contacting employers will be discussed extensively in several parts of this book, only the most important employer groups and employer service organizations will be listed here.

Better Business Bureau
Chamber of Commerce and Junior Chamber of Commerce
Local units of trade and professional associations
    Manufacturers' associations
    Service business associations
    Trade associations

Service clubs
  Kiwanis
  Lions
  Optimists
  Rotary
  Sertoma
  Women's business and professional associations

EMPLOYEES AND EMPLOYEE GROUPS

Few educators, other than teacher-coordinators, appreciate fully the influence of co-workers on beginning workers in an occupational field. Co-workers can make or break a young worker in nearly any occupational area. Every work group has an informal structure with a hierarchy of prestige among its members and unwritten rules of behavior which must be followed. These subgroup behavior patterns have much to do with interpersonal relations among workers and with acceptance of new workers into the work group to which they are assigned (2).

There are always group mores which must be understood if a young worker is to succeed in his job. Hence there are many things that a student-trainee must know about working with others which are not found in textbooks or taught in most vocational education classes. These constitute an important factor in achieving occupational adjustment, a competency area that is as important to a student-trainee's success as is his mastery of the technical skills and knowledge. Co-workers usually are a strong influence in making vocational decisions.

Because of the potential influence of a student-trainee's co-workers on his acceptance in their work-group society and the strong influence they, as individuals and as a group, may have on his career decisions, a cogent teacher-coordinator designs a carefully planned educational program for them. If arrangements can be made he talks to the co-workers as a group, setting the stage for the student-trainee. He keeps them informed about the program and involves them in it when opportunities arise. He also works with the training-sponsors to help establish and maintain good co-worker relations.

SCHOOL PERSONNEL

The cooperation of nearly all school personnel, from the board of education members to the school custodian, is essential in cooperative vocational education. Consistent support of the school administration, the guidance counselors, and the teachers must be present if the program is to persist. Counselor support is especially important because no coordinator can afford to endure for a long period of time anything but goodwill on the part of those in the pupil personnel services. Experienced teacher-coordinators usually are fully aware of the fact that cooperative vocational education is an elective program and consequently a team operation. They recognize the fact that the development of a full-service program requires giving as well as receiving and that it is judicious to compromise in certain situations. They also realize that building an empire of their program is seldom an acceptable practice. Therefore, they do not hesitate to involve their colleagues in important aspects of program operation, and they seize every opportunity to give credit to their co-workers in publicity and in human relations situations.

Inasmuch as the remaining portion of this book will treat in some detail the use of good human relations with school personnel, the subject will not be pursued further at this point except to list in alphabetical order the school personnel usually contacted by teacher-coordinators:

Adult educational personnel
Board of Education
Business office personnel
Coaches
Counselors
Custodians
Department heads
Director of Vocational Education
General, academic, and special education teachers
Junior high school personnel
Post-high school personnel
Principal and assistant principals
School nurse and social worker
Superintendent of Schools
Vocational teachers

GOVERNMENT AGENCIES

A teacher-coordinator usually has more contacts with government agencies than other vocational teachers have, whether or not the program he operates is locally and/or state and federally reimbursed. Student-trainees are subject to all labor laws covering the employment of women and minors. Few of the positions held by student-trainees are not covered under wage and hour, workmen's compensation, and social security rules and regulations. Student-trainees employed in positions covered by interstate commerce laws are subject to additional rules and regulations. Even though teacher-coordinators are not law enforcement officers they should know something about labor laws because they usually feel that they have a moral obligation to protect students and employers of their students from unintentional violations of the law. They also want to avoid publicity which discourages the employment of student-trainees.

Establishing good relations with the State Employment Service is another goal of most teacher-coordinators. There are many ways in which this government agency can cooperate with the public schools. The employment service has excellent data and information on labor demand and supply which is of great value in vocational education program planning and in guidance. Representatives of this service may administer the General Aptitude Test Battery (GATB) to high school students upon request. The local office of the agency also provides placement services and will discuss placement with school personnel.

Coordinators of state and federally reimbursed cooperative vocational education programs have frequent contacts with the staff of the Vocational Division of the State Department of Education. It is essential that they know the rules and regulations covering program operation. They usually must attend state conferences and other official meetings called by the State Department of Education in order to maintain their certification credentials. During some of these meetings they establish relationships with teacher-coordinators in neighboring schools and often cooperate with them on projects of mutual interest or other matters which will be discussed later in this book.

In addition to the state and federal government there are government agencies which are contacted less frequently such as social service agencies, the police department, and local regulatory offices.

COMMUNITY GROUPS

"The community is the classroom" may not be a very accurate statement, but cooperative vocational education approaches this concept of modern school procedure. There are many groups in the community, other than employers and parents, who are interested in the education of future citizen-workers. During the recent upsurge for making education more relevant in the minds of young people, and older ones, too, public attention has turned to vocational education—particularly the type which combines education and work. Alert teacher-coordinators are sensitive to this new interest; consequently they are expanding cooperative vocational education into new occupational fields and serving additional groups of students, many of whom have special needs.

Working with these new community groups results in new experiences which challenge a teacher-coordinator's ability. Much time and effort is needed to learn about the concerns of these groups and to devise means of utilizing their potential inputs into cooperative vocational education and related programs. Careful consideration must be given to the potentialities and limitations of such groups in supporting vocational education programs. They may be grouped as follows:

>Civic or political action groups
>Ethnic group welfare organizations
>Fraternal organizations
>Law enforcement interest groups
>Professional associations
>Social service groups
>Religious organizations

NEWS MEDIA

Accurate, favorable publicity is essential to sound cooperative vocational education. Students who can benefit from this type of education must know what it is and how it relates to their needs. On the surface, this may seem to be a simple matter, but experience with communications media about the program has shown that many false impressions usually emerge and that a carefully planned educational campaign tailored to specific interest groups is essential.

The community news media usually are interested in publicizing cooperative vocational education so their assistance is easy to obtain. However, unless there is a well-coordinated long-range public relations and publicity plan these services are not likely to be used effectively. Also, the teacher-coordinator sometimes experiences difficulty in obtaining news articles which convey an accurate image of the program. School papers are an important part of the public relations program.

THE ADVISORY COMMITTEE

Viable cooperative vocational education programs depend largely on a functional advisory committee composed of representatives of program-supporting groups (1). Employers and employees constitute essential members of these committees, the purpose of which is to help the school make decisions about the program's organization and operation. These committees also act as a liaison with the community and help keep the instruction practical from the standpoint of both employers and student-trainees.

As the name implies, advisory committees are purely advisory in function and have no administrative authority. Organizing an advisory committee and forming its members into a functional group requires careful coordination. Also, using this committee effectively to prevent and/or to solve problems is a coordination function.

TRAINING SPONSORS

Each student-trainee is assigned a training sponsor who serves as his supervisor and teacher during the time he is at work in his training agency. This person, who is sometimes referred to as a member of the "downtown faculty," works closely with the teacher-coordinator in making an occupational training laboratory out of the student-trainee's job. The training sponsor participates in developing a training plan, the purpose of which is to provide the student-trainee with a variety of on-the-job experiences. His/her teaching responsibilities dovetail with the student-trainee's classroom learning insofar as possible. Hence a training-sponsor is aware of and sensitive to what the trainee is studying in the classroom, and the teacher-coordinator is aware of and respondent to what the student is learning at the training agency. Needless to say, this calls for skillful coordination. This part of the teacher-coordinator's responsibilities will be discussed in detail in chapter 8.

In summary, the teacher-coordinator's role as a coordinator is one of bringing into harmonious relationship all of the helpful resources which can assist in a training program designed to meet the needs of present and future student-trainees. His purpose is to improve instruction. It means wearing many hats and being aware of which one of the hats one is wearing at any given moment.

The Curriculum Specialist Role

In almost all cooperative vocational education programs, the teacher-coordinator's role as a curriculum specialist is the most important one because the welfare of the program depends highly on how it is performed. Without relevant and meaningful curriculum content no vocational education program can survive very long, particularly one that is highly sensitive to worker needs and manpower needs and one that is highly accountable to the users of its products.

A teacher-coordinator's curriculum specialist role usually is very challenging and highly rewarding, one which few practitioners feel that they have really mastered. It is challenging because of its relative complexity and rewarding because of the almost immediate feedback that a teacher-coordinator receives from his efforts. These program characteristics are partly responsible for a teacher-coordinator's reputation for being a hard worker.

CURRICULUM CHALLENGES

One factor in making the teacher-coordinator's curriculum specialist role challenging is the dynamic nature of the content for which he is responsible. During no two years is it anywhere near the same. The reason for this is that instruction must conform to the needs of the occupational field(s) for which the training is offered. As occupations change, so does the curriculum; as socioeconomic conditions change, so does the content. Feedback from the work world is continuous.

A second challenging factor is the multilateral character of the curriculum. Each student pursues a curriculum of his own, one which parallels his needs for developing the competencies required for a successful career in the occupational field of his choice. Even in specialized programs, usually offered at the post-secondary level, where student-trainees seek somewhat similar types of careers such as agri-business and electronic data-processing, each student holds a different job that impacts on his curriculum. In addition to differences in the occupational and job-based needs, there usually is a wide range of differences in individual social and personal needs. This is nothing new, except that it assumes special significance in cooperative vocational education where continuous employment by a training agency often depends on these differences.

A third factor which makes the curriculum specialist role provocative is the necessity for articulating the inputs from the several learning sources. A teacher-coordinator continually and concurrently works with four separate sources of curriculum input, each with an organizational structure of its own; namely the classroom, the job, the community, and the youth group organization. Thus he must be able to shift thought patterns rapidly.

The fourth factor relates to the choice and implementation of the approaches used in curriculum development and evaluation. There are three basic ways of viewing cooperative vocational education curricula, each of which serves a particular purpose and complements the other two:

The Vocational Competency Area Approach (discussed in chapter 9) entails viewing the curriculum from the standpoint of three broad categories of instruction that are based on the vocational maturity level(s) of program participants. The three areas are: (1) technical competencies, (2) occupational adjustment competencies, and (3) career development competencies.

The Occupational Competency Area Approach entails viewing the curriculum from the standpoint of the five types of competencies needed for work adjustment in any occupation. They are (1) fundamental skills, (2) personal-social skills, (3) the technology of the occupation, (4) the discipline(s) underlying the occupational field, and (5) economic understandings of the world of work.

The Scope-of-Competency Approach (discussed in chapter 3) entails viewing the curriculum from the standpoint of four categories of competencies that are based on scope or breadth of those competencies. They are (1) individual job competencies, (2) single occupation competencies, (3) occupational cluster competencies, and (4) general vocational competencies.

The teacher-coordinator's curriculum task is to devise and implement a system that will enable him to measure students' achievements and capabilities and to select the most appropriate content-and-methods mix to achieve the desired outcomes. It is not a simple job.

Needless to say, it takes a newcomer to cooperative vocational education considerable time and experience to understand curriculum development, implementation, and evaluation. One saving grace of cooperative vocational education consists of a combination of the tangibility of curriculum outcome and immediacy of feedback on instruction; another is that the relevancy of most vocational content is fairly easy to determine; a third is that the student-trainee's job provides a natural integrating guide of great value in curriculum development and evaluation.

PURPOSE OF THE TRAINING AGENCY

In order to convey a reasonably accurate image of the teacher-coordinator's role in curriculum development, it is necessary to mention some pertinent facts about the purpose of the training agency that were not revealed in the paragraphs above. If the objective of cooperative vocational education were job training only, the curriculum development task would be relatively easy; individual study and personal counseling would serve the need fairly well. On the contrary, the primary goal of cooperative vocational education relates to career development and vocational maturity which demand a wide variety of projects and activities, job training being one of the very essential elements.

The student-trainee's job functions properly when it is a medium for facilitating the development of the student-trainee in his career. It not only provides a medium for applying the skills, knowledge, and attitudes of an occupation but for learning by direct contact about the ways of life in his occupational field and for clarifying his occupational preferences. Equally important is the opportunity it provides for experiences in occupational adjustment, a part of which is mastering the art of learning a job effectively and efficiently. All of these outcomes don't just happen; they must be planned as an integral part of the curriculum, and the teacher-coordinator must follow up on them.

Cooperative vocational education is not job training per se; it utilizes job training as one of several aspects of occupational preparation. Being able to learn a job quickly is a very important competency during these times of need for job mobility. It is an important tool of vocational flexibility. There is general agreement that most of us learn best by thoughtful doing. Sound vocational education includes the application of the competencies to be learned. Therefore, the best way to learn the procedures and techniques of learning a job is to actually learn a job under guidance with proper attention being given to the process of learning. Helping the student-trainee focus on the job learning component of on-the-job training requires considerable insight into the process and constant surveillance.

RESPONSIBILITY FOR NEED SURVEYS

Sound cooperative vocational education programs, like good business operations, begin with a careful study of the need for the offering under consideration. They are not started for the purpose of giving a worthy teacher an opportunity for a new educational venture or because a group of students rejects traditional education and job placement promises to reduce the tension. The study of needs is based on a survey of the manpower needs in the occupations for which the curriculum is to be offered and on a *thorough* examination of the needs of the population (students) to be served.

In small and medium-size communities, the responsibility for occupational and student need determination usually resides with the teacher-coordinator. In large communities, he may be involved in initial data and information gathering, and he is duty bound to help keep the survey information current.

In summary, the teacher-coordinator's role as a curriculum specialist is one of his most challenging assignments because the cooperative vocational education curriculum parallels the individual vocational needs of students each of whom has individual needs and is employed in a different training position. To meet this challenge, the curriculum must be multilateral and the content must be diversified and dynamic. In addition to the custom tailoring of content for rapidly developing youth, there is the necessity of dealing continuously with four different sources of curriculum input and three different locations to implement the instruction; namely the classroom, the job, the youth organization and the community.

On the bright side of the ledger most of the cooperative vocational community education curriculum content is relatively tangible, and its relevance to the learner is easy to establish. Also, the student-trainee's job provides an excellent frame of reference for integrating the curriculum content into his pattern of behavior.

Job training is only one of several aspects of cooperative vocational education. The student-trainee's job makes equally important contributions in the realms of career development and occupational adjustment. Command of the competencies attached to learning a job is very important in preparing students for changing jobs when the need arises. All of these outcomes must be planned and implemented because they do not happen by themselves.

All sound cooperative vocational education begins with studies of manpower and population needs. The teacher-coordinator's responsibility for this task varies with the size of the community.

The Counseling Role

Most conscientious teacher-coordinators spend a large part of their time participating in counseling activities. One reason for this practice is that usually he is the person most responsible for determining whether or not his students can benefit from his particular cooperative vocational education program. The most important reasons, however, are that he has more sources of information about his students than almost any other faculty member and that he must offer a curriculum tailored to the individual needs of each student. Time consuming as the counseling role may be, it is a great source of personal satisfaction to a dedicated teacher-coordinator. The counseling role provides continuous feedback of information to the teacher-coordinator in preparing for employment, entering an occupational field, and adjusting to a job.

CAREER COUNSELING

Career counseling relating to occupations for which a teacher-coordinator prepares his students is his vocational domain. It is he who should know more about the local, state, area, and national manpower needs and worker characteristics of his field than any other staff member, including the professional guidance staff. His frequent contacts with employers provide a continuous source of specific information about the local employment needs, often including the unique qualifications for a particular position. This type of useful information is indispensable in proper placement of students and very helpful in vocational guidance and in instruction.

Career counseling in cooperative vocational education is a teamwork task. Even though the teacher-coordinator may be very sophisticated in occupational information about his field, use of this information is only a part of the career counseling process. Even more important is the matter of obtaining valid information about the students who are interested in entering the program so that they may be helped in making appropriate vocational and educational plans. Usually the guidance counselor is prepared better in this domain than the teacher-coordinator. Then too, the counselor usually has occupational information of a general nature about occupational clusters and specific occupations other than the one represented by the teacher-coordinator.

PERSONAL COUNSELING

Once the students have entered the cooperative vocational education program, personal counseling begins in earnest. An individual who needs no personal counseling is rare indeed. Regardless of academic or social status almost every student needs some personal assistance in preparing for the world of work and then in adjusting to a work environment. Since each training position in which a student-trainee works is a unique environment, often requiring a different type of behavior, student-trainees almost invariably need help in making personal adjustments. Problems of personal adjustment have become more numerous during the past decade because of the declining opportunities to learn to work in the home and because of the general attitude of dissension among many youth.

Frequently the root of the adjustment problem rests with the individual student himself; sometimes it resides in the home; and, of course, it may stem from the job environment. Whatever the cause, it is the teacher-coordinator's responsibility to help solve the problem. He or she may need professional advice or the help of the counselor and occasionally the principal. Sometimes the situation should be referred to a psychiatrist.

RELATIONSHIPS WITH GUIDANCE COUNSELORS

In order to establish the proper relationship between counselors and teacher-coordinators good communication is necessary at the outset of the program. Then it is up to the teacher-coordinator and those who follow him to maintain good working relationships.

Many counselors do not understand the purpose of cooperative vocational education simply because it never was explained very well to them. Even among those who have a general concept of the cooperative plan there are counselors who do not know the singular purpose of the several sections of the program in their school. Every guidance counselor should know the purpose of each program section and the characteristics of students who might or might not benefit from the training in each section.

The first step in establishing desirable coordinator-counselor relations is bringing about a good understanding by both parties of the duties and responsibilities of each in relation to cooperative vocational education in general and to the individual sections of the program. Sometimes a question arises regarding which party should make the initial contact. There is no correct answer to the question, but a good suggestion is that neither should wait for the other and the teacher-coordinator should take the initiative as soon as possible. His reception is likely to be warm. New teacher-coordinators usually discover that guidance counselors are genuinely interested in learning about the program(s) if properly approached. After all, both counselors and coordinators have a common goal in their concern for the vocational welfare of students, and cooperative vocational education has some very attractive features from a guidance viewpoint.

If a teacher-coordinator is to maintain good communication with guidance counselors he must possess some sophistication in the realm of career development and in some of the elements of occupational and vocational guidance. By the same token, guidance counselors may improve their communication with teacher-coordinators through acquiring knowledge of work adjustment. Excellent results have been achieved when the two parties team up in workshop courses.

Much more will be said about the important guidance role of the teacher-coordinator in chapters 4 through 6.

The Placement Role

Master teacher-coordinators are as careful and take as much time in qualifying a training agency for participation in cooperative vocational education as they do in determining the readiness of student applicants for work in remunerative production on cooperative jobs. The importance of this role cannot be stressed enough because a student-trainee's experiences at work are frequently a more important force in shaping his career than those of the classroom or the school. Unless the work environment is compatible with a student's moral and value system and his career goal, the experience can be negative. Work experience can be meaningful or it can be meaningless; it can be helpful or harmful. Unless the probabilities of a positive experience in terms of an individual student's needs are high, a training agency should not be used.

One must keep in mind that the availability of potentially good training agencies is a limitation of cooperative vocational education and that this is an important factor in determining whether or not the cooperative plan should be installed. With this thought in mind we shall scan some of the teacher-coordinator's responsibilities in placement and examine them thoroughly in chapter 7.

TRAINING AGENCY DEVELOPMENT

In light of the discussion above, the reader may wonder whether very many part-time jobs would qualify as good training positions for student-trainees. Perhaps not many would satisfy rigorous criteria at the outset, but this does not mean that with proper guidance they would not become good training positions. The quality of on-the-job education depends almost entirely on the ability and interest of the teacher-coordinator in working with the employer and training sponsor in developing a good occupational experience laboratory. Thus the task of determining the feasibility of installing a cooperative vocational education section depends on the availability of potentially good employment situations and the ability of the teacher-coordinator to develop a bona fide training agency.

Given adequate time during the school day for coordination work and a reasonable teacher-student ratio, a well-trained teacher-coordinator will develop in a community a cadre of excellent training agencies. Most employers are willing and anxious to improve their existing training programs. The role of a teacher-coordinator as a "teacher educator" will be referred to briefly later in this chapter and then treated more fully in chapter 8.

MATCHING STUDENTS AND JOBS

Assuming that there are adequate training agencies available and that there are a number of students interested and qualified for training in the occupational field for which the training is offered, the teacher-coordinator's task is to arrange for the placement of those students in appropriate training agencies. Hopefully they will be employed in positions that are in line with their realistic career goals. At this point in the development of vocational education there are likely to be uncertainties about career goals of some students entering the program—a situation which undoubtedly will be improved with the advent of orientation-to-the-world-of-work and career exploration programs in the elementary and junior high school years. Hence some students will have well-defined career goals while others may only have decided to try out broad occupational clusters. These factors must be taken into consideration when engaging in the placement process. Every effort must be made to have the student employed in a compatible position in which he will put forth his best effort and be successful. Clarification of his career interests should be an outcome of his occupational experience.

PLACEMENT OF UNUSUAL STUDENTS

Since most types of employment are conditioned on worker productivity, certain students may be difficult to place. Many employers hesitate to hire a teenager unless there is a reasonable chance of his employment's being economically justifiable. Although this attitude has prevailed in the private sector for years, it has become more common in the public sector with the current emphasis on accountability. A teacher-coordinator must recognize this phenomenon and to the best of his ability cope with it. One way of providing for students who are difficult to place is to provide alternate types of training, such as the project plan, until the student has demonstrated his readiness to carry his own load in the labor market.

Another way, depending on the degree of the student's vocational maturity, is to persuade an employer that employing a less able person will be a good long-run investment. Many employers are inclined to employ workers with greater capabilities than the positions they fill require, which often results in high personnel turnover. Therefore, a well-trained worker of lesser talents would be more likely to provide longer tenure and therefore lower long-time labor cost.

A third way to provide for a "disadvantaged" worker is possible if, under one of the special government programs, the school is able to obtain funds with which to reimburse employers for additional training costs and for the difference between the student-trainee's productivity and that of a normal producer.

Chapter 7 of this book provides information on placement policies and practices in cooperative vocational education.

The Supervisory Role

Like supervisors in business, industry, and other types of employment in the private sector of the economy, much of what a teacher-coordinator accomplishes is done through others. As was indicated in the section of this chapter on the teacher-coordinator's role as a coordinator, he works with many supporting groups, and those who work for the program usually need some supervision or the job does not get done. Few teachers within the school have as many supervisory responsibilities as the teacher-coordinator. First, any educational program relying so heavily on individual instruction requires a great deal of classroom supervision. Second, the matter of supervising unpaid training sponsors who teach and oversee student-trainees while they are on the job is no easy task. Third, nearly every cooperative vocational education program has a youth organization which really tests the metal of the teacher-coordinator as a supervisor.

CLASSROOM SUPERVISION

The cooperative vocational education classroom usually is a busy place where each student is likely to be doing something different. Even when the class studies general related material, each student usually applies what he learns to his own job, occupation, or personal need pattern. The same holds true when studying occupational group competencies. Individual job competencies are completely a matter of individual learning, and single occupational competencies are almost exclusively acquired through individual study. This means that classroom management and supervision are important elements in the role of a teacher-coordinator.

The most difficult of the four curriculum competency areas from the supervisory standpoint is the single occupational competency area. Since few of the class members are likely to be employed in the same occupation, it is necessary to provide a large variety of individual study materials. Several types of learning packs and job-study guides have been created to meet the need for viable instruction, each having a separate format and recommended procedure for use. This complicates the task of classroom supervision.

Classroom supervision may be viewed as a precursor of job supervision in that the teacher-coordinator prepares student-trainees for learning on their jobs under the supervision of a training sponsor. Thus a teacher-coordinator's supervisory practices are in a sense under the microscope in that the student-trainees compare them with the supervision they receive on their jobs outside of the school.

JOB SUPERVISION

Supervision of unpaid training sponsors requires tact and diplomacy, yet many teacher-coordinators get good results from their training sponsors because there are many nonmaterial rewards from being a training sponsor. One obvious compensation is the satisfaction a training sponsor receives from helping a young person; another is the recognition he may get for performing the service. Less evident, however, is the opportunity to learn how to supervise young workers. Whether or not the latter motive is realized depends entirely on the teacher-coordinator. A teacher-coordinator has much to offer his training sponsors if he takes the time to teach them some of the things he knows about adolescents and the psychology of learning. Much of his supervision of training sponsors is by necessity of a subtle variety; on occasion it may be quite direct. Teacher-coordinators who conscientiously engage in supervisory practices soon learn how to motivate training sponsors and work through them to improve the learning environment of student-trainees when they are on their jobs.

Each vocational education program should include a systematic plan for training-sponsor development. Education is one type of remuneration with which a school woos its cooperating training sponsors and which is of mutual benefit to them and to the school. Sponsor development will be discussed in chapter 8.

YOUTH ORGANIZATION SUPERVISION

Sponsoring a local chapter of a youth organization is a very important part of a teacher-coordinator's role because it has a strong influence on the development of individual and group occupational competencies and on teacher-student relationships. A good youth organization sponsor is able to guide chapter members in becoming self-sufficient citizen-workers. He supervises them in such a manner that they feel they are working for themselves rather than to meet course or program requirements. He guides them in choosing chapter activities which help them develop occupational competencies and become worthy members of a work force.

Obviously, youth organization sponsorship requires a very subtle type of supervision which entails a thorough understanding of interpersonal relations and group dynamics. Fortunately, state and national youth organizations provide a large amount of assistance to local chapters, but the implementation of the practices, procedures, and recommended activities calls for a great deal of assistance by the teacher-coordinator. Young people need much help in interpreting the materials received from the parent units and, of course, need training in assuming responsibility. Even though the demands on the chapter sponsor's time may be great, most teacher-coordinators believe that it is time well spent in preparing their students for adult roles. Supervision of youth organizations will be discussed in chapter 3.

The Public Relations Role

Cooperative vocational education is an elective program. If prospective students do not know about it and the faculty and counselors do not believe in it, the plan is doomed to failure. It also requires the support of employers, parents, and other community groups. Another factor in the need for a strong public relations program is the fact that cooperative vocational education is new to many people. There are still large numbers of youth and adults who think that the only worthwhile education is academic and that the curriculum should be confined to what happens in the classroom.

COMPONENTS OF PUBLIC RELATIONS

A teacher-coordinator strives to achieve good public relations through practicing good human relations in all of his daily activities and through planned publicity, the purpose of which is to reach potential program participants and supporters whom he is unable to contact personally. Both means of achieving good public relations are essential in any community. Publicity becomes more important as the community increases in size.

Teacher-coordinators soon learn the art of good human relations if they do not possess it when they begin work in cooperative vocational education. They realize that cooperative vocational education is never sufficient unto itself and that continued service to students who need the program depends on the cooperation of many other individuals and groups, all of whom have a common interest in the welfare of youth. They do not try to build "empires" within the school system, and they do not describe their cooperative vocational education section as "my program." They try to develop in their associates an identification with the program needs in terms of benefits to students and to the parties addressed rather than in terms of their own needs. In short, they behave as extroverts in the true psychological sense.

Responsibility for planning, directing and/or implementing cooperative vocational education publicity almost invariably rests with the teacher-coordinator. If the assignment is relegated to someone else, false program images are likely to emerge, so normally control of publicity should rest with the teacher-coordinator.

The public relations role is not as simple as appears on the surface because there are many types of "audiences" with whom to communicate, each with somewhat different viewpoints. The "shotgun" approach is not effective; the publicity must be pinpointed. The implication of this principle is that the teacher-coordinator must know the needs of each segment of his market and the benefits of cooperative vocational education that appeal to them most. Selection of the media used depends largely on the recipients of the publicity. Without question, the most effective media are the students who are presently enrolled in the program and, of course, the graduates; both of them can be used to mutual advantage in a wide variety of publicity devices.

SELLING A SERVICE

Successful teacher-coordinators are committed to the concept that the first element of a good public relations program is a good product; no amount of publicity can overcome the ill effects of a poor product. The questions may arise, What is the product of cooperative vocational education? What does it create? From the employer's viewpoint the product is a person who is capable and willing to perform a service, hence it is really the service that the worker performs. From the student's viewpoint the outcome of the program is a sound preparation for the career of his choice or some step along the way to that goal. From either viewpoint the outcome is a service, and the objective of a public relations program is to build a favorable attitude toward that service.

The way a cooperative vocational education program is promoted has a strong influence on the type of student who applies for admission and consequently on the complexity of the guidance and placement roles of a teacher-coordinator. For example, promoting a cooperative vocational education program by extolling the virtues of combining school and work usually attracts students having a wide range of scholastic ability and vocational maturity. Promoting the preparation for a particular occupational field(s) appeals to students of greater vocational maturity and more wholesome attitudes toward school. Therefore, if the goal of the promotional effort is to build a functional occupational training program the teacher-coordinator should focus his campaign on occupational images and advocate the cooperative plan as one of the best ways of launching a career.

Teacher-coordinators must select the media for their program promotions, make the necessary contacts with media personnel, prepare or supervise the content of the message, and perform many other public relations duties which require specific skills and knowledge. This requires considerable sophistication in public relations and publicity.

In conclusion, the public relations role of the teacher-coordinator can hardly be overemphasized. A number of potentially good cooperative vocational education programs have never started because of poor handling of the public relations tasks, and many have never functioned properly because of inadequate or inappropriate efforts.

The Administrative Role

The extent of a teacher-coordinator's administrative load usually varies inversely with the size of the school. As a rule, large school systems employ a vocational director and frequently he is supported by a staff of vocational education supervisors. These people assume the responsibility for much of the administrative work, including cooperative vocational education. Teacher-coordinators furnish data and information through forms and reports, consult with the administrative personnel upon request, and sometimes participate in policy formation.

In smaller school systems a teacher-coordinator may be charged with all vocational education including the administration of the adult vocational education program. Frequently the school administration is inadequately informed about vocational education administration in general and about cooperative vocational education in particular. This places great responsibility on the teacher-coordinator who must know the laws and regulations for program administration and prepare the required reports. It also entails program planning, operation and evaluation, and the administrative competencies attached to management by objectives.

THE VOCATIONAL EDUCATION PROGRAM

Cooperative vocational education is one of several types of vocational education plans which must be articulated in order to provide a total program of vocational education designed to meet the needs of all people in the geographic area(s) served. The units of the program range from the elementary school through the adult evening school. Education for out-of-school youth and adults must be included in the plan, and vocational education offered outside of the public school domain must be taken into consideration.

In this age of accountability, vocational education planning and administration is fast becoming a highly systematized operation similar to those of the National Space Administration and of private business and industry. Planning, Programming and Budgeting Systems (PPBS) have been developed in several states. The effect of this movement on the vocational education administrators and many teacher-coordinators has been challenging and stimulating. To learn to use the new planning and administrative systems requires in-service training of implementers of the process.

INTERDISCIPLINARY COOPERATION

Another characteristic of the new direction in vocational education is the emphasis placed on interdisciplinary cooperation among the vocational education areas. As indicated earlier, recent legislation forces the formerly independent vocational education departments to cooperate in providing vocational education for large groups of occupations which transcend the traditional vocational education fields and provide vocational training for groups of people who have been neglected heretofore. This new obligation has brought about changes in administrative relationships and organization which affect teacher-coordinators who must serve new groups and contribute, within the realm of their expertise, to offerings in related occupational areas.

Section one of the following chapter explains the teacher-coordinator's managerial role, a very important concept.

The Recording and Research Role

Every teacher-coordinator must be a record keeper and a researcher if his program is to persist and maintain its viability. This double role is becoming more essential as we progress into an accountability period which probably is here to stay. One reason that a teacher-coordinator must be a good record-keeper is that usually he must prepare required program records which call for the collection of data and information. A more important reason is that his activities are so numerous and varied that no one could possibly hold all the necessary details in his mind and recall them when needed. He must be a researcher simply because the dynamic nature of cooperative vocational education mandates it. It is the only way he can keep abreast of the needs concerning the several facets of his program.

RECORDING

The recording role may seem dull and even disagreeable to some very active teacher-coordinators, but it need not be so if they view their record-keeping tasks in the proper light. The purpose of the records should be to facilitate program establishment, operation, and evaluation. Records tell the story of the program and pass the word along to interested parties who use them—sometimes to the teacher-coordinator's successor. (Fortunate indeed is the new coordinator who inherits a good set of records, and fortunate are the students who are served by a teacher-coordinator who keeps good records because it is unlikely that he repeats his mistakes.) Record keeping becomes an enjoyable task when the records are used for constructive purposes and when they bring about favorable recognition.

Preparing Required Reports. A teacher-coordinator normally spends more time keeping records than regular classroom teachers do because usually he is required to file a number of reports with the State Department of Education. Such applications and reports provide subtle opportunities for good program operators to get the recognition they deserve. They are one of the few means available to the local school for comparing its operations with those of similar programs in other communities. Creative teacher-coordinators use the information from a number of required reports they prepare for their state departments of education to inform local program participants and supporters about their programs. They find that it isn't much work to tailor the data and information to the interests of these groups.

Keeping Voluntary Records. The value of voluntary records is grossly underrated by most teacher-coordinators. Nevertheless, such records can be one of a teacher-coordinator's most effective tools in program operation and in his public relations work. The required records are helpful insofar as they go, but they have definite limitations in that they are usually too global to manifest many of the real achievements of the program and the benefits to individual members. Nor are the usual required reports very useful in spotting potential problem areas.

It was mentioned earlier that there are wide differences in the nature of the objectives of cooperative vocational education programs and that the goals of individual sections within the total cooperative education program may vary a great deal. This being the case, each teacher-coordinator needs his own set of records in addition to those that are common with other sections of the total program. A teacher-coordinator's records are designed to facilitate the development of the unique occupational competencies in his area of training.

RESEARCH ACTIVITIES

The need for continuous informal cooperative vocational education program research cannot be disputed. Changes in operational practices, personnel qualifications, and career opportunities point to the fact that those in cooperative vocational education must recognize and accept responsibility for practical research as a necessary part of their jobs. Gathering data on, and finding solutions to, everyday problems in the classroom, training agencies, and youth organizations must be done systematically if a cooperative vocational education program is to move ahead in preparing youth for satisfying careers. Unless solutions are found to everyday problems quickly, they may become acute and costly.

Two types of practical research are needed—short-term studies to which quick solutions may be found and long-term projects that are broader in scope. The majority of the average teacher-coordinator's research responsibilities are of the short-term variety. Short- or long-term investigations deal with a wide assortment of problems relating to manpower, population and enrollment figures, and statistical data; coordination activities, program policies and procedures, physical facilities, teaching methods and learning activities, curriculum content and evaluation, student motivation, youth group, supervisory practices, public relations, and others.

Most people who are concerned with cooperative vocational education place more confidence in information that is supported by statistical data

Roles Of A Teacher-Coordinator 53

and supporting facts than individual opinions of persons associated with the program. New teacher-coordinators soon realize this situation and find themselves engaged in informal research which improves in quality as they gain experience.

TIME MANAGEMENT

Closely related to a teacher-coordinator's recording and research role is the management of his time. The relationship stems from the fact that time management involves the use of records and research. Time management usually is one of a teacher-coordinator's most frustrating problems, and it is probably the most important factor in determining his effectiveness.

Without time planning, the teacher-coordinator's job begins to run the person instead of the person running the job. As his responsibilities and pressures increase, it is natural for him to fall into the habit of simply doing whatever seems most pressing at the moment, and doing these things keeps him very busy. Yet there are more important things that need to be done. Unless they are scheduled, they will be pushed aside for less important matters which seem to be more urgent at the time.

Successful teacher-coordinators make time for important tasks and for creative thinking and problem solving which is essential to cooperative vocational education. They take all the time they need to do a task, but they take no more. They are respectful of the time of others. The person who does not set aside time for problem solving and creative thinking will not do as much of either as one should or could. Good time planning is the only way a teacher-coordinator can free himself from the little problems that squeal the loudest, the only way he can get more time to do the things he really needs to do.

There are a number of techniques for managing one's time, and various devices have been used to facilitate the process. They are simple to understand and require no special talents. Time planning is more habit than anything else. One's success in performing the operation depends mostly on his willingness to assume the responsibility.

Role as a Professional Educator

Offhand, one might think that a teacher-coordinator's role as a professional educator is no different from that of other teaching staff members. From the viewpoint of loyalty to the teaching profession this should be true. However, when viewed from the standpoint of the teacher-coordinator's position in relation to the school and the community, he occupies a unique station, and on occasion some confusion exists. Sometimes the school staff sees the teacher-coordinator as a practitioner from the work world outside the school. Conversely, employers may think of the teacher-coordinator as being a school person from outside of business and industry. In theory, the teacher-coordinator acts as a liaison between the school and the occupational field(s) in which he teaches.

A teacher-coordinator may feel that his liaison position between the school and the employment community is desirable or undesirable, depending on his personal outlook. For example, one may assume the attitude that he is not completely at home either among his fellow teachers at school or among the employers and workers of his occupational field and that no one really understands his problems. On the other hand, he may feel that his position as an intermediary between school and the employment community offers a perspective available to no other staff member and that because of his position he can do much to improve education, both in the school and in the business community. Which of these outlooks, if either, a particular individual adopts usually is related to his background of education and occupational experience outside of education. Some teacher-coordinators who entered teaching directly from an occupational field think that it took them about as long to feel completely at home in education as they spent in the occupational field from which they came.

LIAISON WITH EMPLOYERS

A teacher-coordinator must have sufficient competency in the occupation(s) in which he teaches to command the respect of practitioners in the field. In order to keep up-to-date on the technology of his occupational field and to maintain his occupational status, he should participate in selected professional activities of that field. One's professional behavior in his occupational field(s) usually sets an example for his students. It also enables him to become aware of the need for curriculum adjustments and helps him improve his competence in vocational guidance.

LIAISON WITH EDUCATORS

The dependence of cooperative vocational education on the cooperation of all teaching staff members provides the clue to a teacher-coordinator's need for high professional standing among his colleagues. Partly because of this need, but also because of the human relations competencies teacher-coordinators develop during their work in the community, they are inclined to become leaders in the professional activities of the school faculty. They usually participate in school activities, assume their fair share of nonteaching assignments, and participate actively in professional education association activities.

Concluding Statement

The necessity of wearing different hats when working with individuals and groups of people who seem to seek opposing goals may sound threatening to a person contemplating a position as a teacher-coordinator. Granted that it is possible for a novice to work himself into an awkward position by trying to please everyone, this seldom happens to a properly prepared teacher-coordinator. His understanding of the purposes and objectives of his particular cooperative vocational education program unit and his sound student-oriented philosophy of vocational education serve him as reliable guidelines for making rational decisions consistently, thus precluding many problems.

Every teacher-coordinator makes an occasional mistake of some kind. If he is judged as being sincere, he usually is surprised at how understanding the supporters of his program really are. On the other hand, if he seems spurious, he will probably be appalled at their sadism.

A legitimate apprehension of many potential teacher-coordinators relates to the numerous tasks which they apparently are expected to perform and to the probability of their being able to perform them well in the allotted time. Although being a teacher-coordinator is not a logical occupational choice for a clock watcher, these responsibilities can be performed expeditiously if the teacher-student ratio is reasonable and if the teacher-coordinator manages his time well. A neophyte may be inclined to accept more duties and responsibilities than he can manage because he finds it difficult to refuse requests of almost any kind. The key to the solution of the logistics problem lies in good planning of the use of one's time and in one's ability to refuse judiciously and diplomatically the extraneous tasks that interfere unnecessarily with fulfilling the mission of cooperative vocational education. Good planning of the use of his time, plus the efficiency that he develops from his experience, enable a business-like teacher-coordinator to do more than he ever thought possible. A sincere novice soon learns that he must delegate responsibility if he is to achieve his goals.

In conclusion, *mastery* of the occupation of vocational teacher-coordinator usually requires sound occupational and professional education preparation together with several years of cooperative vocational education experience. The occupation is much more rewarding to most conscientious, energetic vocational educators than most regular teaching assignments. In addition, it is a common stepping stone for those who aspire to higher positions in education or in the occupational field taught. To most practicing teacher-coordinators the most appealing feature of the occupation is the satisfaction derived from the achievements of present student-trainees and program graduates.

REFERENCES

1. Burt, Samuel M. "If You Want Me to Serve on a School Advisory Committee," *News from NACVE*, Special Edition, July 1974. Washington, D.C.: National Advisory Council on Special Education.
2. Crawford, Lucy C. *A Competency Pattern Approach to Curriculum Construction in Distributive Education, Volume I.* Blacksburg, Va.: Virginia Polytechnic Institute and State University, 1967, p. 16.
3. Lombard, George F. *Behavior in a Selling Group.* Boston: Harvard University, Division of Research, Graduate School of Business Administration, 1955, 359pp.

ADDITIONAL REFERENCES

Ashmun, Richard D., and Mary K. Klaurens. "Essentials in Educating the Teacher-Coordinator." *American Vocational Journal* 44 (May 1969): 28-29, 62.

Bernard, Louise. "The Proper Allocation of Priorities." *Business Education Forum* 23 (April 1969): 6-9.

Eck, Marilyn J. "Occupational Experience—A Business Teacher's Asset." *Business Education Forum* 24 (December 1969): 30-31.

Haines, Peter G., Betty L. Schroeder and Janice Danford. *Applying the Cooperative Plan of Instruction to Manpower Programs.* East Lansing, Mich.: Michigan State University College of Education, 1970, 155pp.

Home Economics Materials Center. *Orientation to the World of Work, Part I and Part II.* Lubbock: Texas Technical University, January, 1971, 219pp. and 212pp.

Mosbacker, Wanda. "The Role of the Coordinator." *Journal of Cooperative Education,* May 1969, pp. 29-37.

Miller, George H. "The Coordinator—His Job." *Journal of Cooperative Education,* November 1965, pp. 30-32.

Wray, Ralph D. "Resolving the Teacher-Coordinator's Dilemma." *Journal of Business Education* 49 (October 1973): 17-18.

Roles Of A Teacher-Coordinator

SUGGESTED ACTIVITIES

1. Write a two-page narrative description of the job of a teacher-coordinator which could be used to inform a person from business or industry who may be interested in a career in education.

2. Arrange to observe or "shadow" a cooperative vocational education teacher-coordinator for a day and make notations of the different roles performed in his or her activities.

3. Prepare a profile or resume' of your own qualifications, experiences, and/or professional preparation for each of the ten roles performed by a teacher-coordinator. Develop a plan for acquiring competencies for the roles in which you need further education or experience.

Chapter 3   TASKS OF A TEACHER-COORDINATOR

Comprehending the many roles performed by teacher-coordinators is the first phase of learning that job, but it alone is not enough to become an effective practitioner. The second phase in the study of this cluster of occupations consists of acquiring a working knowledge of the daily tasks one performs and how these tasks relate to the purposes and goals of the program that he manages. In order to learn a job well and keep pace with inevitable changes in job-related assignments, one needs a viable concept of the functions and tasks of persons occupying such positions. Having an organizational framework of the job in mind facilitates orderly professional growth and the development of a well-adjusted vocational educator.

One who holds an accurate mental picture of the organizational structure of his job is able to see its many tasks in perspective and to attach values to individual tasks which are not realized when those tasks are viewed individually. He or she can assign learning priorities to the various task categories and round out the preparation needed in certain competency areas. Newly assigned tasks can be placed in the proper context with other related duties and responsibilities. Without a clear picture of the organizational structure of their jobs, few people become well-balanced performers; they tend to concentrate on the things they

Tasks Of A Teacher-Coordinator 59

like to do best and neglect some essential competencies about which they are unconsciously incompetent.

A teacher coordinator's job may be structured in a variety of ways depending on how the person who organizes the information and data sees the roles of an incumbent. For example, a job analyst may take the viewpoint of a traditional school administrator and see this job as primarily that of a classroom teacher. Conversely, he may perceive it through the eyes of an expert teacher-coordinator of cooperative vocational education as the job of a program manager. In light of the numerous roles of a teacher-coordinator discussed in chapter 2, it is evident that persons in this occupation have many duties and responsibilities in addition to those of regular classroom and in-school laboratory teachers. Researchers have proved that "teacher-coordinator" is a separate and distinct occupational category (1). Now that more is known about the teacher-coordinator's job through research and sophisticated literature, it seems appropriate to approach the organizational structure of a teacher-coordinator's job from the viewpoint of an expert teacher-coordinator.

The objectives of this chapter are to enable a prospective or practicing in-service teacher-coordinator to:

1. Hold in high regard the importance of adhering to a viable job structure when preparing for or practicing the occupation of teacher-coordinator;
2. Conceive the teacher-coordinator's job as that of a program manager;
3. Accept the concept that an effective teacher-coordinator, as a program manger, achieves his objectives through others and serves as a leader of an instruction-learning team;
4. Identify the seventeen component elements in Sullivan's Cooperative Vocational Education Management Model;
5. Describe the teaching career analysis prepared by Cotrell and associates;
6. Explain the difference in the assigned tasks of teacher-coordinators and those of classroom teachers or in-school library teachers;
7. Discuss the uses of the list of performance requirements of teacher-coordinators;
8. Explain the relationship between task analysis and career development;
9. Enumerate the unique characteristics of student-trainees and explain how they influence the teacher-coordinator's selection of content and teaching-learning activities;
10. Explain how a teacher-coordinator's use of the four major

sources of learning differs from that of other vocational education teachers;
11. Define the four categories of cooperative vocational education content and show why a teacher-coordinator is responsible for teaching all of them;
12. Identify the factors and kinds of information that an effective teacher-coordinator considers when choosing learning activities for his student-trainees.

The Teacher-Coordinator as a Program Manager

In order to gain insight into the scope and responsibility level of a teacher-coordinator's job, one must think of the person who fills the position as more of a program manager and administrator with teaching responsibilities than as a school teacher who spends part of his work day in the community checking on his students. The teacher-coordinator *manages* the cooperative vocational education program. He or she and the school administrator are the "responsible party," accountable for the outcomes resulting from the instructional processes. They are responsible for directing the teaching and supervisory activities of others—the training agency employers and training sponsors in particular—so that student-trainees will master the designated occupational competencies.

In cooperative vocational education, the increased amount of community involvement and direct participation of laymen in the instructional process places the teacher-coordinator in a managerial role. The school's decreased proportion of all the instruction received by student-trainees in cooperative vocational education in no way lessens the school's responsibility for the amount and quality of instruction needed to achieve a program's objectives. The school management is accountable for *all* the instruction under the supervision of the school.

A teacher-coordinator obviously functions as a manager when he calls on the employer and/or training sponsor to facilitate the student's on-the-job learning. He functions indirectly as a manager when he teaches the student-trainee to be more responsible for his own learning and gives him assignments which call for assistance from the training sponsor and from other personnel employed by the training agency. The teacher-coordinator adds to his managerial functions when the student assumes an expanded self-instructional role in comparison to other students who receive instruction exclusively at school. The student-trainee accepts the added responsibility associated with the greater freedom of choice of

Tasks Of A Teacher-Coordinator

learning activities as he learns the essential skills, knowledge, and attitudes at the training agency where he is employed.

MANAGERIAL FUNCTIONS OF A TEACHER-COORDINATOR

Specifically, how does a teacher-coordinator function as a manager? In order to answer this question, we must first define management. Management is a process of getting things done through other people.

> Management is a social process. It is a process because it comprises a series of actions that lead to the accomplishment of objectives. It is a social process because these actions are principally concerned with relations between people. (3)

Management entails the decision-making process in activities such as planning, organizing, staffing, coordinating, controlling, and evaluating. A teacher-coordinator engages in these activities in conjunction with many aspects of his cooperative vocational education program, such as the stated career goals of his student-trainees, pay and school credit, related vocational instruction, stated paid work assignments at the place of employment, signed training agreements, written training plans, sophisticated guidance procedures, and placement of students in training agencies and positions.

SULLIVAN'S MANAGEMENT PROCESS MODEL FOR COOPERATIVE VOCATIONAL EDUCATION

A management process model aids effective management. It helps the manager in the following ways (5):

1. In establishing and communicating direction toward mutually agreeable objectives;
2. In organizing human and other community resources;
3. In isolating instances where decisions are to be made;
4. In making possible the assignment of components of the management model as work tasks on a systematic basis;
5. In making possible systematic evaluation of the process;
6. In communicating the manner in which the process is to occur.

Models also help when communicating program intent, thus facilitating time planning and in some cases helping to justify additional costs when comparing instructional plans.

Sullivan (5) presented a management model which is helpful in describing the cooperative vocational education management process (figure 3-1). It enables a reader to get acquainted with the component functions of events and to see where the teacher-coordinator is intro-

FIGURE 3-1

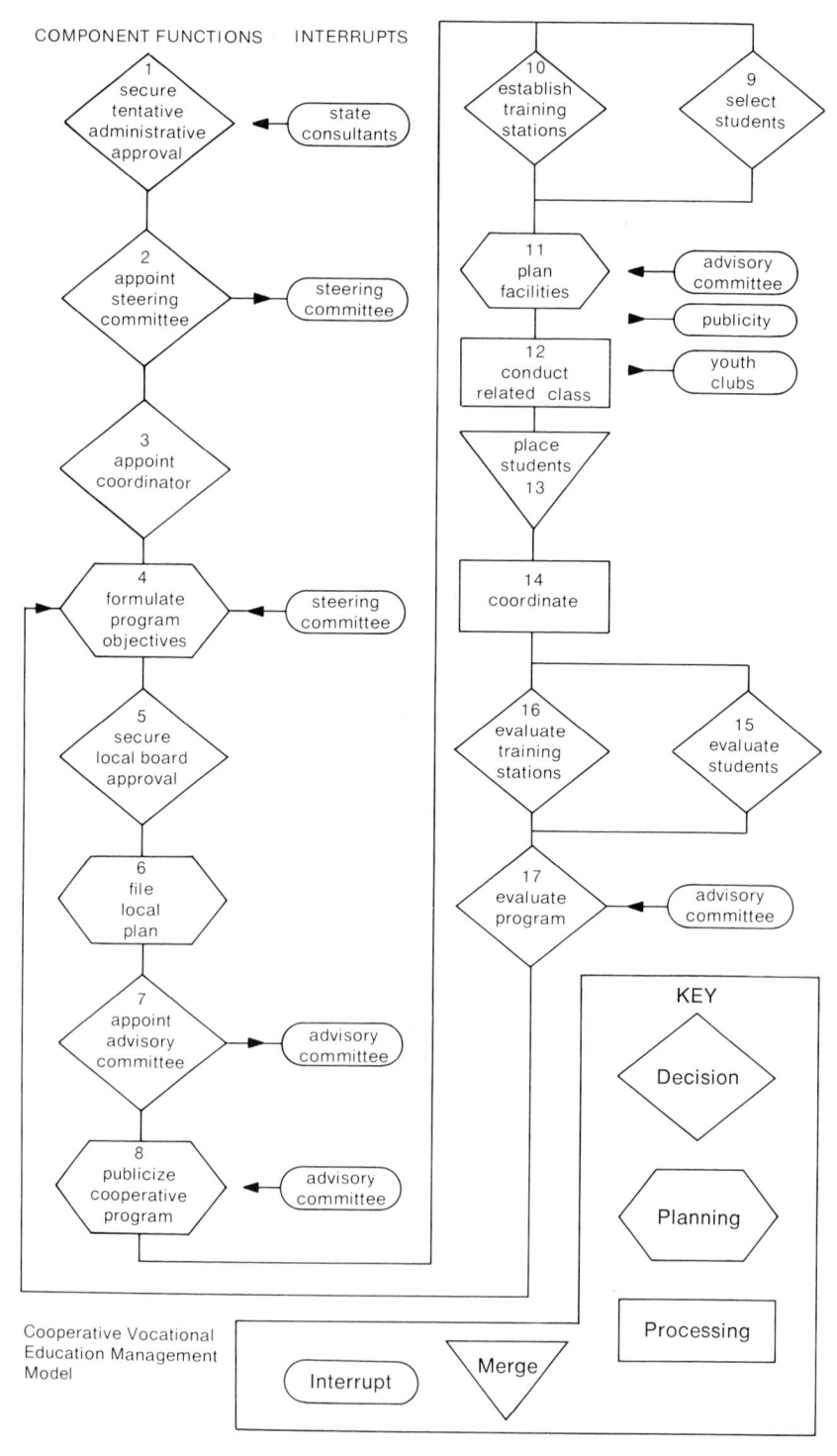

COMPONENT FUNCTIONS   INTERRUPTS

1. secure tentative administrative approval ← state consultants
2. appoint steering committee → steering committee
3. appoint coordinator
4. formulate program objectives ← steering committee
5. secure local board approval
6. file local plan
7. appoint advisory committee → advisory committee
8. publicize cooperative program ← advisory committee
9. select students
10. establish training stations
11. plan facilities ← advisory committee / → publicity
12. conduct related class / → youth clubs
13. place students
14. coordinate
15. evaluate students
16. evaluate training stations
17. evaluate program ← advisory committee

Cooperative Vocational Education Management Model

KEY
- Decision (diamond)
- Planning (hexagon)
- Processing (rectangle)
- Interrupt (oval)
- Merge (triangle)

62

duced into the program functions. Standard symbols are used to designate the type of function utilized—decision, planning, process, and merge. (See symbol key on model.) The off-line functions—steering committee, advisory committee, publicity, and youth clubs—which act as resources are designated as input and output "interrupts" or ancillary functions.

Readers are reminded that this is only one process model and that youth organizations, for example, may be designated as a component function in some models.

Component Functions. The seventeen component functions of the Sullivan management model are broken down into smaller parts which may vary, depending upon and according to the role assigned to the local administrator and teacher-coordinator, according to the objectives of the program, and according to the characteristics of the community. The concept of the component function breakdown presented by Sullivan follows:

COMPONENT FUNCTION BREAKDOWN
Cooperative Vocational-Education Management Model

1. *Secure Administrative Approval*
   a. Administrative letter
   b. Board tentative approval
   c. Administrator implementation
   d. Preliminary community survey
2. *Appoint Steering Committee*
   a. Local community business and other leaders organized to complete a temporary assignment, including completion of community survey, feasibility study, and program objectives
3. *Appoint Teacher-Coordinator*
   a. Potential teacher-coordinator isolated from teacher ranks, or outside teacher-coordinator identified
   b. New teacher coordinator assigned to job with specified duties, one of which is to be a part of the steering committee
4. *Formulate Program Objectives*
   a. Steering committee formulated objectives
5. *Secure Local Board Approval*
   a. Board acts in light of community survey, feasibility study, and objectives formulated for the program
6. *File Local Plan for Vocational Education*
   a. Potential student isolated by priority and other factors which determine local reimbursement

7. *Appoint Advisory Committee*
    a. Steering committee is disbanded
    b. Advisory committee composition is determined (age and length of term)
    c. Advisory committee member recommendations made to board by administrator
    d. Advisory committee members appointed by board to terms
8. *Publicize Program*
    a. Local business, community, parents, students, and teachers informed by various media available about program, goals, and curriculum operation
9. *Select Students*
    a. Teacher-coordinator, guidance counselor, parents, and students involved in selection process
    b. Permanent record and other test and counseling data used to establish with the student a tentative career objective
    c. Students classified by career objectives and training station needs
10. *Establish Training Stations*
    a. Training station interviews conducted to determine possible work stations and task assignments
    b. Wage, hour, safety, and other legal requirements standards checked
    c. Tentative training plans and training memoranda constructed
11. *Plan Facilities*
    a. Tentative match made between student career objectives and training station availability
    b. Laboratory and classroom training facility needs isolated
    c. Hardware and software materials listed by area
    d. Floor plan for teaching layout constructed
    e. Cost and procurement factors estimated
12. *Conduct Related Class*
    a. Related materials for each training plan secured
    b. General related instruction materials secured
    c. Training plans constructed
    d. Related class conducted using general and specific information directed by training plans
    e. Student youth organizations started
    f. Publicize program
13. *Place Students*
    a. Student interviews with employers
    b. Training memoranda are signed by four parties
    c. Training plans completed
    d. Students begin cooperative work experience
14. *Coordinate*
    a. Teacher-coordinator visits students at training station
15. *Evaluate Student Progress*
    a. Student performance is compared to training plan objectives by student, teacher-coordinator, and employer

Tasks Of A Teacher-Coordinator 65

16. *Evaluate Training Station*
    a. Safety and occupational hazards checked
    b. Instructional benefits evaluated
    c. Employment outlook and opportunities evaluated
17. *Evaluate Program*
    a. Student performance within program
    b. Student performance upon graduation
    c. Training station value and employment effectiveness
    d. Program goals with established goals set by steering committee

Ongoing Activities Which Act as System Interrupts
   a. State Consultant Services
   b. Publicity
   c. Advisory committee meetings on a scheduled basis
   d. Youth club activities
   e. Coordination between the training station and the school-related class

Variance in the breakdown of the component functions may be illustrated by function 13, "Place Students," which might vary between programs serving regular students and one serving a special group of culturally disadvantaged students, or between urban and rural communities, or between one occupational field and another.

Time Frames. As mentioned on page 61, the model can be used as a basis for establishing a time schedule for completing the various functions. Time frames can be devised to account for the total available time, the delegation of responsibility of personnel, and to construct a schedule for the teacher-coordinator when he enters the scene to establish the program (function 4), and later when he operates it. For example, in the latter case the evaluation component (number 17) would take into consideration the performance of students while participating in the program, their performance after graduation, and the evaluation of the training agency. A report which compares the student performance outcomes with stated program objectives would be made.

Program Operation Functions. In this book, the functions relating to program installation (Sullivan's component functions 1 through 7) will not be discussed; however, frequent mention will be made to program objectives. The intent of this book is to aid practitioners in learning to carry out functions 8 through 17 which relate to an on-going program. Particular attention has been given to the development of the theoretical base that can be used in decision making and to relate that theory to the daily activities of a teacher-coordinator so that he or she can make reasoned judgments concerning activities beyond those discussed in this textbook.

THE TEAM APPROACH

In cooperative vocational education, the school uses the team approach to achieve its pervading purpose, that of facilitating career development. During the time that students participate in the program they are guided in the pursuit of either established or emerging career goals; they learn to adjust to an adult work environment; and they apply classroom-learned occupational skills as well as learn new ones. Their objective is employability in an occupation which offers them the particular rewards they seek from work.

In order to realize these program goals and student expectations, there must be an effective teaching team—competent practitioners in the occupations and other school and community personnel—providing hands-on experiences in a real-life work environment. Obviously, the teacher-coordinator must coordinate the activities of this teaching team—a management function. Some of the team members participate directly in the instructional process; others act in an ancillary role.

The Instructional Staff. The teacher-coordinator is the lead instructor of the teaching team, in addition to being the operating manager of the instructional process. As a teacher, he engages in group and individual instruction designed to meet the group and individual goals of his students. As an operating manager of on-the-job instruction, he serves as an initiator of activities, as a consultant to training sponsors and students, and as an evaluator of student and program progress.

Initiating the activities necessary for good instruction at the training agency is of utmost importance. Unless the teacher-coordinator takes the initiative (a management function), little learning is likely to take place in the student's on-the-job laboratory. A teacher-coordinator must be given sufficient training and time to perform this managerial task.

Students and training sponsors need help in analyzing and organizing their learning and teaching tasks; usually neither one has much knowledge of the teaching-learning process—therefore, a teacher-coordinator spends much of his time consulting with and advising both parties. Sometimes misunderstandings between student-trainee and training sponsor arise and the teacher-coordinator acts as a supervisor in reconciling them. Many teacher-coordinators engage in informal sponsor training and some carry on formal sponsor-training classes. These too are managerial tasks.

Teacher-coordinators continously engage in evaluating the results of learning that takes place at the students' training agencies; then appropriate action is taken. These are managerial activities. Also the program evaluation activities performed by the teacher-coordinator are located in this category.

The Ancillary Service Members. Cooperative vocational education is highly dependent on good ancillary services, particularly on those performed by advisory committees. Organizing and maintaining a functional advisory committee calls for a high degree of managerial skill. Operating a cooperative vocational education program also includes a variety of managerial type tasks relating to labor laws, licensing, labor union rules and regulations, city ordinances, and relations with trade associations, civic organizations, and service clubs. In addition, there are the usual program application forms, activities reports, claims for reimbursement, and evaluation reports required of state and federally reimbursed programs which are prepared by most teacher-coordinators.

There are other ancillary service personnel, both within and outside of the school, who influence a student-trainee's learning of vocational competencies. Logically, a rational teacher-coordinator would rely on the pupil-personnel-service staff members, and other personnel, particularly vocational teachers, to participate in teaching some of the vocational competencies in the areas of their expertise. A teacher-coordinator who thinks that he can supply the instruction for all of the competencies necessary to bring a deficient student up to standard is soon disillusioned, so other general and vocational education teachers and the counselors are called upon to participate in instruction.

Members of a student-trainee's family can do a great deal to augment a student-trainee's career development. They can support the teacher-coordinator and training sponsor in helping a neophyte student-trainee to master work-related habits in the social adjustment competency area. It is a good practice for the teacher-coordinator to visit the home of new student-trainees in order to enlist the cooperation of influential family members in this training and to gain an insight into the family's work-value system and interpersonal relationships. Parents should cooperate in cooperative vocational education by permitting their daughters and sons to be a part of this pragmatic instructional process, condoning its practices—sometimes by supplying transportation and by tolerating some of the interference with family routines.

When one considers all of the managerial duties of a teacher-coordinator it is easy to see why he should be identified as a manager first and then a teacher—the educational process is implemented as much or more through others as through his own teaching. It must be remembered, however, that he is the lead teacher and that the classroom is the nucleus of the instructional program.

Task Analysis of the Teacher-Coordinator's Job

Sullivan's cooperative vocational education management model described above provides a systematic explanation of the way a cooperative vocational education program functions. It also enables a reader to see where a teacher-coordinator fits into the total cooperative education process. But it does not furnish a detailed list of teacher-coordinator tasks that is needed to plan the systematic learning of the job. For the latter, we must turn to a task analysis. The Center for Vocational and Technical Education, The Ohio State University, has sponsored several research studies which help meet this need. These studies, which were directed by Cotrell (1), produced a vocational teaching career analysis and a teacher-coordinator task analysis which have been selected for use in this book because they are based on the opinions of practitioners representing six vocational fields. Before examining the teacher-coordinator task analysis, it may be appropriate to make some comparisons between the jobs of teacher-coordinators and regular classroom and in-school laboratory instructors that will place the teacher-coordinator's job in perspective.

PERCENTAGE OF UNIQUE TASKS

The Center's research on career analysis of vocational teaching positions in agricultural, business and office, distributive, health occupations, home economics, technical, and trade and industrial education dealt with classroom teachers, in-school laboratory teachers, and teacher-coordinators at the high school level and with classroom and in-school laboratory teachers at the post-secondary level (1). The report is of particular interest to teacher-coordinators because the responses are divided into two groups: (a) those from classroom and in-school laboratory teachers, and (b) teacher-coordinators of cooperative vocational education programs. It also identified the common and unique tasks of the two groups which led to some interesting findings.

Twelve of the fifty clusters of tasks (twenty-four percent) were identified as being unique to the teacher-coordinator and only two clusters were found to be unique to the classroom and in-school laboratory instructor. Seventy-one percent of the competencies were found to be common to all three types of instructional personnel. The fact that roughly *one-fourth* of the tasks of a teacher-coordinator are unique to that occupation has many implications for the preparation of teacher-coordinators. Even a cursory examination of the unique tasks will reveal that they are relatively complex. Further examination of them will reveal that a large portion is made up of management-oriented responsibilities. A graphic portrayal of the allocation of the clusters of tasks to common and unique responsibilities of teacher-coordinators and of classroom and in-school laboratory teachers will be found in appendix B.

PERFORMANCE REQUIREMENTS OF TEACHER-COORDINATORS

Experience with the teaching career task analysis revealed the need for an independent study of the teacher-coordinator's job. Therefore, another study (2) which was limited to teacher-coordinator respondents was funded by the Center for Vocational and Technical Education. Three hundred experts, fifty from each of six established fields, reacted to 385 elements or tasks (the terms are synomymous here). The types of programs represented were off-farm agricultural education, office occupations, distributive education, wage-earning home economics education, trade and industrial education, and special needs education.

At this time, it seems appropriate to use the Center's task analysis for career planning that is oriented toward careers in the teacher-coordinator realm. Therefore, the task analysis developed by the Center will be presented here in part. A complete list of tasks will be found in appendix C.

In this analysis, the teacher-coordinator tasks have been divided into categories and clusters which aid the user in perceiving the characteristics of the tasks. The study revealed 385 tasks which were divided into ten categories and eighty-two clusters. The number of tasks in each cluster is shown in parentheses. Clarification of cluster titles may be gained from reading the list of tasks in the appendix.

CATEGORY A
Program Planning, Development and Evaluation

1. Vocational survey (11)
2. Survey preparation (3)
3. Consultation for survey (3)
4. Administrative approval of advisory committee (2)
5. Advisory committee (9)
6. Occupational selection (4)
7. Utilization of advisory committee and labor for occupational analysis (2)
8. Follow-up of graduates (2)
9. Planning and evaluation of vocational education program (10)
10. Long-range planning (6)

CATEGORY B
Instruction—Planning

11. Objectives and performance goals (3)
12. Unit planning (5)
13. Student involvement in unit planning (1)
14. Unit plans for individualized instruction (2)
15. Preparation of instructional materials (3)
16. Instructional materials, equipment and supplies (5)
17. Lesson planning (8)

CATEGORY C
Instruction—Execution

18. Introduction and closure of lesson (2)
19. Teacher-centered techniques (5)
20. Teaching techniques (7)
21. Traditional educational technology (2)
22. Educational technology (8)
23. Visual aids (5)
24. Directed study (2)
25. Individualized instruction (3)
26. Laboratory instruction (6)
27. Interaction techniques (11)
28. Instruction by students (2)
29. Outside resources (3)
30. Educational innovations (6)

CATEGORY D
Instruction—Evaluation

31. Student performance criteria and evaluation (7)
32. Student involvement in evaluation (5)
33. Evaluation of on-the-job experiences (3)
34. Laboratory tests and rating sheets (2)
35. Formulation of test items (6)
36. Administration and analysis of tests (4)
37. Evaluating instruction (3)
38. Teacher self-evaluation (2)

CATEGORY E
Management

39. Budgeting and supplies (7)
40. Fees and gratuities (2)
41. Reference books and supplies (3)
42. Data and records (8)
43. Laboratory management (9)
44. Safety measures (3)
45. Student behavior (6)

CATEGORY F
Guidance

46. Teacher-student rapport (3)
47. Personal concern for student (4)
48. Student records (5)
50. Student counseling (6)
51. Occupational counseling (7)

Tasks Of A Teacher-Coordinator

49. Administering standardized tests (4)
52. Student referral (5)

CATEGORY G
School-Community Relations

53. Planning school-commumity relations (3)
54. Feedback on vocational programs (8)
55. School and community service (6)
56. School-student-community activities (3)
57. Unions (labor and management) (1)
58. Staff relationships (3)
59. Program publicity (7)

CATEGORY H
Student Vocational Organization

60. Establishing student vocational organization (4)
61. Management of student vocational organization (15)
62. Cooperation with state and national organization (7)
63. Books and publications (3)
64. Chapter parents (1)

CATEGORY I
Professional Role and Development

65. Philosophy and goals (6)
66. General school duties (2)
67. Professional service (6)
68. School problems (2)
69. Student teaching (8)
70. Self-evaluation (3)
71. Upgrading competencies (4)

CATEGORY J
Coordination

72. Resource materials (1)
73. Student-learner selection (7)
74. Training station (3)
75. Union (1)
76. Employment regulation (federal and state) (5)
77. Safety (3)
78. Persuasion (1)
79. Training agreement (4)
80. Coordination of on-the-job training (13)
81. Student control on the job (3)
82. Related on-the-job instruction (6)

TASK ANALYSES AND CAREER DEVELOPMENT

A teacher-coordinator task analysis may be a valuable source of information for persons preparing for positions in cooperative vocational education, either as undergraduates in a teacher-education program or as persons with content-field or teaching degrees that did not include study of cooperative education. It can also serve in-service personnel who want to update their professional competencies or earn promotions. Lastly, it can serve as a valuable tool for those who are charged with the responsibility of training teacher-coordinators.

Anyone considering a career that involves cooperative vocational education can gain much insight into the type of work a teacher-coordinator does by examining a good task analysis. He or she can acquire a feeling for the nature of the work from examining the ten categories of a coordinator's activities. The clusters can be used to become better acquainted with the categories, and the elements or tasks can point up the specific activities included in the clusters.

If, after studying the teacher-coordinator task analysis, an individual decides to prepare for a job in this occupation, he or she can use the task analysis as a planning aid when selecting college courses and technical field occupational experiences that will contribute to competency development in various task categories or clusters. In a similar manner, in-service teacher-coordinators who are aware of their need for updating can identify needed areas of training.

Although any list of tasks is never complete, it still may serve as a guide for educational planning. Additional competencies and/or competency clusters may be added as they are discovered. A logical sequence for mastery of the competencies and a timetable should be made. State supervisors and teacher-educators can be helpful resources in the preparation of such professional improvement plans.

The Teaching-Learning Tasks

In the first section of this chapter the concept of a teacher-coordinator's being a manager of an instructional program was explained, and in the preceding section, ten categories of specific tasks were identified. The uniqueness of the tasks included in the category, coordination, is manifest, but those tasks belonging to the categories, instruction—planning, instruction—execution, and instruction—evaluation embody important differences from regular classroom and school laboratory teaching which need clarification. As a precursor to the chapters that follow, something must be said about the ways in which the characteristics of the student-trainees affect the nature of instruction. In a nutshell, instruction given in successful cooperative vocational education programs has much in common with adult vocational pedagogy. Cooperative vocational education usually serves young people who are entering an adult environment. Nearly all of them want to be recognized and treated as adults. That is why adult-type methods and activities, when properly executed, have proved to be the most productive.

CHARACTERISTICS OF STUDENT-TRAINEES

Student-trainees may differ from other students in certain respects depending on the type of individuals a given program is designed to serve, but all of them differ in some ways from regular classroom and in-school laboratory students because of the nature and purposes of cooperative vocational education. For example, all of them combine formal school work with remunerative employment. This condition augments certain types of instruction and restricts the use of others.

Nearly all student-trainees experience close contact with adults, a condition which affects their behavior in a variety of ways. With good guidance, they learn to cope with an adult work environment and to some extent they may modify their own behavior. Many of them associate with co-workers and other people who possess highly diverse work personalities and life styles. The purpose of this discussion is not to explore the kinds of outcomes these associations may invoke in students but rather to point up a condition which impacts on the selection of instructional methods and content.

Student-trainees soon learn that there usually is more than one authority on the particular type of competency they hope to master, a point that was alluded to earlier. Therefore, when appropriate instructional methods are used, they learn to locate source persons for the type of truth they seek. During the course of their inquiries and their daily associations with co-workers, a number of them consciously or inadvertently adopt work models who exert strong influence on their behavior. Many of these resource people are appropriately chosen, but this is not always the case. It is the responsibility of a teacher-coordinator to guide his students in their selection of information sources and in weighing the merits of the information gathered. Considerable knowledge about the sources of information utilized by the student-trainee may be required. The situation may be particularly difficult when a conflict of opinion exists between a position held by the teacher-coordinator and/or a textbook author and the student's resource person. Thus the kind of relationship that exists between the teacher-coordinator and each student-trainee (as well as to the class as a whole) has a bearing on an instructor's planning and execution of instruction. Selection of proper instructional methods and content for the variety of situations encountered by members of a cooperative vocational education class requires special applications of teaching skills.

Another characteristic of a large majority of student-trainees is their preference for work activities on a regular job in contrast with sedentary academic study. Usually the teacher-coordinator's objective is to help his students cultivate a reasonable blend of study and occupational experience and to develop study habits that will persist in adult life. Such goals call for especially skillful instructional planning, a topic which will be investigated more fully in later chapters of this book.

There are a number of other characteristics of student-trainees which affect a teacher-coordinator's teaching-learning tasks that will not be discussed at this juncture. For example, student-trainees usually do not have much free time; they earn money which opens doors in designing special learning activities; they have the opportunity for almost immediate feedback in applying the learning; each class member has a unique experience in his job environment that he can draw on for class discussions; and students have the privilege of free help from a specially selected tutor, the training sponsor.

LEARNING RESOURCES

The teaching-learning tasks of a teacher-coordinator include the use of four major sources of learning: (1) those taking place in a regular classroom or school laboratory, (2) those associated with the student-trainees' jobs, (3) those that utilize the community at large, and (4) those emanating from a youth group organization (club). Each source should be used in the development of a well-balanced worker. There are two important differences between teacher-coordinators and other vocational teachers that relate to the use of these learning resources: (a) the extent to which each of these four sources is utilized, and (b) the need for articulating and regulating their input for individual students and for the class as a whole. When learning input from any one of these sources becomes disproportionate in terms of its impact on an individual student's vocational development, teaching-learning problems arise.

Most vocational teacher-coordinators recognize the importance of a student's job as a rich source of learning and as a strong motivational force. It is without question the most effective medium for infusing reality into a student-trainee's curriculum if the student's place of employment is compatible with his career goals and work personality. His job serves as the integrating element for the learning he obtains from other sources—he continuously relates it to his job. On the contrary, when classroom or laboratory instruction and/or youth group activities lose their relevance to a student-trainee's progress toward his career goal, the job likely will become the dominant source of learning, sometimes to the point where the student-trainee rejects the other sources. Thus the teacher-coordinator as a manager has larger responsibility for maintaining a balance of the learning sources.

The skill of articulating the four sources of learning requires close attention to the balance in vocational development of individual student-

Tasks Of A Teacher-Coordinator 75

trainees. Skilled teacher-coordinators sense each student's attitude toward each of the learning sources, as well as that of the class as a whole toward these sources. They work with their training sponsors, youth group leaders, and their advisory committee to obtain help in bolstering needed resources and they are astute in helping students appreciate the value of the contributions from the various sources of learning.

TYPES OF CONTENT

As you have read, each student-trainee has a curriculum of his own. He joins the entire class in some content areas; in others he works in a small group with students possessing similar interests; and in a number of context areas he is on his own, working individually. A cooperative vocational education classroom is *not* one in which all students at all times do the same thing in the same way. This situation calls for careful planning of instruction based on a thorough understanding of each student's needs at all times. It invites "teacher-pupil" planning, at least for a portion of the curriculum. It suggests that students should become increasingly responsible for self-directed learning.

One perspective in categorizing the learnings in which a student-trainee engages is to classify them on a four-point scale based on the uniqueness or commonality of the competency to be learned: (1) individual job competency, (2) single occupation competency, (3) occupational cluster competency, and (4) general vocational competency (see figure 3-2).

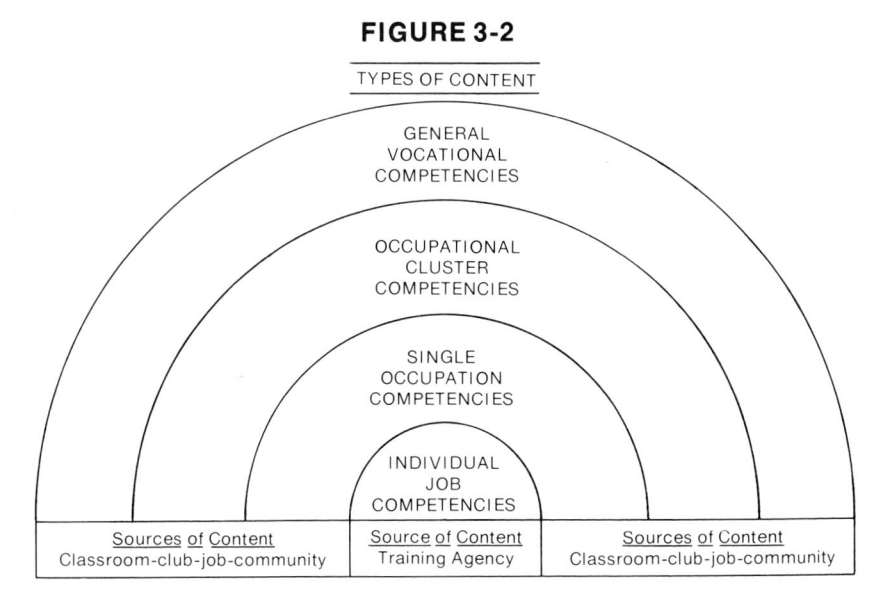

FIGURE 3-2

TYPES OF CONTENT

GENERAL VOCATIONAL COMPETENCIES

OCCUPATIONAL CLUSTER COMPETENCIES

SINGLE OCCUPATION COMPETENCIES

INDIVIDUAL JOB COMPETENCIES

Sources of Content	Source of Content	Sources of Content
Classroom-club-job-community	Training Agency	Classroom-club-job-community

Individual Job Competencies. Competencies that are unique to the student-trainee's training agency and to his particular position in that training agency, e.g., company policies, procedures, practices.

Single Occupation Competencies. Competencies that are unique to the particular occupation in which the student-trainee works, but are common to all other persons who work in that occupation, e.g., perform the technical tasks and/or use technical information unique to that particular occupation.

Occupational Cluster Competencies. Competencies common to the occupations in a particular occupational cluster such as one of the fifteen occupational clusters in the U.S. Office of Education instructional code.

Agri-Business and Natural Resources	Health
	Hospitality and Recreation
Fine Arts and Humanities	Manufacturing
Business and Office	Marine Science
Communication and Media	Marketing and Distribution
Construction	Personal Services Occupations
Consumer and Homemaking— Related Occupations	
	Public Service
Environment	Transportation

General Vocational Competencies. Competencies which by definition are common to all workers regardless of the training agency, the occupation, or the occupational cluster, e.g., employer-employee relationship competencies, co-worker relationship competencies, and competencies involved in learning a job.

Content classification according to the broad categories above can be applied to vocational instruction in plans other than cooperative vocational education, but a teacher-coordinator finds himself responsible for the four types of learning content to a greater extent than most other vocational education teachers. Employers are interested in well-balanced competency patterns regardless of the type of teaching-learning content it may take to develop them. As shown in figure 3-2, the teaching of individual job competencies is delegated largely to training sponsors, but the teacher-coordinator plans his classroom instruction pertaining to the other three types according to the individual and group needs of his class members. Such planning will be discussed in more detail later in this textbook.

Classes of students with heterogeneous occupational goals tend to gravitate toward the general vocational competency type of content largely because common learnings are compatible with large groups. For example, the content treated in a diversified occupations (DO) class usually is more general than that of classes for students whose goals are in one of the occupational clusters. Content in post-secondary programs tends to be of a more specific type.

CHOICE OF LEARNING ACTIVITIES

Ability to select appropriate learning activities for student-trainees is one of the most important criteria for measuring a teacher-coordinator's teaching competency because it involves the consideration of so many factors and depends on such a large amount of information. This task entails the weighing of large amounts of information about individual student-trainees' needs, their jobs and training environments, the nature of the content to be taught, and the types of outcomes that reasonably may be expected from the various learning activities. It also calls for skillful use of human relations because the student-trainee and training sponsor frequently are included in the selection process, and learning outcomes may affect other people. Judgmental errors are reflected in student attitudes and morale.

Recall that cooperative vocational education student-trainees usually want adult status and that the program objectives usually include helping students bridge the gap between adolescent and adult life. Also call to mind the fact that an important strut in this bridge is to help students develop learning skills that will persist into adult life after the student has completed the program and is on his own, so to speak. These two purposes must be kept in mind throughout the process of selecting learning activities. Fortunately the training agency, if properly used, is a wonderful laboratory for implementing these purposes.

Another concern when choosing learning activities for student-trainees is the relevance of content and learning activities to the needs of the learners. The real-life environment afforded by a training agency is a boon when it is used to support classroom learning, but it can also be a curse if what is taught in school doesn't hold true on the job.

A final suggestion at this point regarding the selection of learning activities is recognition of cooperative education students' need for activity and variety. Usually student-trainees are action-oriented individuals, a characteristic which will be discussed in relation to learning activities later.

Concluding Statement

When one first discovers the large number of tasks a teacher-coordinator performs and the heavy responsibilities he carries, he or she wonders how this is possible. The fact that twenty-four percent of the tasks he performs are in addition to those performed by regular vocational classroom and school laboratory teachers and that a teacher-coordinator is a manager who is responsible for the productivity of other individuals seems frightening if not impossible. Do some of the teacher-coordinators take the job without realizing the demands of the competencies required in order to maintain high standards of performance? Do some of them go about their daily tasks indefinitely without learning what the teacher-coordinator's job entails? Perhaps so. Fortunately, cooperative vocational education has some very strong features which, when compared to traditional systems, are attractive enough to maintain its existence (4).

For a moment, let's look at what usually happens to a neophyte teacher-coordinator. At first he is overwhelmed by the magnitude of the job, but he sees others who operate successful programs and enjoy their work, so he says, "Why not give it a trial?" He doesn't accomplish everything he sets out to do the first year, but during that year he learns something about management of learning and sees how he can accomplish more the next year with the same amount of effort. So it is. Each year is more productive until, finally, high standards are achieved.

REFERENCES

1. Cotrell, Calvin J., et al. *Model Curricula for Vocational and Technical Teacher Education: Report No. I. Performance Requirements for Teachers, Final Report.* Columbus: Center for Vocational and Technical Education, The Ohio State University, 1971, 143pp.
2. Cotrell, Calvin J., et al. *Model Curricula for Vocational and Technical Teacher Education: Report No. III. Performance Requirements for Teacher-Coordinators.* Research and Development Series No. 66 Columbus: Center for Vocational and Technical Education, The Ohio State University, 1972, 148pp.
3. Newman, William H., Charles E. Summer, and Warren E. Kirby. *The Process of Management.* Englewood Cliffs, New Jersey: Prentice-Hall, Inc., 1967, p. 9.
4. "School Supervised Work Education Programs." *Research and Practice Curriculum Report* 3, No. 2. (December 1973). Washington, D.C. National Ass'n. Secondary School Principals, Curriculum Service Center.
5. Sullivan, James A. "Managing Cooperative Vocational Education Programs." *Occupational Education Quarterly*, 4 No. 3. Carbondale: Department of Occupational Education, Southern Illinois University (Fall 1972), pp. 1-2.

ADDITIONAL REFERENCES

Butler, Roy. *Cooperative Vocational Education Programs: Staff Development.* Information Analysis Series No. 70. Columbus: The Center for Vocational and Technical Education, The Ohio State University, 1970.

Tasks Of A Teacher-Coordinator

Carroll, Stephen J., Jr., and Henry L. Tosi, Jr. *Management by Objectives.* New York: Macmillan, 1973.

Hale, James A. *Review and Synthesis of Research on Management Systems for Vocational and Technical Education.* Information Series No. 51. Columbus: The Center for Vocational and Technical Education, The Ohio State University, 1971.

Hamlin, Herbert M. *Policy and Administration Decision Needed When Introducing Vocational and Technical Education in Agriculture Off-Farm Occupations.* Center Related Series No. 8. Columbus: The Center for Vocational and Technical Education, The Ohio State University, 1965.

Huffman, Harry. *Guidelines for Cooperative Education and Selected Materials from the National Seminar Held August 1-5, 1966, A Manual for the Further Development of Cooperative Education.* Leadership Training Series No. 10. Columbus: The Center for Vocational and Technical Education, The Ohio State University, 1967.

McGivney, Joseph H., and William C. Nelson. *Program Planning, Budgeting Systems for Educators, Volume I: An Instructional Outline.* Leadership Training Series No. 18. Columbus: The Center for Vocational and Technical Education, the Ohio State University, 1969.

_____ *Program Planning, Budgeting Systems for Educators, Volume III: An Annotated Bibliography.* Bibliography Series No. 3. Columbus: The Center for Vocational and Technical Education, The Ohio State University, 1969.

SUGGESTED ACTIVITIES

1. Prepare a two-column chart, and in the left-hand column list what you think are characteristics of student-trainees who would be enrolled in a program in your vocational field (e.g., busy schedule of school and work hours). In the right-hand column indicate how the characteristics may influence your selection of content and teaching-learning activities (e.g., teach students to manage their time; avoid giving assignments which require considerable amount of homework).

2. For each of the four types of content that are shown in figure 3-2 identify four competencies that would be taught to student-trainees in your vocational field.

3. From the list of eighty-two competency clusters, prepare a list of those for which you feel you need additional education or training. From your listing develop a plan for acquiring the needed training including courses to be taken, observations and hands-on experiences, self-study materials, and other methods of learning.

4. Study the detailed list of performance requirements shown in appendix C. Make a light pencil mark after those tasks which you feel you know how to do now. As you gain competencies in the other areas, check off the items.

Chapter 4   FACILITATING CAREER DEVELOPMENT

Facilitating career development is the pervading purpose of cooperative vocational education. Though the emphases on particular program objectives may vary widely from one vocational field or level to another, each objective will contribute in some way to the career development of the students enrolled.

Career development is a developmental process that everyone experiences, whether it is planned or whether it just happens. Some careers are satisfying and enjoyable, and some are not. Much depends on the outcomes of many career decisions that are made as a person goes through life.

Cooperative vocational education, when properly implemented, provides an excellent environment in which to make rational career decisions. It can serve as a laboratory for learning how to make satisfying career decisions. Whether such skills are actually acquired depends on the sophistication and attitudes of the teacher-coordinator in the realm of career development.

If a teacher-coordinator makes a conscious effort to facilitate career development, his students will be better prepared to make vocational plans and to cope with the work adjustments that are mandatory in our rapidly changing world of work. The search for self-fulfillment and personal satisfaction through one's work is a life-long process. The purpose of this chapter is to help the conscientious teacher-coordinator expand his repertory of career development competencies such as the ability to:

1. Describe the process of career development;
2. Identify the developmental tasks that are related to vocational choice and to occupational entry and adjustment;
3. Describe typical career patterns;
4. Plan instructional activities which facilitate career development;
5. Explain how the classroom, the job laboratory, and the youth organization should contribute to career development.

The Career Development Process

There is a rapidly growing body of literature on career development which begins with the research studies of Donald E. Super in the 1950s (4). Before that time, developmental psychologists wrote about the stages in an individual's vocational growth and about career patterns. Careers were viewed largely in terms of patterns of jobs which individuals held during their working life. In contrast with these early interests, current efforts in career education are focused on helping individuals find satisfying occupational roles and on preparing them for a productive work life. Whereas the pioneers in educational personnel work were concerned mostly with the economic aspects of vocational guidance (placing round pegs in round holes and square pegs in square holes so to speak), today's concerns revolve around the task of helping an individual make plans and decisions which lead to self-fulfillment and satisfaction with his work.

The modern concept of the career development process will be described in the pages that follow, starting with a definition of career development, then career patterns, life stages, and finally the developmental tasks that individuals perform during their career development.

DEFINITION OF THE CAREER DEVELOPMENT PROCESS

Career development is self-development viewed in relation with orientation, choice, entry and progress in educational and vocational pursuits. It is a developmental process which begins in infancy and continues through retirement. It includes all of the behaviors that are associated (1) with becoming aware of one's own interests, aptitudes and needs, (2) with choosing and preparing for an occupation, (3) with entering employment and adjusting to a job and (4) with changing jobs.

This definition has numerous implications for teacher-coordinators, several of which are presented here. It helps to place vocational education in perspective as a facilitator and guide in the total career development process because it includes experiences other than those which usually are thought of as being vocational. Also, it allows for precursors to vocational training in the elementary school and middle school and for continuing education at the adult level. If this definition is accepted, a vocational educator should be concerned with the total career education program and he should identify his unique role as a teacher, teacher-coordinator and so on, and then cooperate with guidance personnel and others involved in education for careers.

Further, the definition mandates implicitly that it is the vocational educator's responsibility to focus on the individual interests, aptitudes, and needs of learners (1) when they choose an occupation, (2) when they enter employment in that occupation or occupational field, and (3) during the adjustment period that follows entering into employment. Conscientious teacher-coordinators are vitally concerned about all of these facets of career development, particularly with assisting student-trainees in making adjustments to their jobs.

The fourth dimension of the definition, relating to behaviors associated with changing jobs, infers that cooperative vocational education teacher-coordinators have a responsibility to prepare students for being flexible enough to change jobs and to know how to make job changes. This proposition will be discussed later.

CAREER PATTERNS

A working knowledge of career patterns has a definite place in a teacher-coordinator's repertory of career development competencies. This type of knowledge enables him to understand better the subgroup structure and interpersonal relationships in the work environment of potential or existing training stations—an essential competency in placing and counseling student-trainees. Generally, an acquaintanceship with career patterns should also become a part of the students' career awareness, the main reason being that they associate with fellow workers who follow, unknowingly, various work patterns and whose work motivation may be a reflection of their satisfaction or dissatisfaction with their present employment. Identification of other uses for a command of the career pattern concept will be discussed later in this section.

How Individual Career Patterns Evolve. There are four commonly recognized career patterns which are identified as (1) conventional, (2) stable, (3) unstable, and (4) multiple-trial. In addition, there are women who combine homemaking and working outside the home (a double-track), and some who interrupt their normal career employment to raise a family and then return to their original career occupations (interrupted pattern).

One career pattern is not necessarily superior to another. Preferences for career patterns rest with the personality and aspirations of an individual. The circumstances under which a person chooses or gravitates toward one pattern or another vary widely (See table 4-1).

TABLE 4-1

CAREER PATTERNS

Conventional	School or College	Job 1	Job 2	Job 3	Job 4	Stable Occupation or Career	
Stable	School or College	Stable Occupation or Career					
Unstable	School or College	Job 1	Stable Occupation or Career	Job 2 or School	Stable Occupation or Career	Job 3	
Multiple-Trial	School or College	Job 1	Job 2	Job 3	Job 4	Job 5	No Stable Occupation
Double-Track (Women)	School or College	Job 1	Stable Career + Homemaking				
Interrupted (Women)	School or College	Job 1	Stable Occupation or Career	Homemaking	Stable Occupation or Career		

Conventional Career Pattern. The conventional pattern is typical of a large number of high school graduates and dropouts. It is one in which an individual may have three or four trial jobs prior to his becoming established in an occupation or career. After age twenty-five, most individuals tend to stabilize in an occupational field even though they may change jobs and move vertically in their careers.

Many jobs today require extensive training and special preparation, and changing from one field to another is costly to the individual and to society. Even though we must anticipate that individuals will make a number of changes during their working lives, they can be taught to be more effective in making vocational decisions and plans which lead to receiving satisfactions from their work and being satisfactory in their job performance. Effective vocational decisions would reduce the amount of unnecessary floundering and expedite self-fulfillment.

Stable Career Pattern. A stable career pattern is one in which an individual enters a field of work directly from school or college and continues in that type of work throughout most of his working life. This is likely to happen to persons who pursue professional careers; however, it is not uncommon for highly trained individuals to find that the careers they spent several years preparing for are not as gratifying as they had expected. This situation frequently occurs when some other person has unduly influenced an individual's occupational choice, or when vocational plans were made without adequate consideration of the individual's needs and the characteristics of the occupation.

Unstable Career Pattern. A person who experiences a series of career changes after several attempts to stabilize may be characterized as having an unstable career pattern. This is not necessarily bad, unless the changes from one field to another fail to bring satisfaction and a sense of progress. Those individuals who thought they were established in their lifetime work and are forced to leave due to changes in occupations may seem to have unstable career patterns, but this pattern has become quite common with the rapid changes in occupations and employment opportunities. The vocational education program must prepare future workers for a changing world of work, and it must provide continuing education to retrain individuals for emerging occupations.

Multiple-Trial Pattern. A fourth career pattern is one in which the individual makes frequent changes from one type of work to another. This sequence of horizontal changes in entry level jobs is referred to as a multiple-trial career pattern. In recent years, it has become more difficult to subsist on this type of work because most jobs that pay well require special preparation. Few young people seem to realize that in order to earn a family-supporting income, or even to support themselves adequately, they will need to choose an occupational field and acquire the specialized skills and knowledge required for the occupation.

Career Patterns for Women. Women may have career patterns which fall into one of the four categories just described, but they may also have double-track or interrupted career patterns. It is reasonably safe to assume that in the future more girls will have career patterns similar to those of males, or career patterns which combine homemaking with careers outside of the home. Girls should be made aware of the high probability that they will have careers in addition to being homemakers, and that they will need vocational preparation to qualify for satisfying jobs. Those who leave their careers to raise a family, and later seek to re-enter the work world may anticipate retraining and updating of their job skills. Boys also need to be apprised of these changing roles of women and how the roles of men and their careers are affected by the increasing number of women pursuing lifetime careers.

Applications of Career Pattern Knowledge. In addition to using knowledge of career patterns for guiding and counseling students concerning career decisions mentioned in the introduction to this discussion, there

Facilitating Career Development

are other important applications of this competency area in cooperative vocational education. For example, a knowledge of career patterns is very useful in curriculum planning and evaluation. An examination of the career patterns of workers in the industry served and an analysis of the career patterns of workers in the occupations for which training is being offered should provide obvious clues for general and individual instruction. Moreover, such instruction is essential to accurate measurement of group and/or individual job progress.

A good knowledge of career patterns enables a teacher-coordinator to understand better the need for career guidance and for flexibility in occupational education. When he knows the dynamics of career patterns in the work force both nationally and locally he becomes more tolerant of some worker behaviors and more sensitive to the need for flexibility in occupational training. For example, usually he is more inclined to stress the process of learning a job as an occupational competency which has transferability rather than being satisfied with teaching student-trainees how to learn a single job.

LIFE STAGES IN CAREER DEVELOPMENT

A competent teacher-coordinator must understand the stages of an individual's career development, referred to as life stages, in order to provide good guidance and to be able to select appropriate learning experiences for the developmental stages of his students, both collectively and individually.

One way of looking at the career development process is to consider the life stages which individuals experience as they progress from early childhood through their working lives. As shown in table 4-2, the period from birth through the elementary years is seen as a stage of *growth* in which aptitudes, interests, values, and skills are formulated, at least tentatively, but subject to modification in later stages. During junior and senior high years, and in the first years of employment, or even while in college, individuals are in an *exploration* stage as they are searching for an acceptable adult role. In the period from the middle twenties until age forty or fifty, most individuals are trying to establish their place in the community and the work world. This is referred to as the *establishment* stage.

The stages of "growth," "exploration," and "establishment" are followed by a stage of *maintenance* in which the major task is one of maintaining one's place in the work world until retirement. The final stage of work life, *decline*, is one in which individuals relinquish their work roles and live out their lives in less demanding forms of work activity. Even though there are many individuals whose development will deviate from the stages described, it is reasonable to assume that students enrolled in cooperative vocational education are primarily in the exploration stage. Career exploration during the period that students participate in cooperative vocational education is facilitated by providing them with a wide variety of experiences and directing their observations to significant characteristics of the occupations represented by workers in the training agency.

TABLE 4-2

Life Stages

Stages	Age Range	Characteristics
Growth	0-14	Orientation and awareness of world of work Identification with workers Fantasy about careers Development of aptitudes, interests, and skills
Exploration	15-25	Development of a self-concept Part-time employment Testing aptitudes, interests and skills Trial work period, floundering Attempt to implement a self-concept
Establishment	25-45	Stabilization within an occupational field Drive for achievement and advancement Self-concept modified and implemented Establishment of a home, family, and community role
Maintenance	45-65	Preservation of a self-concept Sense of self-fulfillment for some and frustration for others Concern for security Tapering off of creative productivity
Decline	65-Beyond	Slowing down Seeking less demanding activity Development of new roles and means of self-fulfillment Retirement

DEVELOPMENTAL TASKS

Competent teacher-coordinators are sensitive to each student's level of career development, and they plan individual learning experiences that help their students progress to higher levels of vocational maturity.

In recent years most educators have become more aware and appreciative of the need for facilitating the career development process. They know that the casual or unplanned encounters of youngsters with work and the work ethic often lead to misconceptions about work values and attitudes which at a later date interfere with their self-fulfillment. They are beginning to realize the importance of planned career development experiences beginning as early as pre-school years and continuing throughout one's work life. Teacher-coordinators are particularly cognizant of the student's need for a series of well-planned career development experiences prior to entry into a vocational education curriculum. They claim that the senior high school level is frequently too late for them to provide much help in correcting deeply entrenched detrimental work attitudes and habits, and the career exploration experiences in broad occupational clusters could do a great deal to improve the motivation of students who pursue cooperative vocational education.

A Career Development Task List. Able educational and occupational psychologists have been studying vocational behavior for several decades. The work of Piaget (6), Havighurst (2), Super (5), and others contributed to the identification of a series of career-related developmental tasks in a study by Antholz (1) as part of a curriculum development project at the University of Minnesota (7). In this study, career development tasks were identified and associated with educational grade levels for curriculum planning purposes. The list derived from this study is given in table 4-3. This list of developmental tasks has helped teacher-coordinators to clarify the meaning of career development and to identify their role in a K-12 career education program. Unfortunately, it does not extend beyond the senior high school level.

The facts that individuals progress in their career development at different rates and that there is considerable overlapping from one stage of development to the next are well recognized, nevertheless the list is a suitable guide for counselors and teacher-coordinators in curriculum planning and in general program operation. If students enter cooperative vocational education with a background of instruction in the tasks listed in the chart under levels one, two, and three, the teacher-coordinator's role in facilitating career development should be much easier. Students entering the program will have made at least a tentative choice of an occupation they want to learn, and they will have acquired an accurate self-concept as well as some background information about careers in their occupational field. Teacher-coordinators should recognize the tentative career choices of students and provide opportunities for student-trainees to continue exploring, reality-testing, and revising their goals.

Level Four Developmental Tasks. Cooperative vocational education provides nearly ideal situations for the students to interact with workers and work environments and to test out their perceived interests, apti-

TABLE 4-3

DEVELOPMENTAL TASKS RELATED TO CAREERS (1) (7)

Level 1—Primary Grades	Level 2—Intermediate Grades	Level 3—Junior High	Level 4—Senior High
Becoming aware of self-characteristics	Developing a positive self-concept	Clarifying one's self-concept	Reality-testing of a self-concept
Acquiring a sense of agency (control) over one's own destiny	Acquiring the discipline of work	Assuming responsibility for vocational planning	Formulating ideas about preferred life styles
Identifying with workers	Valuing work as a personal goal	Formulating career hypotheses (tentative goal setting)	Revising career hypotheses
Acquiring knowledge about workers	Increasing knowledge about workers	Acquiring knowledge of occupations and work settings	Considering educational and vocational paths
Acquiring interpersonal skills	Increasing interpersonal skills	Acquiring knowledge of educational and vocational resources	Learning to make decisions
Relating and revealing one's self to others	Increasing willingness to reveal one's true self to others	Becoming aware of the decision-making process	Working toward tentative goals and commitments
Acquiring respect for other people and the work they do	Valuing human dignity	Acquiring a sense of independence and self-control	Acquiring vocational skills, knowledge, and attitudes

tudes and values. The teacher-coordinator works with training sponsors and with individual students in arranging appropriate experiences which bring out the more subtle aspects of an occupation or a work setting. Students come to know themselves through planned interaction with others and the feedback received during that interaction. The student-trainee's on-the-job encounters with people, ideas, objects, and activities should be followed up with discussion, analysis, and evaluation of what the student experiences. Interpretations of experiences are as important in career development as the actual experiences themselves. The teacher-coordinator must help his students analyze and interpret the meaning of their experiences for further career planning and occupational preparation. (See Level 4-Senior High, table 4-3.)

Outcomes of Career Education

In order to plan experiences that will facilitate career development, the teacher-coordinator needs to identify the kinds of performance outcomes which will indicate that this development is taking place. There are a number of curriculum models in which outcomes of career education have been identified and described. Due to the developmental nature of career behavior and the value-attitude kinds of outcomes that are associated with it, stated objectives usually focus more on the process of career planning and decision making than on the actual plans and decisions each student makes.

The Comprehensive Career Education Model developed at the Center for Vocational and Technical Education, The Ohio State University (3), contains elements and outcomes of career education K-14 as shown in table 4-4.

The Career Development Curriculum (CDC) projects at the University of Minnesota (7) have emphasized the self or human-development aspects in career education. Career development is viewed as a process in which students clarify values and meanings about themselves through planned encounters with occupational dilemmas and expectations of industrialized society. Outcomes are stated in terms of tasks or dimensions of vocational behavior associated with choosing, entering, adjusting, and progressing in one's career.

TABLE 4-4

Elements	Leading to	Outcomes
Career Awareness	K 1 2 3 4 5 6 7 8 9 10 11 12 13 14	Career Identity
Self-Awareness		Self-Identity
Decision-making Skills		Career Decisions
Appreciation and Attitudes		Self and Social Fulfillment
Economic Awareness		Economic Understandings
Skill Awareness and Beginner's Competence		Employment Skills
Employability Skills		Career Placement
Educational Awareness		Educational Identity

Dimensions of Career Development. The student will:

1. *Self-Concept Dimension.* Identify his interests, abilities, values, needs, and other self characteristics as they relate to occupational roles.
2. *Occupational Awareness Dimension.* Explore occupational areas and describe opportunities, potential satisfactions, required roles of workers, and related dimensions.
3. *Psychological Meaning of Work Dimension.* Describe the psychological meaning of work and its value in the human experience.
4. *Organizational Structure Dimension.* Describe modern work structure and its organizational milieu.
5. *Social Contribution of Work Dimension.* Tell how the individual's role in work is tied to the well-being of the community.
6. *Planfulness Dimension.* Demonstrate planfulness in striving to achieve occupational goals and objectives.
7. *Work Ethic Dimension.* Demonstrate through his work-relevant behavior that he is acquiring a concept of self as a productive person in a work-centered society.
8. *Education-Work Relationships Dimension.* Describe the relationship which exists between basic skills and the jobs he can reasonably aspire to in adult life.
9. *Occupational Preparation Dimension.* Demonstrate possession of a reasonable degree of basic skills, knowledge, and behavioral characteristics associated with work of some type or an occupational area.
10. *Employability Dimension.* Demonstrate through his work-relevant behavior an ability to learn, adjust to, and advance in his chosen occupation.

Facilitating Career Development

Students seeking cooperative vocational education admission are frequently young people who feel a need to be employed. The need to be employed may be caused by a desire for spending money, a disenchantment with the traditional school environment, or a desire for independence and a sense of maturity. Whether the need to be employed is real or imagined, the young person who wants a job is likely to view cooperative vocational education as a means of getting a job and earning some money while going to school.

Many students apply for admission to a program without knowing very much about the occupations for which the training is given or about their own chances of being satisfied and successful in different occupational fields. One of the goals of career education and a part of the career development process is learning to make vocational and educational decisions and plans that will lead to satisfying and successful careers.

CHOOSING AN OCCUPATION TO STUDY

The student must have an interest in the career field for which the training is offered, however tentative that interest may be, in order to channel his efforts toward learning the technical information and the related occupational skills. When the student has a motivation that goes beyond just being employed, the classroom instruction becomes more meaningful, and the training given by the participating employer is more thorough and extensive.

In the near future a comprehensive career education curriculum, from kindergarten on, shall have prepared high school students to select occupations that they would want to explore in depth. However, if students have not had adequate opportunities to explore careers and their own interests prior to enrolling in a cooperative program, some form of intensive guidance and career exploration must be provided to help the students select occupations or career fields that they want to study. The first step in facilitating career development in cooperative vocational education is to help students identify occupational areas or career clusters in which they are likely to find satisfaction and be able to perform satisfactorily, and which afford them a reasonably good chance of being employed. The benefits of cooperative education are maximized when the instruction and training are related to the interests and goals of the students and the availability of opportunities for employment.

EXPLORING CAREERS IN A PRE-EMPLOYMENT CLASS

Students who participate in a pre-employment class before entering a cooperative training program can explore many different occupational opportunities before selecting an area for more intensive training. Directed observations, field interviews, and other activities and projects which bring students into contact with different workers, work settings, and types of work activity help students to clarify their interests and goals. Then, when they enter a cooperative program, the students are better prepared to select the occupational areas that they want to study. The training sponsor or the cooperating employer is more enthusiastic and committed to training when the student-trainee shows sincere interest in the occupational field. Even though the student's career goal is

Facilitating Career Development

tentative, it is very important that he has selected an area which is of interest to him prior to placement in a cooperative training situation.

EXPLORING CAREERS WHILE PARTICIPATING IN COOPERATIVE VOCATIONAL EDUCATION

Once the student is enrolled in a cooperative vocational education program, the classroom instruction and the related on-the-job training should help him to further clarify his own occupational interests, abilities, and needs and to comprehend his chances for satisfaction and success in the career field being studied. Career exploration and interest clarification must be planned experiences in order to achieve the desired outcomes. Planned experiences focus the student's attention on facets of a career that he would never consider until he had spent many years in that career field. By helping the student gain a more comprehensive and accurate perspective of the career field in which he is receiving training, the teacher can stimulate the desire to learn the required knowledge and skills, or provide the student with the information he needs to change his goals and redirect his learning efforts.

On-the-Job Experiences. Career exploration experiences should be included in the on-the-job training plan. Even though most of their training and experiences are in specific jobs or areas within their places of employment, it is usually possible to arrange for students to observe or interview workers employed in other job areas. In many job placement situations the students can be rotated from one job or department to another. Whether or not the student has the opportunity to experience productive work in all facets of a business or industry, he should be aware of the various alternatives that will be available to him at a later date. Through directed observation and his contacts with workers he should learn about the requirements for satisfactory job performance, the satisfactions workers get from their jobs, the life styles and career patterns of individuals in different jobs, the physical and psychological stresses of different jobs, and other factors that are important in career planning.

Periodic evaluations and reviews of progress on the job by the training sponsors provide students with feedback and knowledge about their potentials for success and advancement. Students are motivated when achievement and good performance are recognized. Suggestions for improvement can be attended to before problems become serious enough to call for dismissal or to cause the student to abandon his career goals in that occupation. Reinforcement, recognition, and constructive criticism are important in helping students discover where they may fit within an occupational field.

Classroom Experiences. Career development of students in cooperative vocational education is facilitated by planned experiences in the classroom which cause students to assess their own interests, abilities, and other career related characteristics. These experiences may include interest and needs inventories and measures of aptitude and achievement combined with discussion and interpretation of the meaning of tests and their congruence with how students see themselves. Through discussions and shared perceptions by classmates, the students clarify their own values and needs. Students learn about occupations and about themselves from sharing their experiences with one another.

Student-trainees frequently do not have the opportunity to work in all departments or tasks at their cooperative training stations. Experience and reality-testing in the performance of some occupational tasks should be provided in the classroom. Students can experience a managerial role by having responsibility for managing or coordinating a class project. Youth organization activities and projects are valuable means of providing occupationally related experiences and allowing students to try out new roles. When the classroom is furnished with the equipment and materials that are used in the occupations being studied, students can get some feeling about their own interests and skills in working with the equipment and materials. These experiences supplement what they learn on the job, or serve as stimuli for students to seek further practice and performance in the on-the-job setting.

Resource speakers who represent various occupations or career patterns may be utilized in the classroom to provide students with additional role models and occupational information. Speakers must be carefully selected and adequately oriented for the assignment of giving students relevant career information. It is usually better to select speakers who are engaged in the occupation to which students can reasonably aspire, and who can talk about their own work and career patterns. Students should be involved in selecting the resource speakers and in formulating questions that are of interest to them in their search for role models and career goals.

Individual Counseling Experiences. Each individual's career development is a personal thing and likely to be quite unique for each one even though groups of students tend to be in the same general stages of career development. The uniqueness of individual interests, abilities, needs, and other background factors calls for individual guidance and assistance in career exploration and planning. The teacher-coordinator must provide individual counseling for students to discuss their on-the-job experiences and to help them interpret the meanings of these experiences. Sometimes students encounter adverse conditions on the job, experience failure; or, on the other hand, see only the positive factors in the jobs they have. Through individual counseling, the teacher-coordinator helps the students put their experiences in the right perspective, avoiding over-generalizations and weighing factors that are important in decision making and career planning. This individual counseling is more a matter of listening to the student verbalize about his experiences and feelings, and the teacher-coordinator asking questions that cause the student to think about alternative ways of interpreting his experiences, than it is giving the student advice. Eventually, the student learns to ask the questions himself and to discern what is relevant for his own plans and progress.

Vocational Student Organization Experiences. Career development can be enriched greatly through the student-planned activities of a vocational student organization, such as FFA, VICA, and DECA. As students experience leadership roles and participate in group activities they discover their individual capabilities, interests, and values. The vocational student organizations develop personal and professional skills that help them to perform more effectively as leaders and as group members working toward common goals.

The use of resource speakers at student-planned meetings, field trips, and state and national conferences bring student members into contact with representatives from business and industry, thus providing more information on career opportunities and exposure to many outstanding role models. Other activities, such as sales projects and community service programs, supplement the learning that takes place on the job and in the classroom. Self-direction and the ability to organize group efforts are developed in the student-centered vocational organization.

Concluding Statement

The teacher-coordinator's role in the career development of students is to facilitate the exploration of adult working roles through planned experiences and encounters with realities of the world of work. In addition to having the skills needed to enter, adjust to, and advance in a recognized occupation, students who have completed a cooperative vocational education program should know more about themselves, about the career options available to them, and how to reach their expectations. This is not to suggest that they should have necessarily narrowed their choices, but that they should become more skillful and efficient in making career plans and decisions that lead to self-fullfillment and satisfaction.

REFERENCES

1. Antholz, Mary B. "Conceptualization of a Model Career Development Program, K-12." Master's paper, University of Minnesota, 1972.
2. Havighurst, Robert. *Human Development and Education.* New York: Longmans, Green, 1953.
3. Miller, Aaron J. "The Emerging School-Based Comprehensive Career Education Model." A paper presented at the National Conference on Career Education for Deans of Colleges of Education. Columbus, Ohio, April 24, 1972.
4. Super, Donald E. *Career Development: Self-Concept Theory.* New York: College Entrance Examination Board, 1963.
5. Super, Donald, et al. *Vocational Development, A Framework for Research.* New York: Teachers College, Columbia University, 1957, 142pp.
6. Sylvester, Robert. "Piaget: His Ideas Are Changing Our Schools." *The Instructor* 78 (February 1969): 59.
7. Tennyson, W. Wes, L. Sunny Hansen, and Mary K. Klaurens. *Teacher Education for Career Education.* Minneapolis: University of Minnesota, 1973, 105pp. (Mimeograph)

ADDITIONAL REFERENCES

Gibson, Robert. *Career Development in the Elementary School.* Columbus: Charles E. Merrill, 1972, 81pp.

Goldhammer, Keith, and Robert E. Taylor. *Career Education—Perspective and Promise.* Columbus: Charles E. Merrill, 1972, 296 pp.

Hoyt, Kenneth, Rupert Evans, Edward F. Mackin, and Garth L. Mangum. *Career Education—What It Is and How to Do It.* Salt Lake City: Olympus, 1972, 190 pp.

Magisos, Joel H., ed. *Career Education.* Washington, D.C.: American Vocational Association, 1974, 397 pp.

SUGGESTED ACTIVITIES

1. Visit a school in which there has been a concerted effort to infuse career education into the total curriculum. Interview one or two teachers to find out what they are doing in their classrooms to facilitate career development.

Facilitating Career Development

2. Prepare a graphic illustration or a narrative description of your own career development showing the significant factors, experiences, and decisions that led up to your present status and goals.

3. Design a learning activity for three of the dimensions of career development given in chapter 4, utilizing a classroom activity for one, an on-the-job experience for another, and a youth organization activity for the third.

4. Prepare an explanation of how a teacher-coordinator uses his knowledge of career patterns while performing his tasks as a teacher-coordinator. Do the same for life stages. Use illustrative situations to make your points.

5. Make a list of the uses to a teacher-coordinator of a working knowledge of career development when operating a cooperative vocational education program.

Chapter 5   TEACHING WORK-ADJUSTMENT COMPETENCIES

The primary purpose of cooperative vocational education is to help individuals learn the competencies needed in making *satisfying* and *satisfactory* work adjustments. This is its contribution to the individual's career development. Hopefully, those who complete the training will not only be satisfactory to their employers but will receive adequate satisfactions from their work. In order to achieve work adjustments, individuals must have the skills, knowledge, and attitudes (competencies) that are required to perform the work well; and the work they do must provide the incentives and rewards which will satisfy their individual needs.

Student-trainees, like other young people beginning their work lives, are likely to hold a number of jobs during their careers. Changes in positions, or occupations brought about by promotions, transfers, voluntary job terminations or other shifts in job assignments are efforts on the part of employers and employees to make more satisfactory work adjustments. Helping student-trainees make a satisfactory and satisfying adjustment in their initial cooperative vocational education positions will, when properly guided, prepare them to make future changes and adjustments more easily. Learning how to adjust to a new type of work in a new job setting among co-workers and supervisors whom he does

Teaching Work-Adjustment Competencies

not know is an important competency for a young worker to possess, particularly during this period of high employment mobility.

This chapter (1) describes the relevance of work adjustment to career development and to cooperative vocational education, (2) explains a viable theory of work adjustment, (3) discusses the measurement of the components of work adjustment, and (4) provides the teacher-coordinator with some guidelines for assisting students in making satisfactory and satisfying transitions from school to work.

A careful study of this chapter should help the prospective teacher-coordinator to:

1. Describe the relevance of work adjustment to career development and cooperative vocational education;
2. Explain the theory of work adjustment in terms of job satisfaction and satisfactory job performance;
3. Identify the factors and dimensions of work that are related to work adjustment;
4. Explain why satisfactory job performance is a function of matching individual abilities with the ability requirements of the jobs;
5. Explain why job satisfaction is a function of matching individual needs with jobs that provide the corresponding reinforcers;
6. Describe techniques the teacher-coordinator employs to aid students in work adjustment;
7. Explain the interaction between job satisfaction and satisfactory job performance;
8. Identify some work adjustment problems that student-trainees encounter and describe how the teacher-coordinator assists student-trainees in overcoming these problems.

Current Interest in Work Adjustment

The thrust in vocational education during the second half of this century has shifted from one of primarily satisfying the needs of the employers to one of satisfying the needs of both employers and workers. Cooperative vocational education has contributed to this change in emphasis. When school and work were combined in cooperative vocational education it gradually became apparent that technical skills and knowledge alone were not adequate and that more attention should be given to the worker's needs and the satisfactions he seeks from his work. Placement in a training agency position which offers the rewards or satisfactions sought by the student-trainee is also necessary to ensure proper vocational growth. This precept augments the concern of educators for curricula and instruction tailored to the individual needs of learners and the foundation of their career-related values.

Educators are not the only parties interested in the worker side of the productivity coin. Vocational psychologists, industrial relations consultants, and employers have shown great interest in the work adjustment of employees. Obviously, a well-adjusted worker is more productive and contented than is one who is poorly adjusted.

Knowledge about work adjustment has increased greatly during recent years. Vocational psychologists (1) have formulated a theory of work adjustment and developed test instruments which promise to be of great value in helping teacher-coordinators improve their vocational guidance, job placement, and instructional activities.

The Relevance of Work Adjustment

Where does work adjustment fit into the vocational education program, and how does it relate to cooperative vocational education? These are pertinent questions in the study of coordination principles and practices. To answer them adequately, the aim and scope of work adjustment must be understood.

DEFINITION OF WORK ADJUSTMENT

In a broad sense, the work adjustment of an individual is a condition in which he is in harmony with his entire work-related world. It encompasses his attunement with the entire socioeconomic culture in which he operates. Work adjustment has several facets which include:

1. The worker's concept of the role of work in our socioeconomic system;
2. His ability to perform satisfactorily in his occupation and on his job;
3. The satisfaction which he derives from his work;
4. His adaptation to the life style and personal-social roles that his work allows him to perform—at home, in the community, and among his peers.

In short, a person doesn't achieve complete work adjustment at a given point in time unless he values the idea of working, he is satisfactory to his employer, he is well satisfied with working for his employer, and he is reasonably content with his daily life outside of work.

The broad definition above seems to fit all current types of educational programs dealing with work, and it appears to be a satisfactory goal for a total program of education for work. Practitioners who operate cooperative vocational education units as the capstone experience in occupational preparation will tend to place more emphasis on the job satisfactoriness and job satisfaction (facets two and three) on the assumption that students enrolled in such programs have already developed positive attitudes toward work and the ability to adapt to the life style and personal-social roles their work allows them to perform. On the other hand, there are many new work-experience-type programs which have as their primary focus the improvement of work attitudes and personal-social skills that workers need to function effectively in their daily living. Although it may always be necessary to give some attention to the worker's concept of the role of work in our socioeconomic system and to the personal-social competencies, hopefully, career awareness and orientation experiences at the early grade levels will minimize this task in the future.

RELATIONSHIP TO CAREER EDUCATION

Work adjustment may be considered to be an element of career development. Since work adjustment is not a discrete block of the career education dimensions, and some of the dimensions are present in more than one aspect of work adjustment, the relationship can be explained best in chart form (see table 5-1).

Adjustment to the Socioeconomic System. Since work adjustment includes the possession of certain attitudes and values concerning work in our socioeconomic system, education for work adjustment should begin very early in the curriculum of the school system. As part of the child's early "adjustment" to the socioeconomic system in his orientation to the world of work, the psychological meaning of work, the social contribution of work, and the work ethic are introduced. (See table 5-1 and chapter 4.) The clarification of such values and the development of attitudes toward work continue as long as necessary—including the cooperative education period and beyond.

Satisfactory Work Performance. Satisfactory work performance depends in large measure on the worker's command of the basic or fundamental skills and the social skills which are very important elements of career education. In a career education curriculum, pupils, beginning in kindergarten and continuing throughout their educational program,

TABLE 5-1

Relationships Of Aspects Of Work Adjustment To Dimensions Of Career Education

Aspects of Work Adjustment	Dimension of Career Education
1. Adjustment to the Socioeconomic System	Social Contribution of Work Psychological Meaning of Work Work Ethic
2. Satisfactory Work Performance	Occupational Preparation Employability Education-Work Relationships
3. Job Satisfaction	Occupational Awareness Self-Concept Organizational Structure Planning
4. Personal-Social Adjustment	Self-Concept Work Ethic Planning

learn basic skills which are essential for employability and are made aware of the relationship of education to their future roles as workers. When their career interests crystallize and their need to be employed becomes imminent, the career education curriculum provides opportunities to develop skills and knowledges that may be associated with specific occupations or occupational fields.

Job Satisfaction. Similarly, it is important that individuals begin at an early age to perceive work as a source of satisfaction and realize that people choose occupations in which they are likely to be satisfied. Since the job satisfaction aspect of work adjustment largely depends on the suitable selection of an occupation, the dimensions of career education that focus on self-concept, occupational awareness, the organizational structure of work, and on planning are very important. At the junior high school level pupils clarify and refine self-concepts, occupational images, and vocational plans through exploratory experiences as a part of the career education curriculum.

Personal Social Adjustment. Career education also encompasses the aspect of work adjustment that depends on the worker's ability to adapt to the life style and personal-social roles his work requires or allows him to engage in. In their orientation to the world of work during the elementary grades and exploration of careers during the junior high years, students examine work and occupations in terms of opportunities to implement a self-concept outside of work, to contribute to the well-being of the community through one's work, and to exercise control over one's destiny through making wise choices and plans. The role of workers as family members, citizens in the community, and members of social groups, is considered part of career education because one's career and personal-social life are highly interdependent.

Obviously, work adjustment is not the exclusive responsibility of cooperative vocational education or even of vocational education, but is to a high degree dependent on general education, and its roots are found in institutions serving the early school years. Work adjustment is one of the primary goals of career education and an important criterion in its assessment.

RELATIONSHIP TO COOPERATIVE VOCATIONAL EDUCATION

If work adjustment is an important criterion in the assessment of career education and it is also the primary purpose of cooperative vocational education, cooperative vocational education is a very critical element in career education. This being the case, what are the work adjustment objectives of cooperative vocational education?

Adjustment to the Socioeconomic System. The degree to which a cooperative vocational education unit is involved in helping student-trainees understand and adapt to societal attitudes toward work in our socioeconomic system depends on the vocational maturity of the student-trainees. When a cooperative vocational education unit serves as a capstone of training for a specific occupational cluster or field, generally students will have already developed mature concepts of work and will have realized its importance to their own welfare and to the socioeconomic system. On the other hand, program units serving students who are somewhat alienated by our educational and economic system may have as their primary purpose the cultivation of appropriate work attitudes and an improved understanding of our economic system.

Satisfactory Work Performance. Development of the skills, knowledge, and attitudes to perform satisfactorily in the student-trainee's occupation is a criterion of most *capstone* twelfth-grade and post-secondary cooperative vocational education programs. Such program units vary in their dependence on job experiences for the student's learning specialized technical skills. Achieving work adjustment without possessing specialized technical competencies is difficult, except in very low-level skill positions.

Job Satisfaction. The third aspect of work adjustment is the forte of cooperative vocational education. Proper coordination of classroom, job, community and youth organization learnings can help student-trainees to acquire well-balanced competency patterns which lay the groundwork for continuing work adjustment.

Personal-Social Adjustment. The fourth aspect of work adjustment, which deals with the worker's adaptation to the life style and personal-social roles he plays outside of work, can be served very effectively through cooperative vocational education. The teacher-coordinator can provide guidance and directed experiences which help students in their personal development and clarification of values relating to community participation, use of leisure time, social activities, money management, and other facets of daily living. The co-workers whom students encounter serve as examples, good and bad, for exploring different life styles. They demonstrate how others adapt to roles outside of work. The youth organization activities can greatly enhance the student's participation in community life and provide opportunities for leadership and satisfying social experiences.

PREPARATION FOR FUTURE WORK ADJUSTMENTS

Work adjustment over a period of time calls for the use of skills needed in changing jobs. Work adjustment is a state of being or a human condition, and when job changes are made an individual usually is in the process of trying to achieve work adjustment. Changing jobs requires the use of a number of competencies not practiced in the performance of one's regular work. Among these infrequently used capabilities are those practiced when locating vacancies, applying for a job, learning a job efficiently and effectively, and terminating a position.

Cooperative vocational education makes possible real-life experiences in all these infrequent tasks. Many coordinators have given some attention to the matter of locating vacancies and to terminating employment, and a great deal of attention to applying for a job, but they have expended very little effort in teaching the process of how to learn a job rapidly and effectively.

One can safely say that no other vocational education plan of instruction offers as good an environment for teaching young people how to learn a job as does cooperative vocational education. This instructional plan affords a real-life laboratory for each task involved in the process. It provides an opportunity to learn the process and techniques of learning a job by actually learning one—learning by doing. But one does not learn the process merely by doing it. Thus the learner must participate in the planning of the learning, discover and identify the alternative procedures, and so on. Knowing how to learn a job is an important element in work adjustment and will be discussed in more detail later in chapter 9.

A Theory of Work Adjustment (4)

There are several theories of work adjustment. The theory referred to in this book is taken from the research and writings of a group of vocational psychologists at the University of Minnesota. This theory seems to be particularly relevant to achievement of the desired outcomes in cooperative vocational education. Mastery of the work adjustment theory can be of great value in the organization, operation, and evaluation of cooperative vocational education. It can be a useful conceptual framework for decisions concerning the teacher-coordinator's duties and responsibilities in helping student-trainees "bridge the gap" between school and work life. When this concept is accepted, the effectiveness of a particular cooperative vocational education program may be assessed largely in terms of the work adjustment of present and former student-trainees.

The theory of work adjustment described below deals primarily with aspects two and three in the definition given earlier. It treats job "satisfactoriness" and job "satisfaction," but it does not highlight the worker's attitudes and values concerning the work ethic in our socioeconomic system or the worker's adaptation to the personal-social roles outside of work.

This restricted definition of work adjustment corresponds more closely with the functions of the teacher-coordinator of a cooperative vocational education unit designed to prepare students for a specific occupation or occupational field. It focuses particularly on the adjustment of the individual to his employer, his supervisor, and his co-workers, as well as to demands of the job itself. It also subsumes the individual's understanding of his own attitudes, interests, and temperament. It should not be interpreted as an attempt to make individuals conform to the work situation, but rather to help them obtain satisfaction and achieve success in their work. To some degree the individual adapts to his environment and to some extent he shapes it. The focus is on meeting the needs of individuals and on helping them to become more effective in meeting their own needs. The length of time required to achieve work adjustment varies widely among individuals and according to the work situation.

JOB SATISFACTION AND SATISFACTORINESS

Work adjustment is measured by and inferred from two primary sets of indicators; the "satisfaction" of the individual and the employer's evaluation of the "satisfactoriness" of that individual's work performance. *Satisfaction* includes satisfaction with the job as a whole, overall job satisfaction as well as satisfactions with the several components of the individual's work environment. *Satisfactoriness* is indicated by the individual's productivity and efficiency and by the way he is regarded by his employer, supervisors, co-workers, and clients or customers. An individual who has adjusted to his job is reasonably well satisfied with most aspects of his work. He meets his employer's expectations for productivity and for the quality of his work performance. (See figure 5-1.)

Individual Abilities and Needs. In order to facilitate work adjustment—help individuals achieve "satisfactoriness and satisfaction"—the teacher-coordinator must recognize the unique characteristics of individuals and the variables associated with different jobs. Individuals may be described in terms of having an *ability set*, or skills and knowledge which are observable or can be measured. Each individual possesses some combination or set of abilities which were acquired in the process of growth and education.

Individuals may also be described in terms of a *need set*, or the importance they attach to various kinds of rewards and values which people seek from their work. Individuals vary in their desire for recognition, responsibility, and other "reinforcers" which jobs may offer. Each individual has a unique pattern of vocational needs which may be inferred to some extent from his occupational aspirations. These needs are measurable with the *Minnesota Importance Questionnaire* which is described later in the chapter.

Job Requirements and Reinforcers. Jobs may be described in terms of "ability requirements" and "reinforcer systems." *Ability requirements* refer to the abilities required to perform the work or the job. Satisfactory performance, *satisfactoriness*, depends on the congruence of the individual's ability set with the occupational ability requirements of the job. Jobs may also be described in terms of the *reinforcer system* or rewards that are available when working on the job. Job *satisfaction* for an individual is dependent on the congruence of the occupational reinforcer system in the job with the individual's pattern of job-related needs or need set.

THE INTERDEPENDENCE OF SATISFACTION AND SATISFACTORINESS

Job satisfaction and satisfactoriness are interdependent. When a worker performs the work satisfactorily he is more likely to receive the rewards or reinforcers that are important to his satisfactions. Recognition, added responsibility, higher compensation, advancement, and

FIGURE 5-1

Work Adjustment

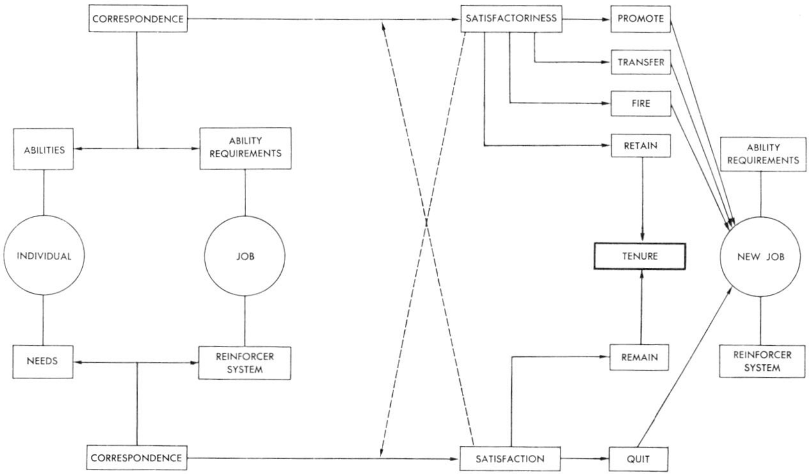

EXPLANATORY NOTES:

1. Jobs can be described in terms of the abilities required to perform the work (e.g., clerical skills, verbal skills, mathematical ability).
2. Individuals can be described in terms of the abilities they possess (e.g., clerical skills, verbal skills, mathematical ability).
3. "Satisfactoriness"—the employer's evaluation of the employee—depends on the correspondence between the employee's abilities and the ability requirements of the job.
4. Jobs can be described in terms of the "reinforcers" or rewards that are available to workers (e.g., responsibility, variety, social service).
5. Individuals can be described in terms of the work-related needs they have, or what they consider to be important in an ideal job (e.g., variety, responsibility, social service).
6. Job "satisfaction" depends on the correspondence between the worker's needs and the "reinforcers" the job provides.
7. "Satisfactoriness" and "satisfaction" are interdependent. If one performs the job satisfactorily, he is likely to receive the reinforcers; if one receives the reinforcers he is likely to be motivated to develop his abilities and perform the job satisfactorily.
8. When there is lack of correspondence between the individual's ability set and the ability requirements of the job, or between the individual's needs and the reinforcer system, he may be expected to move to another job, either as a result of the employer's action or the employee's pursuit of reinforcers.
9. CONCLUSION: In choosing an occupation, one should consider whether or not he has the abilities the occupation requires, and whether or not the occupation offers the reinforcers or rewards that are important to him.

107

many of the other dimensions of satisfaction accrue to the worker when he meets the performance expectations of the employer. Thus, in helping students find satisfaction in their jobs, the teacher-coordinator needs to make certain that students are placed in jobs where they can succeed, and that they acquire the abilities they need to insure continued success and satisfaction.

Conversely, satisfactory performance is more likely to be achieved if the young worker's needs are being met. Rewards and reinforcers have a motivating effect when the student-trainee realizes that satisfactory performance is usually followed by reinforcers such as recognition, added responsibility, esteem from co-workers, and more challenging work. Young workers are not likely to possess the art of prolonged effort without applause and in order to maintain satisfactory performance, the reinforcers must be present.

In the early stages of adjusting to the first jobs, the teacher-coordinator may have to remind employers of the student-trainees' needs for immediate reinforcement and some indication that rewards and reinforcers are available. Even though the initial jobs are not very satisfying, the student-trainees must feel that present efforts to do their jobs well will lead to satisfaction of their needs at some reasonable future time. Without promise of achieving job satisfaction, there is little incentive to develop occupational competencies or to perform their jobs satisfactorily.

Measures of Work Adjustment Factors

An individual's need set and a job's reinforcer system are not easily measured; however, there are instruments which attempt to measure them. Even though the measuring instruments may need further refinement, an awareness of the variables can be helpful to the teacher-coordinator and his student-trainees in making more realistic decisions and plans for occupational choice making, placement, and instruction. Measurement of abilities and needs can be utilized to stimulate the student's thinking about his self-characteristics and the characteristics of various occupations and jobs, as well as being used when trying to match individuals and available jobs and predicting the outcomes. (See Figure 5-2.)

ASSESSMENT OF INDIVIDUAL ABILITIES

Teacher-coordinators are cautioned not to depend entirely on testing as a means of determining occupational choices and placement. Test

FIGURE 5-2

The Theory Of Work Adjustment In Operational Terms (4)

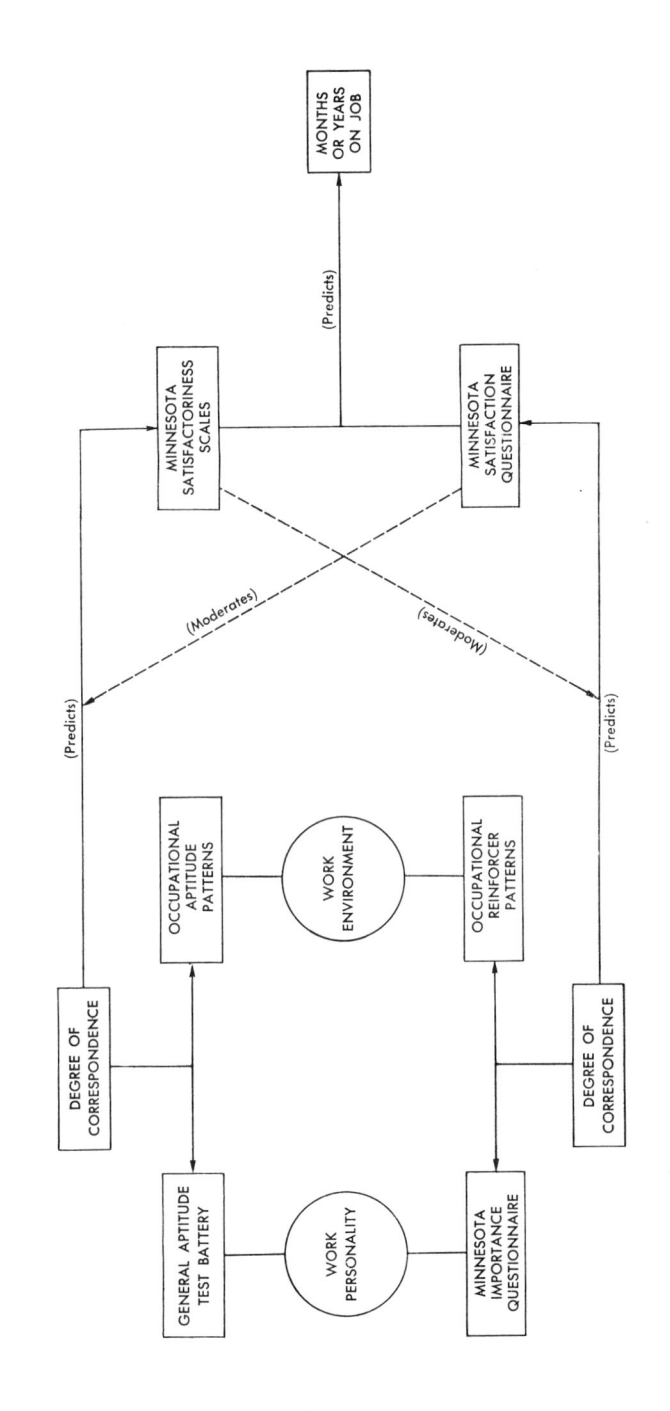

scores are a means of verifying their judgment and helping students to conceptualize their own individual patterns of abilities and needs. Jobs may call for specific abilities for which there are no available tests, yet one might make some common sense inferences about an individual's ability to perform a job based on previous experiences or a simulated trial performance.

General Aptitude Test Battery. The most widely known instrument for measuring vocational abilities is the General Aptitude Test Battery (GATB) administered by the U.S. Employment Service. The GATB consists of eight pencil-and-paper ability tests and four apparatus tests which yield scores on the following dimensions:

1. General intelligence
2. Verbal ability
3. Numerical ability
4. Spatial ability
5. Perceptual ability
6. Clerical ability
7. Eye and hand coordination
8. Manual dexterity
9. Finger dexterity

The Employment Service has standardized scores and profiles of the ability patterns for workers in different occupations so that they can refer applicants to jobs that require a particular combination of the measured abilities. The U.S. Employment Service personnel will assist the school in administering the GATB and will provide data on the ability requirements of different occupations.

Other Ability Tests. In addition to the GATB, there are other ability tests which provide similar measures of individual abilities and have standardized scores for workers in various occupations. Many large organizations or firms have ability tests and standardized scores for the jobs within their organization. Smaller firms can usually give a rough idea of what abilities are needed for the jobs they have. In the absence of measurement tools they rely on the individual's self-estimate of his own abilities and his record of achievement in school and previous jobs.

The most important idea here is for the teacher-coordinator and the student to recognize that "satisfactoriness" is related to the degree of correspondence between the ability requirements of the job and the student-trainee's ability set. This concept should be understood and considered in placement, instruction, guidance, and supervision of on-the-job training.

ASSESSMENT OF INDIVIDUAL NEEDS

Job satisfaction is the result of having one's needs or values reinforced in the job he holds. While it is generally assumed that every individual

Teaching Work-Adjustment Competencies

gets satisfaction from a sense of achievement and from recognition for performance, individuals vary in the degree of importance they attach to various "dimensions" of needs and reinforcers. Jobs and work environments also vary as to the different kinds of reinforcers and rewards available to the people who perform the work.

The Minnesota Importance Questionnaire. One of the most significant contributions of the Minnesota studies of work adjustment has been an instrument to assess individual needs patterns—*The Minnesota Importance Questionnaire*. This assessment yields an individual profile of one's work-related needs on the following dimensions:

1. Ability utilization—the job makes use of the worker's individual abilities.
2. Achievement—the job gives the worker a feeling of accomplishment.
3. Activity—the worker is kept busy all the time.
4. Advancement—the job provides opportunities for advancement.
5. Authority—the worker tells other people what to do.
6. Company policies and practices—the company administers its policies fairly.
7. Compensation—the wages or pay compare well with that of other workers.
8. Co-workers—relations with co-workers are friendly.
9. Creativity—the worker can try out some of his own ideas.
10. Independence—the worker can do the work alone.
11. Moral values—the worker can do the work without feeling it is morally wrong.
12. Recognition—the worker can get recognition for the work he does.
13. Responsibility—the worker can make decisions on his own.
14. Security—the job provides for steady employment.
15. Social service—the worker is doing things for other people.
16. Social status—the worker is regarded as being "somebody" in the community.
17. Supervision: human relations—the supervisor or foreman backs up the employees with top management.
18. Supervision: technical—the supervisor trains the workers well.
19. Variety—the worker has something different to do every day.
20. Working conditions—the job has good working conditions.

An individual's profile of needs is determined by the comparative importance he attaches to each of the above dimensions in considering his ideal job. The *Minnesota Importance Questionnaire* presents the respondent with paired comparisons of these dimensions and when the respondent consistently indicates that certain dimensions are more important than others, the respondent's profile shows what dimensions he has indicated are most important and least important.

Occupational Reinforcer Patterns (1,2,7). An individual's profile of needs, as derived from the *Minnesota Importance Questionnaire,* may be compared with the *Occupational Reinforcer Patterns* of workers in different occupations. (See Sample Profile, figure 5-3.) The Minnesota Industrial Relations Center has standardized profiles for a number of occupations and for occupational clusters. Comparison of an individual's profile with the *Occupational Reinforcer Patterns* yields some indication of the likelihood of the individual's overall satisfaction in different occupations.

A teacher-coordinator may choose not to use the instrument described above; however, some method of assessing students' needs and placing them in jobs where they will be satisfied is important. Student-trainees should be aware of the dimensions of needs that lead to satisfaction, and they should examine themselves and selected occupations within this framework.

ASSESSMENT OF JOB SATISFACTION (3)

The job the student has while he is enrolled in a cooperative vocational education program may offer only a limited or tentative kind of job satisfaction. It is a mistake, however, to overlook potential job satisfaction when placing student-trainees in training jobs because their motivation and continued interest in the occupational field are affected by the reinforcers which they receive on the cooperative job. The teacher-coordinator should place student-trainees in jobs that seem to be matched to the student-trainees' needs as well as to their abilities, and then maintain a continuous check on job satisfaction, as well as job performance and progress.

How Tests Are Used. Job satisfaction can be measured by instruments, such as the *Minnesota Satisfaction Questionnaire.* In addition the coordinator works closely with individual students so that he knows whether or not the student's needs are met. When a student-trainee completes a questionnaire, or when he is asked to reflect on his evaluation of many aspects of his job, he is learning more about himself and about the process of making realistic career decisions. The results of a job satisfaction assessment provide the teacher-coordinator with cues for further counseling with the student-trainee or conferring with the employer about providing reinforcers on the job. The student may need help in human relations skills in order to elicit satisfying relationships with co-

FIGURE 5-3

SAMPLE PROFILE
OCCUPATIONAL REINFORCER PATTERNS (2)

Salesperson, General (Department Store)
(N = 95 Supervisors)

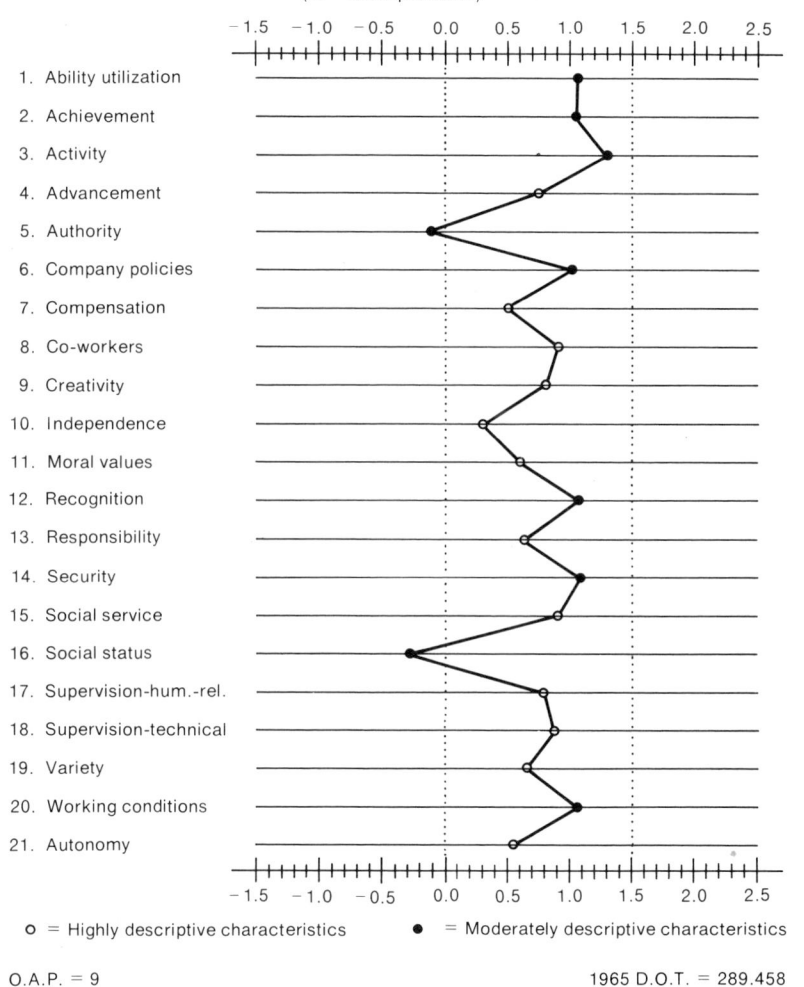

	Scale	Value
1.	Ability utilization	● ~1.0
2.	Achievement	● ~1.0
3.	Activity	● ~1.2
4.	Advancement	○ ~0.8
5.	Authority	● ~-0.3
6.	Company policies	● ~1.0
7.	Compensation	○ ~0.4
8.	Co-workers	○ ~0.5
9.	Creativity	● ~0.8
10.	Independence	○ ~0.3
11.	Moral values	○ ~0.5
12.	Recognition	● ~1.0
13.	Responsibility	● ~0.7
14.	Security	● ~1.0
15.	Social service	○ ~0.7
16.	Social status	● ~-0.3
17.	Supervision-hum.-rel.	○ ~0.9
18.	Supervision-technical	● ~0.7
19.	Variety	○ ~0.6
20.	Working conditions	● ~0.8
21.	Autonomy	○ ~0.5

○ = Highly descriptive characteristics   ● = Moderately descriptive characteristics

O.A.P. = 9   1965 D.O.T. = 289.458

Descriptive Characteristics
 Are busy all the time
 Make use of their individual abilities
 Have steady employment
 Receive recognition for the work they do
 Get a feeling of accomplishment
 Have good working conditions
 Have a company which administers its policies fairly
 Do not have the position of somebody in the community
 Do not tell other workers what to do

Occupations with Similar ORPs
 Accounting Clerk, Manufacturing
 Assembler, Small Parts
 Draftsman, Architectural
 Electrical Technician
 Electronics Mechanic
 Marker
 Painter/Paperhanger
 Production Helper (Food)
 Sheet Metal Worker
 Television Service-and-Repairman

workers, or he may need certain technical skills in order to receive recognition and additional responsibilities. The employer or training sponsor may need to be reminded that the student needs certain kinds of reinforcers during this period of transition from school to work; or the outcome may be a decision to place the student in a different job.

Alternative Methods. Another way of providing for job satisfaction is considering the aspects of a job that are potentially satisfying to most individuals and making certain that the satisfiers are present in all the jobs where the students are placed. The job satisfaction studies of Frederick Herzberg (6), and further studies applying the Herzberg theory, suggest that achievement, recognition, responsibility, and the work itself are the most important factors in job satisfaction. According to the Herzberg theory, extrinsic rewards such as compensation and working conditions have to be maintained at an acceptable level; but the intrinsic characteristics of the work itself have a greater effect on the workers' satisfaction and motivation.

This theory can be applied in cooperative vocational education by placing students in jobs that are interesting and challenging and by helping the employers maintain both the extrinsic and intrinsic rewards in the jobs. Even though the initial jobs may not be satisfying to the student-trainees later in their careers, job satisfaction from a cooperative job is important in maintaining the student-trainee's motivation to learn and to perform well enough to qualify for more satisfying jobs. The most commonly sought rewards are more likely to be experienced when the student-trainee has the technical skills and knowledges that are required for advancement or promotion beyond the entry job.

ASSESSMENT OF JOB SATISFACTORINESS

A sense of achievement and success is essential in the student's motivation to learn. Failure or a feeling that the work is not important causes the student-trainee to consider other jobs or occupations to satisfy work-related needs.

Need for Achievement. Lack of correspondence between one's abilities and the ability requirements of a job may be due to the individual's lacking the required abilities or his having more abilities than the job requires. Either condition calls for some adjustment in which the teacher-coordinator takes action.

If the student-trainee lacks the required abilities, the teacher-coordinator provides instruction to develop the necessary skills, knowledge, or attitudes; or he places the student-trainee in a different job for which the ability requirements correspond to the student-trainee's ability set. If the student-trainee has more abilities than the job requires, the teacher-coordinator should work with the employer in arranging for work activity that utilizes the ability set of the student-trainee; or he should consider placing the student-trainee in a different training agency.

Measuring Work Performance. The teacher-coordinator is responsible for checking the student-trainees' job performance and progress. He may employ various types of rating sheets and evaluation forms which are discussed in chapters 10 and 11; and obtain verbal reactions or feedback from the training sponsor during the regular coordination calls to the student's training agency. The Minnesota Studies in Vocational Rehabilitation includes an evaluation instrument called the *Minnesota Satisfactoriness Scales,* which appears in figure 5-4, p. 116.

The *Minnesota Satisfactoriness Scales* (5) is an instrument which is useful in comparing the student-trainee's performance with that of other employees in the same place of employment and with workers in the same job. It answers the question of how satisfactory the student-trainee's performance is from the employer or training sponsor's point-of-view. The teacher-coordinator may want to use this type of rating sheet in combination with another form that lists the specific occupational skills, knowledges, and attitudes for which instruction was given and which were applied or practiced on the job.

Student-trainees should be aware of the criteria that are used in evaluating satisfactory performance. This awareness is accomplished in the follow-up reviews of the employers' evaluations and by having the student-trainees evaluate themselves using the *Minnesota Satisfactoriness Scales,* or the same evaluation forms that the employers complete.

Some Basic Problems in Work Adjustment

Work adjustment begins with placement in the right job, but this does not mean there will not be problems. Even though a teacher-coordinator makes a concerted effort to select good training agencies, to place students in jobs that are compatible with their abilities and needs, to provide needed instruction and guidance and to maintain continuous contact with on-the-job supervisors, student-trainees often encounter problems in adjusting to their work. The majority of the problems can be attributed to the discontinuity caused by the change of status from student to adult worker. The sociocultural environment of work calls for a whole range of new values, attitudes, and behaviors. Adolescents, who enjoyed a certain degree of dependency, irresponsi-

FIGURE 5-4

Minnesota Satisfactoriness Scales

Employee Name _____ No. _____
Rated by _____ Date _____

> Please check the best answer for each question
> Be sure to answer all questions

		not as well	about the same	better
Compared to others in his work group, how well does he . . .				
1.	follow company policies and practices?	☐	☐	☐
2.	accept the direction of his supervisor?	☐	☐	☐
3.	follow standard work rules and procedures?	☐	☐	☐
4.	perform tasks requiring repetitive movements?	☐	☐	☐
5.	accept the responsibility of his job?	☐	☐	☐
6.	adapt to changes in procedures or methods?	☐	☐	☐
7.	respect the authority of his supervisor?	☐	☐	☐
8.	work as a member of a team?	☐	☐	☐
9.	get along with his supervisors?	☐	☐	☐
10.	perform repetitive tasks?	☐	☐	☐
11.	get along with his co-workers?	☐	☐	☐
12.	perform tasks requiring variety and change in methods?	☐	☐	☐

		not as good	about the same	better
Compared to others in his work group . . .				
1.	how good is the quality of his work?	☐	☐	☐
2.	how good is the quantity of his work?	☐	☐	☐

		yes	not sure	no
If you could make the decision, would you . . .				
1.	give him a pay raise?	☐	☐	☐
2.	transfer him to a job at a higher level?	☐	☐	☐
3.	promote him to a position of more responsibility?	☐	☐	☐

> Please check the best answer for each question
> Be sure to answer all questions

FIGURE 5-4, cont'd.

Compared to others in his work group, how often does he . . .   less   about the same   more

1. come late for work? ☐ ☐ ☐
2. become overexcited? ☐ ☐ ☐
3. become upset and unhappy? ☐ ☐ ☐
4. need disciplinary action? ☐ ☐ ☐
5. stay absent from work? ☐ ☐ ☐
6. seem bothered by something? ☐ ☐ ☐
7. complain about physical ailments? ☐ ☐ ☐
8. say 'odd' things? ☐ ☐ ☐
9. seem to tire easily? ☐ ☐ ☐
10. act as if he is not listening when spoken to? ☐ ☐ ☐
11. wander from subject to subject when talking? ☐ ☐ ☐

Now will you please consider this worker with respect to his over-all competence, the effectiveness with which he performs his job, his proficiency, his general over-all value. Take into account all the elements of successful job performance, such as knowledge of the job and functions performed, quantity and quality of output, relations with other people (subordinates, equals, superiors), ability to get the work done, intelligence, interest, response to training, and the like. In other words, how closely does he approximate the ideal, the kind of worker you want more of? With all these factors in mind, where would you rank this worker as compared with the other people whom you now have doing the same work? (or, if he is the only one, how does he compare with those who have done the same work in the past?)

In the top 1/4 ☐
In the top half but not among the top 1/4 ☐
In the bottom half but not among the lowest 1/4 ☐
In the lowest 1/4 ☐

Vocational Psychology Research
University of Minnesota
Copyright 1965

---

bility, acceptance, and frivolity in the school setting are suddenly thrust into adult work roles, in which they are expected to be responsible, independent, serious, and diligent workers. Table 5-2 lists some basic problems of work adjustment.

The student-trainees in cooperative vocational education must make the same status transformation as other youth starting their first jobs. They encounter similar problems; however, cooperative student-trainees receive the help of a teacher-coordinator and usually make a smoother

TABLE 5-2
Basic Problems Of Work Adjustment

Needs	Typical Problems
Ability Utilization	Low-level entry jobs and failure to challenge student-trainee's ability.
Achievement	Lack of technical knowledge and skills needed to perform the work satisfactorily or inability to see the importance of the work performed.
Activity	Failure to keep the student-trainees engaged in meaningful work at all times.
Advancement	Unrealistic expectations on the part of student-trainnes or their inability to perceive the relationship of their present job to a future career.
Authority	Impatience to assume authority role and lack of understanding of how authority is delegated.
Company policies and practices	Lack of understanding of why policies and practices are in effect.
Compensation	Impatience and lack of skills to qualify for more lucrative jobs.
Co-workers	Inability to relate to the other employees or gain their esteem due to differences in age, values, and vocational maturity.
Creativity	Lack of necessary competencies to do creative work or the job does not provide opportunities for creativity and innovation.
Independence	Student's inability to work without close supervision or to appreciate the interdependence of workers in the performance of the work.
Moral values	Aspects of the job or the work environment that conflict with student's value orientation.
Recognition	Lack of recognition or unrealistic expectations for recognition due to differences in reinforcement between the school setting and the work setting.
Responsibility	Lack of competencies and experiences to assume responsibilities or the employer's failure to assign responsibilities as students achieve the competencies.
Security	Insecurity inherent in the job being learned or failure to provide student with information about his prospects for steady employment in the future.
Social service	Student's inability to perceive the social significance of his job or the lack of contact with people who benefit from performance of the job.
Social status	Impatience to hold a higher status job or disparity between student's expectations and the prestige the job affords.

TABLE 5-2 Cont'd.

Needs	Typical Problems
Supervision —human relations	Inability to understand the supervisor's behavior or supervisor's inability to enlist student's confidence.
Supervision —technical	Failure to provide adequate instruction on the job.
Variety	Assignment to repetitive work and student's unrealistic expectations for changes of activity, settings, and work groups.
Working Conditions	Truly poor working conditions or disparity between student expectations or values and the working conditions that exist.

transition and status transformation. The competent teacher-coordinator does not try to eliminate the problems, nor does he solve them for the student-trainees. Rather, he assists them in analyzing their problems and in finding their own solutions.

The teacher-coordinator must be sensitive to the work adjustment problems that student-trainees encounter so that solutions other than termination are explored and considered. Three types of problems are those relating to the organization, to the work itself and to personal factors outside of work.

ADJUSTING TO THE ORGANIZATION

As the number of large-scale organizations continues to increase, more student-trainees will be placed in work settings where there are many employees and highly structured work groups. The student-trainee is confronted with both the expectations of the formal administrative organization and the demands of his co-workers in the informal work group on his job. The teacher-coordinator must consider the probability of a student's being able to measure up to the expectations of the organization and to gain acceptance among the workers when selecting training agencies and placing each student.

The Formal Structure. The formal organization of a large business, industry, or government agency may evoke a negative attitude toward work in general because of its impersonality and the inevitable conflict between organizational demands and individual desires. The teacher-coordinator must help the student-trainees understand the rationale for company policies and procedures and for supervisory practices. The student-trainee learns how to work with a system or structure to satisfy his own needs and the expectations of the organization. The desired outcome is for students to master the process of adjustment, a skill which they will use throughout their working lives.

The Informal Structure. Adjusting to the informal structure may be more difficult for student-trainees, especially if the majority of the members in the informal work group are older, experienced workers who have negative stereotypes of youthful beginners. The informal work group has its own norms of how to dress, how the work should be performed, how hard one should work and a myriad of other values and attitudes which one must demonstrate before he is accepted as a group member.

In a sense, the informal work group has control over the intangible rewards of work—recognition, esteem, sense of belonging, interesting work activity, and sociability. The student-trainees have to learn the "ropes," so to speak, and the teacher-coordinator can facilitate this process by having students analyze the characteristics of the informal work group and how an individual gains acceptance and esteem from his co-workers.

Human relations and group process instruction are a part of the student-trainees' related classroom instruction because satisfaction and satisfactory performance are closely tied to how well the student-trainees get along with co-workers. The daily experiences of student-trainees frequently provide examples of human relations problems which the teacher-coordinator uses as a basis for classroom discussion.

ADJUSTING TO THE WORK ITSELF

An individual's needs for variety and activity usually are satisfied by the nature of the work itself. Many student-trainees will experience frustration from the routine of doing the same type of work several hours at a time, day after day, and possibly for weeks or months. They have been conditioned in school to changes in activities, surroundings, and work groups at the signal of bells every hour. The teacher-coordinator should place student-trainees in jobs that offer sufficient variety, but they must also realize that most jobs have a degree of routine which workers learn to tolerate in order to satisfy other needs. A training plan, developed cooperatively by the teacher-coordinator and the training sponsor, usually provides a variety of tasks and activities. The teacher-coordinator makes suggestions to the training sponsor when a change of jobs or routine seems justified and feasible.

The school environment also reinforces student needs for recognition of satisfactory work performance; however, workers are not rewarded or recognized as frequently, or in the same ways. In school, the students get continuous feedback in the form of grades and verbal reactions from their teachers. During this period of job adjustment, while sudents are enrolled in cooperative vocational education, the teacher-coordinator teaches student-trainees to appraise their own work. Sometimes the teacher-coordinator recommends to a training sponsor that a student-trainee be given recognition or more feedback while he is learning a job. Recognition for satisfactory performance usually motivates student-trainees to become more proficient and to continue pursuing their career goals.

Individuals need some form of recreation and social life outside of work and school to maintain their physical and emotional well-being. If student-trainees are encouraged to participate in the social and civic activities of the youth organization and to use leisure time in personally satisfying ways while enrolled in the program, they are likely to continue this practice when they are "on their own." Learning to manage one's personal and private life is essential to making a satisfying and satisfactory adjustment to work.

Concluding Statement

Work adjustment, as presented here, encompasses much more than helping individuals to conform to the expectations of their jobs and the realities of the world of work. The work adjustment studies and the instruments for assessing individual needs, abilities, satisfaction, and satisfactoriness, can be useful tools for teacher-coordinators in guiding and placing student-trainees, in planning appropriate instruction, and in working with cooperating employers. Even though the teacher-coordinators may not use the specific instruments described in this chapter, the principles of work adjustment can be applied in the guidance, placement, instruction, and coordination of cooperative vocational education programs.

The teacher-coordinator aids cooperative student-trainees in work adjustment by:

1. Assessing individual needs and abilities;
2. Placing students in training jobs that correspond to their individual needs and abilities;
3. Teaching students to examine jobs and occupations in terms of the abilities required and the reinforcers available;
4. Checking continuously on student-trainees' satisfaction and satisfactoriness;
5. Providing necessary guidance, instruction, coordination, and feedback to student-trainees in such a way that students learn to understand the process of work adjustment and how to achieve it themselves;

6. Recognizing work adjustment problems and working with employers and training sponsors to improve the conditions which contribute to a satisfactory and satisfying adjustment.

REFERENCES

1. Borgen, Fred H., David J. Weiss, Howard E. A. Tinsley, Rene V. Dawis. *The Measurement of Occupational Reinforcer Patterns,* Bulletin 49. Minnesota Studies in Vocational Rehabilitation. Minneapolis: University of Minnesota, Industrial Relations Center, 1968, 89pp.
2. Borgen, Fred H., David J. Weiss, Howard E. A. Tinsley, Rene V. Dawis, and Lloyd H. Lofquist. *Occupational Reinforcer Patterns (First Volume),* Bulletin 48. Minnesota Studies in Vocational Rehabilitation. Minneapolis: University of Minnesota, Industrial Relations Center, 1968, 263pp.
3. Carlson, R. E., Rene V. Dawis, R. V. England, and Lloyd H. Lofquist. *The Measurement of Employment Satisfaction,* Bulletin 35. Minnesota Studies in Vocational Rehabilitation. Minneapolis: University of Minnesota, Industrial Relations Center, 1962.
4. Dawis, Rene V., Lloyd H. Lofquist, and David A. Weiss. *A Theory of Work Adjustment (A Revision),* Bulletin 47. Minnesota Studies in Vocational Rehabilitation. Minneapolis: University of Minnesota, Industrial Relations Center, 1968, 15pp.
5. Gibson, Dennis L., David J. Weiss, Rene F. Dawis, and Lloyd H. Lofquist. *Manual for the Minnesota Satisfactoriness Scales,* Bulletin 53. Minnesota Studies in Vocational Rehabilitation. Minneapolis: University of Minnesota, Industrial Relations Center, 1970, 51pp.
6. Herzberg, Frederick. *Work and the Nature of Man.* Cleveland: World, 1966, 203pp.
7. Rosen, Stuart D., David J. Weiss, Darwin D. Hendel, Rene V. Dawis, and Lloyd H. Lofquist. *Occupational Reinforcer Patterns (Second Volume),* Bulletin 57. Minnesota Studies in Vocational Rehabilitation. Minneapolis: University of Minnesota, Industrial Relations Center, 1972, 313pp.
8. Weiss, David J., Rene V. Dawis, Lloyd H. Lofquist, and George W. England. *Instrumentation for the Theory of Work Adjustment,* Bulletin 44. Minnesota Studies in Vocational Rehabilitation. Minneapolis: University of Minnesota, Industrial Relations Center, 1966.

ADDITIONAL REFERENCES

Buros, O. K., ed. *Mental Measurements Yearbook.* Highland Park, N.J.: Gryphon, 1972.

Garbin, A.P., Dorothy P. Jackson, and Robert E. Campbell. *Worker Adjustment: Youth in Transition, An Annotated Bibliography of Recent Literature.* Columbus: Ohio State University, The Center for Vocational and Technical Education, 1967.

Klaurens, Mary K. "The Underlying Sources of Job Satisfaction of Distributive Education Student-Trainees." Doctoral dissertation. Minneapolis: University of Minnesota, 1967.

Lofquist, Lloyd H., and Rene V. Dawis. *Adjustment to Work.* New York: Appleton-Century-Crofts, Educational Division, Meredith Corporation, 1969, 187pp.

SUGGESTED ACTIVITIES

1. Analyze the relative importance to you of the twenty dimensions of work in what you would consider your ideal job (very important, important, neither important or unimportant, unimportant, very unimportant).

2. Analyze a job you have held or one that you are seeking in terms of how satisfying the job was or is likely to be on each of the twenty dimensions (very satisfying, satisfying, neither satisfying or dissatisfying, dissatisfying, very dissatisfying).

3. Interview one or two employers of workers in your occupational field to find out (a) what testing they do for assessing worker abilities and interests, and (b) what rating scales or methods they use for evaluating worker performance.

4. For each of the "Basic Problems of Work Adjustment" (table 5-2) briefly describe how a teacher-coordinator can assist a student-trainee in resolving the problem or in making a satisfactory and satisfying adjustment.

5. Prepare a list of the ways teacher-coordinators can use their knowledge of the theory of work adjustment in performing their tasks under each of the ten categories in the teaching career analysis in Appendix B.

Chapter 6   RECRUITING AND GUIDING STUDENT-TRAINEES

The teacher-coordinator is responsible for recruiting and guiding students who are interested in a cooperative vocational education program. Unless a student advances toward his occupational goals through the experiences that the program provides, the school does the student an injustice and thereby misappropriates educational resources. One of the most challenging tasks of the teacher-coordinator is determining which individuals the program shall serve and then helping them decide whether or not to enroll in the program.

This chapter is intended to help the reader:

1. Describe the process of recruiting and admitting students into a cooperative vocational education program;
2. Identify the audiences which should be informed about the goals and objectives of the program and devise means of communicating this information;
3. Describe the type of information students need about themselves and occupations before they select a vocational program;
4. Apply several techniques for gathering data about program applicants and using the data in the student admission process;
5. Describe how application forms, personal interviews, cumulative records, prognostic tests, and recommendations by others are used to aid the teacher-coordinator and the student in making decisions about enrolling in the program;

6. Develop a set of guidelines which could be used in the recruitment and admission process.

Overview of the Task

The task of recruiting and guiding student-trainees consists of (1) publicizing and interpreting the program goals and objectives, (2) providing realistic occupational information and exploratory experiences, (3) helping students appraise their interests and capabilities, (4) enrolling those students whose interests and capabilities can be enhanced by the particular program offered. An ideal situation would be for students to seek a cooperative vocational education program with a tentative career goal in the occupational field being taught; however, many students lack knowledge of the career opportunities and are even less knowledgeable about their own capabilities and interests. Thus recruitment and guidance are critical tasks in the operation of a program.

RECRUITMENT VERSUS SELECTION

The term "selection" often has a negative connotation to individuals who interpret it to mean that students who do not measure up to some arbitrary standards will be rejected. Without doubt, there are instances where students who want to enroll in a cooperative program cannot be accommodated due to the limitations of staff, facilities, or training agencies. Then the teacher-coordinator must "select," so to speak, the students whom he feels can benefit most from the particular program offered.

Although it may appear that a teacher-coordinator selects only the students who have good school records and are likely to succeed in any type of career, his intentions are to select students whose interests and capabilities are related to the occupational field for which the training is offered. If, on the other hand, the teacher-coordinator "recruits" or "selects into" the program students whom he believes can benefit from the training that is offered, rejection is not as obvious or damaging to the self-images of those who appear to be left out.

Those who may be critical of selection or admission practices are often misled by the notion that all students can benefit from a cooperative vocational education program. Although it may be true that occupational experience and the practical aspects of on-the-job learning are beneficial to most people, the goals and instructional focus of each cooperative program are different and students should be guided into programs which are in line with their individual needs and readiness for employment experiences.

STUDENT READINESS TO MAKE CHOICES

Ideally, a school should have a variety of programs that combine school and work—those primarily for preparation in various occupations, those primarily for exploration and guidance, and those primarily for personal-social adjustment. Then students can select the programs which are best suited to their needs and stages of career development. Students are not always realistic in appraising their own needs and readiness, so it is essential that they have adequate opportunities for exploration and self-assessment before they are faced with making critical choices.

Publicizing Program Goals and Objectives

A program is usually initiated because there are students who need help in making the transition from school to the world of work. A closer examination of this need may indicate that students will need specialized skills and technical knowledge in the occupational fields for which there are employment possibilities, or in which they are likely to be employed. The school administration should decide which occupational fields should be taught using the cooperative plan. The goals and objectives of an occupational program center on providing preparation for entry, adjustment, and advancement in one or more of the occupational clusters. The intent is to serve students who are likely to be satisfied and satisfactory workers in the occupational fields for which the school has decided to provide instruction. Frequently students, parents, and even school personnel have a very limited perception of the wide range of occupations within an occupational field. Publicizing the program usually means providing information about occupations and career opportunities within a broad occupational field.

When a teacher-coordinator is employed to supervise this program, he usually is the one who is expected to develop the program goals and objectives and to communicate them. When the program purpose is to prepare young people for careers in a specific occupational field, students, parents, employers, counselors, and other faculty members should understand that purpose and know something about the occupations and career opportunities associated with that field.

If the primary purposes of a program are career exploration and/or personal-social adjustment, this also must be understood so that those who are seeking these kinds of experiences are drawn to the program or are referred to it. Problems arise in planning instruction and in developing on-the-job experiences when the students' needs and readiness are not in harmony with the program goals and objectives.

Publicizing the program goals and objectives may include a variety of methods, depending on the audience to which the publicity is directed and the way it is involved in the program.

INFORMING STUDENTS

Students need to understand how a particular cooperative vocational education program is related to their goals and aspirations. Their initial reason for seeking a cooperative program may be a real or imagined need to be employed, or simply to get out of school in the afternoon. Sometimes it is a rude awakening for a student to find himself in a program where he is expected to study the technical information that is related to his job or to develop occupational skills that may be quite unrelated to his future plans.

Thus a teacher-coordinator must present the program as preparation for an occupational field—if that is the purpose—and make certain that students are aware of the career opportunities in that field. The cooperative plan is a vehicle for developing the competencies that are required.

Students may be reached through printed materials which describe the occupations to be learned as well as the learning advantages of the cooperative plan. The intent is to have students identify with an occupational field rather than simply an opportunity to be employed, even though that objective is an important motivation in the initial stages.

Studies have shown that many students are attracted to programs by knowing or observing students who are already enrolled in cooperative vocational education. This being true, it becomes very important to make certain that the students who are enrolled are achieving the intended goals and objectives. Program publicity should communicate student accomplishments that are related to program purposes. The students enrolled in a program serve as models with whom other students may identify, or they may reject the program because they do not see themselves as having interests, capabilities, and needs similar to those who are enrolled.

Students also become aware of the program through the personal contacts made by the teacher-coordinator, e.g., in a homeroom or school assembly presentation. Here again the teacher-coordinator emphasizes the purposes and objectives of the program and the nature of the occupations which it teaches so students can decide if the program is suited to their interests, capabilities, and needs.

INFORMING PARENTS

Parents need to be informed about the goals and objectives of a program before they encourage their children to enroll. They may view the program as serving other purposes, such as to provide spending money or to occupy students who cannot succeed in academic work. The teacher-coordinator communicates with parents through letters and mailed brochures and through presentations at meetings attended by parents. An advisory committee or group of cooperating employers can be effective in communicating with parents regarding the employer's responsibilities to provide training opportunities.

INFORMING SCHOOL PERSONNEL

The administration, counselors, and other faculty must be informed about the goals and purposes of the program because they are in unique positions to encourage students to enroll. In addition to having printed literature spelling out the objectives of a program, the teacher-coordinator for a particular program should inform other school personnel of what the program is about through daily contacts and faculty meetings. School faculties are very much aware of the fact that students leave the school early to go to work, and they have witnessed remarkable changes in some of those students who did not do well scholastically until they were enrolled in a cooperative program. When they understand program purposes and objectives, other faculty members know which students to refer to a program, and they can be helpful to students who are trying to decide if the program is suited to their needs.

INFORMING EMPLOYERS

There are many reasons why employers should understand the goals and objectives of the program, and it is equally important that they work toward those goals. It is very important that the employer, the student, and the teacher-coordinator are focusing on the same goals and objectives in order that each of these parties knows where to direct his efforts. When a student enrolls to obtain specific occupational training and the employer sees his role only as providing a part-time job, the student may be disappointed in the breadth of experience he receives. On the other hand, if the student has enrolled only because he needs a part-time job and the employer thinks the program is intended to serve students who are interested in his field of endeavor, the employer may be disappointed. The teacher-coordinator develops in employers an understanding of program goals and purposes through presentations at meetings attended by employers, through printed materials, and during personal calls in which on-the-job learning experiences for student-trainees are developed. One of the best ways to develop understanding of the goals of the program is through a sponsor development program, discussed in chapter 8, "Developing the Occupational Experience Laboratory." All publicity for the program should emphasize the program goals and objectives so that the people—students, parents, employers, and other school personnel—see the program in its true perspective and know the "target at which to shoot."

If any of the principal parties fail to grasp the purposes and objectives prior to the time when the student is actually enrolled, the teacher-coordinator clarifies and confirms their understanding of purposes and objectives by having a written training memorandum or agreement which will be discussed in chapter 7.

Providing Realistic Occupational Information

The teacher-coordinator of a particular cooperative education class in a school is probably the best source of occupational information for the occupations he or she teaches. Students are expected to have explored occupations and to have selected some tentative career goals when they enter cooperative training; however, at best their knowledge of the occupations they have chosen to study is rather limited. A teacher-coordinator must find ways to share his knowledge of the occupational field with students who are entering the program and with the individuals who have a significant role in influencing the students' decisions to apply for a particular occupational preparation program—counselors, parents, other school personnel.

PRE-COOP CLASSES

One of the best ways of providing realistic occupational information is to have a pre-coop or pre-employment class in which students explore the many options within an occupational field and clarify their own interests and assess their abilities as they relate to a variety of options.

The career exploration in a pre-coop class includes examination of printed materials such as the *Dictionary of Occupational Titles,* the *Occupational Outlook Handbook*, and various published monographs on careers. The school may have a career resource center or library where such materials are made available, and teacher-coordinators can assist in developing a selection of occupational information materials about their fields of instruction. Similar or supplemental materials may also be found in the classroom where the pre-coop class is held.

A more stimulating kind of exploration is for students to observe and analyze workers and work settings where the occupations are performed. Field trips and field interviews are the obvious ways of learning more about occupations; however, these methods are only effective when students are adequately prepared to observe the right things and ask the right questions. The exploratory experiences should provide the students with information about the psychosocial dimensions of the work and the characteristics of workers as well as the economic and job descriptive data usually sought.

The more accurately students perceive an occupational field and the more they have thought about their own interests and capabilities in relation to an occupation, the less difficult it is to plan a relevant cooperative vocational education experience. Even though occupational aspirations and career goals may change, the student is more likely to benefit from classroom instruction and on-the-job training when the things he learns are congruent with tentative aspirations and reasonably accurate perceptions of self and occupations.

The K-Adult career education curriculum is designed to provide planned exploration of a broad range of occupations. It also provides experiences which prepare students to make rational decisions as they mature and reach an age when they must choose an educational program that prepares them for job entry. The pre-coop course is an opportunity to test the reality and appropriateness of a chosen field, and to develop some entry level skills before the student, the employer, and the teacher-coordinator have made extensive long-range plans to engage in specialized on-the-job training.

NATURE OF OCCUPATIONAL INFORMATION

What does one need to know about an occupational field before making a tentative choice and entering a cooperative program?

The Work Performed. Studies have shown that workers are more satisfied, motivated, and satisfactory when their jobs or occupations allow them to perform work that is interesting and provides a sense of achievement and opportunities for recognition and increasing responsibility. The kinds of work tasks which may be interesting and satisfying will vary widely among individuals; nevertheless, this kind of information is needed to adequately appraise one's potential satisfaction and success in an occupational field.

Recruiting And Guiding Student-Trainees

The Dictionary of Occupational Titles uses a functional classification scheme for designating the level of complexity or type of activity performed in relationship to data, people, or things as dealt with by workers in the various occupations. The classifications are as follows:

DATA	PEOPLE	THINGS
0 Synthesizing	0 Mentoring	0 Setting-Up
1 Coordinating	1 Negotiating	1 Precision Working
2 Analyzing	2 Instructing	2 Operating-Controlling
3 Compiling	3 Supervising	3 Driving-Operating
4 Computing	4 Diverting	4 Manipulating
5 Copying	5 Persuading	5 Tending
6 Comparing	6 Speaking-Signaling	6 Feeding-Offbearing
7	7 Serving	7 Handling
8 No Significant Relationship	8 No Significant Relationship	8 No Significant Relationship

In addition to using the *Dictionary of Occupational Titles* to learn what kinds of tasks are performed in various occupations, students can be taught to analyze the jobs that they explore using the classifications above.

Opportunities for Employment. It is questionable whether programs should even be offered for occupations in which employment opportunities are limited because student needs are not well served when learners are trained for jobs which they cannot obtain. There are wide variations in the availability of employment and different projections of future manpower needs within the occupational fields for which training is offered. Students must be aware of these variables in order to make realistic choices. They should also be appraised of employment opportunities in related occupations which utilize the skills learned in the chosen occupation.

Some of this information is available in the *Occupational Outlook Handbook* and in other literature available from the U.S. Department of Labor and from state manpower services. A local employment service or chamber of commerce may supply data on local employment. Even so, the teacher-coordinator conducts surveys and determines what the local employment opportunities are for the occupations being taught. The information which is obtained from government reports and other literature should be interpreted in light of current trends and local situations. In addition to using employment information for current career planning, students should be learning how to utilize various sources of this information for future planning and decision making.

Life Styles and Jobs. Most of us learn to make some compromises in achieving expected life styles; however, one is more likely to set realistic and satisfying goals if he has some notion of the life styles associated with various occupations. Occupational literature usually is rather vague in describing the life styles of workers. This information is best learned by observing and interviewing workers.

Life style can encompass many dimensions of a worker's pattern of living and might include such things as the following:

1. Amount of leisure time;
2. The standard of living the job can provide;
3. Access to social groups;
4. Expectations for civic service and responsibilities;
5. Time to be with a family or to be away from home;
6. The ways one is expected to dress, talk, or conduct himself;
7. The values, attitudes, and ethics that characterize satisfied and successful workers in the occupational field;
8. Relationships with co-workers and customers or clients.

At one time, much of the occupational literature and guidance services focused on helping individuals match their abilities with job requirements. In recent years employers, counselors, vocational educators, and the young workers themselves have come to realize the importance of finding a satisfying occupational role. This encompasses much more than working to earn a living, or falling into a line of work by accident, or following parental influence. In order to make satisfying decisions and plans, students must know a great deal about the psychological rewards of occupations, as well as the economic rewards, working conditions, and skill requirements.

Working Conditions and Skill Requirements. These dimensions are mentioned together and last because they usually are the most readily available, and equally important.

It makes little sense to prepare students for jobs in which they cannot expect to advance to a level of self-support or in which their abilities are not fully utilized. Wage and salary information usually is of vital interest to students who have immediate needs, even to the extent that some of them would overlook other considerations and long-term gains when choosing a cooperative training job.

In addition to supplying information about income, the teacher-coordinator must help students look at income potentials beyond entry level wages. Some entry level jobs that have relatively low beginning wages may offer better training and higher income over the long run or opportunities to use skills acquired in the initial job for high income-producing jobs as the worker gains experience. Students need help in weighing short- and long-term benefits.

Other working conditions, such as physical surroundings, hours of work, and industrial relations vary so much among individual firms that students get the most realistic picture by visiting work settings and investigating working conditions. Students should examine a number of work situations, however, because of the variations among jobs and youth's tendency to overgeneralize from limited experiences.

Ability and skill requirements of occupations usually are found in the occupational literature, but much of this type of information for the occupational field taught should be known by the teacher-coordinator. Lacking information about specific skills or needed abilities, he should be adept in analyzing jobs and informing students about job requirements. In the cooperative arrangement with employers, the teacher-coordinator has responsibility for referring students who have a reasonably good chance of performing a job satisfactorily. Students can judge better their own potential success when they know what the jobs require. They are more likely to seek training for occupations in which they have some expectation of success. The students should be acquiring job analysis skills too, so they can continue to make realistic choices as their careers develop.

Gathering Information about Students

The purpose for gathering information about prospective students is not limited to being able to select students whose interests and capabilities are matched to the program objectives. Information about the student is needed to help a student appraise himself so he can make satisfying decisions. It also aids the teacher-coordinator in advising a student and in planning an appropriate program of instruction and training.

TYPES OF INFORMATION NEEDED

Keeping in mind that information about students also is used for planning instruction and training, the following types of information are helpful in determining if a particular program is likely to benefit a student:

Vocational Interests
1. Stated occupational preferences
2. Measured vocational interests
3. Avocational interests
4. Preferred activities and school subject matter areas

5. Values and attitudes toward work and different occupations

Aptitudes
1. Artistic abilities
2. Clerical abilities
3. Creativity
4. Manual dexterity

5. Mechanical aptitude
6. Scholastic aptitude

Physical Characteristics
1. Physical stamina
2. Skeletal structure
3. Restrictions or handicaps
4. Health record

Home Environment
1. Socioeconomic status
2. Family interpersonal relationships
3. Responsibilities
4. Parental aspirations
5. Family values, attitudes, life style

Personality Factors
1. General outlook on life
2. Sense of humor
3. Appearance
4. Interpersonal relations
5. Self-direction and drive
6. Emotional stability

Behavior Traits
1. Response to direction
2. Persistence
3. Initiative
4. Reliability and integrity
5. Work habits
6. Health habits
7. Mode of communication

Vocational Maturity
1. Knowledge of occupations and world of work
2. Attitude toward career planning
3. Work experience
4. Future orientation

When a teacher-coordinator has information such as we have outlined here he is in a position to determine whether or not the student is likely to benefit from a program. More importantly, given certain interests, capabilities, characteristics, and so forth, the teacher-coordinator can provide appropriate experiences and instruction to help a student advance toward self-fulfillment and a satisfying career. The student participates in this appraisal and thereby learns to make better predictions about himself and to make realistic choices of his own.

Any deficiencies or negative factors about a student should be viewed, not necessarily as reasons for rejecting the student, but as clues to what is the best course of action for him. Such factors may call for remedying a health problem, giving special instruction, placement in a pre-employment program until the student demonstrates readiness to enter a cooperative vocational education program, or placement with a particularly understanding employer.

In some cases it will be clear to the teacher-coordinator and the student that enrolling in a particular cooperative program is not the best course of action. Then the teacher-coordinator, frequently with the help of a school counselor, helps the student to explore the other options and alternative programs.

Recruiting And Guiding Student-Trainees

SOURCES OF INFORMATION ABOUT STUDENTS

The teacher-coordinator has a variety of sources and means of learning about students. No single source is sufficient in itself because of the many different types of information needed and the danger of overgeneralizing from a single piece of data. One source of information may validate another source or it may give the teacher-coordinator reason to seek further information. The student's participation in gathering and revealing information about himself has important benefits to him.

The Application Form. After the teacher-coordinator has publicized the program and students have been informed of its purposes and objectives, occupational preference and application forms are given to interested students. Schools that have a variety of programs may use the same forms or set of forms for all the occupational fields. The questions on the forms will vary with the type of information sought and with the total process of identifying and enrolling students in programs. A preliminary form such as the occupational preference forms in figure 6-1 may be used to identify which occupational fields students are interested in exploring and to divide the total group among the teacher-coordinators of the various programs for preliminary counseling.

At some point in the admission procedure the teacher-coordinator must obtain personal data, similar to what is found on an application for employment (figure 6-2, p. 138). The application form is a reliable, efficient way to gather information on the following items:

1. Student's full name, sex, date of birth
2. Home address and telephone number
3. Social Security number
4. Parents' names, occupations, places of employment
5. Hobbies, interests, and activities
6. Work experience
7. Courses taken in school
8. Physical handicaps or health problems
9. Homeroom teacher and counselor

In addition to the factual information above, the application form may contain questions which cause students to think about their interests and capabilities with regard to choosing an occupational field. The answers to the questions may suggest topics to be explored in greater detail during a personal interview. These may be questions such as:

1. Which school subjects do you enjoy most? Like least?
2. What do you plan to do following graduation?
3. Why do you want to enter this program?

FIGURE 6-1

Occupational Preference Form

Name _____ HR _____ Home Phone _____
     Last   First   Middle

In order to place you in the proper program (DE, OE, HE, T & I, Ag,) and secure training in the occupational area of your choice, please check carefully the following occupational areas and indicate your first (1), second (2), and third (3) choices.

Advertising and Display
_____ Advertising Assistant
_____ Advertising Copy-writer
_____ Display Assistant
_____ Display Helper

Child Care Aide
_____ Nursery School
_____ Day Care
_____ Retarded Child Care
_____ Head Start Programs
_____ Day School

Clothing Care, Construction, and Services
_____ Sewing Machine Opr.
_____ Cutter/Inspector
_____ Dry Cleaning or Laundry Aide
_____ Apprentice Dressmaker
_____ Bridal Shop Aide

Food Services
_____ Chef's Helper
_____ Cook Helper
_____ Salad Girl
_____ Dietary Aide
_____ Bakery Aide
_____ Test Kitchen Technician
_____ Utility Home Economist Aide
_____ Apprentice Caterer
_____ Meat Cutter Helper
_____ Line Server
_____ Tray Server
_____ Hostess
_____ Busboy
_____ Waiter/Waitress

Florist
_____ Floral Design Aide

Health
_____ Dental Assistant
_____ Dental Lab. Tech.
_____ Medical Lab. Asst.
_____ Nurse's Aide
_____ X-ray Technician
_____ Occupational Therapist Asst.
_____ Physical Therapist
_____ EKG Technician
_____ Orderly
_____ Veterinarian's Asst.

Home Furnishings
_____ Interior Designer's Aide
_____ Paint/Wallpaper Aide
_____ Drapery Workroom Aide
_____ Upholstery Workroom Aide

Housekeeping Services
_____ Maid/Housekeeper
_____ Custodian

Office & Clerical
_____ Accountant, Jr.
_____ Accounting Machine Opr.
_____ Bookkeeper
_____ Adding Machine Opr.
_____ Recordkeeper
_____ Calculating Machine Operator
_____ Bank Clerk
_____ Clerk, General
_____ Data Processing Clerk
_____ Telephone Operator
_____ Telephone Receptionist
_____ Stenographer
_____ Secretary
_____ Typist
_____ Clerk-typist
_____ Keypunch Operator
_____ Receptionist
_____ File Clerk
_____ Library Clerk
_____ Dictaphone Operator
_____ Word Processing Clerk

Sales and Marketing
_____ Auto Parts
_____ Apparel & Accessories
_____ Children & Infants Wear
_____ Fashion & Boutique
_____ Men's & Boy's Clothing
_____ Women's & Young Girls
_____ Cosmetics
_____ Farm & Garden Supply
_____ Food Products
_____ General Merchandise
_____ Hardware
_____ Home Care Products
_____ Home Furnishings
_____ Sporting Goods/Recreation Supplies
_____ Stockwork and Inventory

Recruiting And Guiding Student-Trainees 137

FIGURE 6-1, cont'd.

Sales (Cont.)
_____ Cashiering
_____ Catalog Sales
_____ Counter Sales
_____ Receiving and Shipping

Service
_____ Insurance
_____ Laundry & Dry Cleaning
_____ Rental Services

Technical
_____ Draftsman, Architectural
_____ Draftsman, Mechanical
_____ Electronic Technician
_____ Photographer

Trade & Industry
_____ Appliance Repair
_____ Auto Mechanic
_____ Attendant-Auto. Service
_____ Body & Fender Repair
_____ Cosmetology
_____ Radio & Television
_____ Printer
_____ Optical Technician
_____ Instrument Tech.
_____ Machinist
_____ Sheet Metal
_____ Welding
_____ Upholstering
_____ Cabinet Making

---

4. What three occupations are of interest to you?
5. What do your parents think of your participation in this program?

If the teacher-coordinator has access to the application form prior to the interview, he can begin gathering other information such as scholastic records, test data, and recommendations from counselors and other teachers. Then too, he can plan what questions or topics should be discussed in a personal interview with the student.

The Personal Interview. The personal interview can be a valuable means of determining the suitability of the program for a particular student. However, the teacher-coordinator must be competent in putting the student at ease, eliciting pertinent information, and in listening and interpreting what the student has said. The interview should help the student learn more about himself, about occupations and the program, and how to conduct himself in an interview situation.

A student should be able to look back on an interview as a positive experience and view the teacher-coordinator as a helping person. The stage is set when the teacher-coordinator is congenial and empathic to the student's needs and concerns. Usually one starts an interview by asking the student questions that are easily answered and pose no threat to his self-confidence. Early in the interview, the teacher-coordinator should attempt to find out whether the student understands the goals and objectives of the program and whether these are congruent with his reasons for applying. Incongruency is a signal to help the student clarify his goals or to help him explore other programs or courses of action.

The teacher-coordinator may discover that the student has personal problems or handicaps which may only be complicated by the cooperative training or which the teacher-coordinator feels inadequate to handle. Then he helps the student identify the best sources of help and makes referrals when appropriate. A decision not to enroll the student in the pro-

FIGURE 6-2

COOPERATIVE VOCATIONAL EDUCATION PROGRAM

STUDENT APPLICATION

Student's Name _____ Home Room _____ Date _____
Student's Address _____ Date of Birth _____
_____ Telephone Number _____
Father's Name _____ Father's Occupation _____
Mother's Name _____ Mother's Occupation _____

PERSONAL

Age next Sept. _____ Sex _____ Height _____ Weight _____ Health _____
Any physical defects: Sight ____ Hearing ____ Speech ____ Limbs ____ Heart ____
What physical injuries have you had? _____ When _____
Indicate any precautions necessary due to above conditions _____
Interest and hobbies _____ Do you have a Soc. Sec. Card? ____

SCHOLASTIC

How do you consider your record as a student? Above average _____
                                      Average _____ Below Average _____
Days absent—This year __ Last year __ Days tardy—This year __ Last year __
What subjects do you like best? _____ _____ _____ _____
What subjects do you like least? _____ _____ _____ _____
In what extra-curricular activities do you participate? _____
What subjects have you taken that will help you in your planned career? ____

Why do you want to enroll in the cooperative vocational education program?

What do your parents think of your participation in the cooperative program?

What are your plans after graduation? _____

WORK EXPERIENCE (begin with most recent position)

Name of employer	Address	Kind of work

Recruiting And Guiding Student-Trainees 139
FIGURE 6-2, cont'd.

PERSONAL REFERENCES (list only one teacher)		
Name	Address	Occupation

Person to notify in case of emergency   Relationship   Address   Phone No.

Can you provide transportation to your job?   Do you have a drivers license?

Job Choice—1st Choice _____ 2nd Choice _____

Choice of Program   My Class Schedule

	Class	Room
_____ Health Occupations		
_____ Trade and Industrial	1st Hour _____	_____
_____ Office Occupations	2nd Hour _____	_____
_____ Home Economics Related	3rd Hour _____	_____
_____ Agriculture	4th Hour _____	_____
_____ Distributive Occupations	5th Hour _____	_____
_____ Undecided (would like to discuss it further)	6th Hour _____	_____

Counselor _____
Homeroom Teacher _____
Applicant's Signature _____ Date _____
Please complete the OCCUPATIONAL PREFERENCE form and hand it in with this form

Comments: Applicant does not write below this line

Personality	Appearance	Character	Interviewer	Date

Final action

---

gram is less painful when the teacher-coordinator has positive acceptable alternative courses of action for him to follow.

In a personal interview the teacher-coordinator attempts to identify the student's attitudes, strengths, interests, and characteristics which will be factors in placement on a job. This will also help the teacher-coordinator to decide whether the program can benefit him. A decision usually is not made at the time of the interview, allowing the student to do more exploring or allowing the teacher-coordinator more time to gather information he needs to make a final recommendation. When the interview ends, however, the teacher-coordinator should convey what steps are to be taken and when the student can expect to hear from the teacher-coordinator again.

Cumulative Records. Most schools maintain a file folder of each student's school record. The information in the record can be helpful in assessing a student's capabilities and behavioral characteristics, as long as the teacher-coordinator recognizes that entries in the record are only samples of the student's behavior and subject to human errors in value judgments.

Standardized test scores, grade records, attendance, health records, referrals for discipline, citizenship ratings, and similar data may suggest areas which the teacher-coordinator may want to explore with the student or with teachers who have him in their classes. Decisions to enroll or not to enroll a student should not be based solely on entries in the student's cumulative record.

Prognostic Tests. The use of prognostic tests, standardized tests and those devised by the teacher-coordinator, have utility in the recruitment and guidance process, but should only be used as a way of verifying other information or to help the student appraise himself. Using tests is complicated by the fact that it is difficult to find tests that truly measure what one needs to know about a student. For example, a timed writing on the typewriter cannot predict whether or not a student can succeed in an office occupation.

On the other hand, when students are subjected to skill tests in typing, mathematics, language arts, etc., the teacher is able to confirm what the student has said about his own abilities or what the teacher-coordinator has read in the cumulative records file. Testing is costly and time-consuming, so one should weigh the process against the utility of the data that the tests provide.

Another possible justification for giving tests is that students will be asked to take tests when they apply for some jobs. If the teacher-coordinator gives tests similar to employment tests, he has some indication of how the student will perform when he encounters an employment test. Inadequate performance on a test given by the teacher-coordinator may indicate the need for remedial work or practice before a student applies for a job.

Before deciding whether or not to do any testing it would be wise to find out what kinds of test scores are recorded in the cumulative record

Recruiting And Guiding Student-Trainees   141

file and to discuss tests with the guidance counselor. The counselor has expertise in interpreting whatever test information may already be available and in selecting other tests to be given.

Keeping in mind that tests are used to learn more about a student's instructional needs and to provide additional information to help the student make realistic plans, some of the following kinds of tests may be considered.

Achievement Tests
> Reading, Vocabulary, Spelling, Grammar, Mathematics, Science, Foreign Language, Occupational Skills (whatever is relevant for the occupations or the instructional program being considered)

Aptitude Tests
> Clerical, Spatial, Manual Dexterity, General Aptitude Test Battery (GATB)

Visual Acuity and Hearing Tests

Vocational Interest Tests

> Needs and Values Inventories
> Personality Tests

General Aptitude Test Battery. One of the most widely used employee testing programs is the GATB which is administered by the U.S. Employment Service and state manpower agencies. The battery consists of eight paper-and-pencil tests and two apparatus tests which yield an occupational ability profile. Individual profiles can be compared with profiles of workers in various types of occupations. This particular aptitude test is mentioned because the teacher-coordinator is encouraged to contact the public employment service representative about giving the tests at the school for prospective vocational education students.

Recommendations by Others. Another source of information about students is recommendations from employers, faculty members, and individuals in the community. These may be in the form of letters of recommendation, a telephone inquiry, or an opinion sheet in the case of faculty recommendations.

The most frequently used form is a faculty opinion sheet, such as shown in figure 6-3, which asks other teachers to indicate their perceptions of students' behavior traits and capabilities that are relevant to their potential success and satisfaction in the program. The teacher-coordinator solicits opinions of more than one teacher because sometimes students are perceived differently by different teachers. Again, it is well to remember that this kind of information alone is not sufficient to make a decision, but it is used to verify other data or as a signal for further study of the student's readiness for the program.

FIGURE 6-3

COOPERATIVE VOCATIONAL EDUCATION

Student _____ Faculty Member _____ Date _____

School _____ Nature of contact (classroom, club, etc.) _____

The student named above has applied for Cooperative Vocational Education. You are asked to appraise him/her on the following traits in order to assist the teacher-coordinator in the guidance, admission and placement of this student in a cooperative vocational education program. Please identify by a check mark the characteristic behavior of the student in respect to each specific trait.
Please return to teacher-coordinator whose name appears below.

1. SERIOUSNESS OF PURPOSE	Aimless	Aims just to "get by"	Has vaguely formed objectives	Directs energies effectively with fairly definite program	Engrossed in realizing well-formulated objectives	No opportunity to observe
2. INDUSTRY	Needs constant pressure	Needs occasional prodding	Prepares assigned work	Completes suggested supplementary work	Seeks and sets for himself additional tasks	No opportunity to observe
3. INITIATIVE	Always waits to be told	Relies heavily on others	Starts some things	Resourceful	Actively creative	No opportunity to observe
4. POWER AND HABIT OF ANALYSIS	Dull, grasps ideas with difficulty	Assimilates fairly readily but goes no further	Average in assimilating and analyzing ideas	Active mind, some independent thinking	Brilliant mind, marked in analyzing and constructing	No opportunity to observe

142

5. LEADERSHIP	Probably unable to lead	Lets others take lead	Leads sometimes in minor affairs	Leads sometimes in important affairs	Marked ability makes things go	No opportunity to observe
6. CONCERN FOR OTHERS	Anti-social	Self-centered	Shows consideration when guided	Somewhat socially concerned	Deeply and generally concerned	No opportunity to observe
7. RESPONSI- BILITY	Irresponsible	Shows responsibility in some things	Usually dependable	Conscientious	Assumes much responsibility	No opportunity to observe
8. COOPERA- TIVENESS	Obstructive	Difficult to handle	Usually cooperative	Enthusiastically cooperative	Leads others to cooperate	No opportunity to observe
9. SOCIAL ACCEPTA- BILITY	Avoided by others	Unnoticed	Liked	Well liked	Sought by others	No opportunity to observe
10. EMOTIONAL STABILITY	Hyper- emotional / Apathetic	Excitable / Unresponsive	Usually well balanced	Well balanced	Exceptionally stable	No opportunity to observe

Comments: _____

_____ Teacher-Coordinator

Admission Policies and Procedures

When the teacher-coordinator has clearly defined policies and well-organized procedures for identifying and enrolling students in the program, student recruitment and admission run smoothly. The responses and attitudes of students, parents, counselors, employers, other faculty, and the administration toward the decisions made are more likely to be positive when policies and procedures for admission are consistent and well known. When there are no consistent policies and procedures, the teacher-coordinator is opening the door to being criticized for discrimination. Depending on the type of program and other variables in the particular school, there should be policies related to:

1. Steps to follow in the application process such as completing an application form, having a personal interview, getting parent's approval, etc.;
2. Completion of prerequisite courses, or alternative ways of meeting requirements for entry;
3. Criteria which are used in screening or decision making as to who is to be admitted;
4. Final selection process—the persons who participate in the final selection.

STEPS IN THE ADMISSION PROCESS

Usually the admission process is started seven to nine months before the students begin their instruction and training—between January and March for enrollment in September. The exact timing may depend on the school's system for programming students' classes for the next year. A typical schedule for the steps in recruiting and guiding students into the program is as follows:

January   Place an announcement in the school paper and notify counselors and teachers that applications are being accepted.

Conduct a school assembly program or visits to homerooms to provide information about career opportunities, program objectives, and admission procedures.

Distribute program literature and application forms—in the homerooms, through the counselor, or upon request by interested students. Send announcements to parents.

Recruiting And Guiding Student-Trainees

February	Review completed application forms, consult with counselors, arrange appointments for personal interviews and gather other information about the students who have applied. Conduct interviews and gather any further information needed. Tests? Recommendations? Faculty opinions?
March	Assemble the data and meet with representative committee (counselor, employers, other teachers) and decide which applicants should be admitted.
March-April	Conduct follow-up interviews with students who have been admitted; conduct follow-up interviews with those not to be admitted in order to explore alternative programs or courses of action.
April-May	Hold an orientation meeting for students who will be enrolled the following September. Parents may be invited to attend also.
May-August	Get to know those who have been admitted, help them refine their interests and goals, and formulate tentative lists of potential training agencies.

The process outlined above may vary when there are prerequisite courses or when the teacher-coordinators for several cooperative programs work together in presenting several options to students. When there are prerequisite courses the recruitment and admission take place within the course. When there are several program options the teacher-coordinators can develop a system for helping students identify which program is related to their interests and needs.

In addition to the formal recruitment and admission schedule there may be students who seek out the teacher-coordinator for information and application earlier in the year, or even after the formal recruitment period. If the teacher-coordinator has not filled the program quota (the number he can reasonably handle), applicants may be considered as late as the date the program begins. Counselors frequently make referrals and they should be appraised when there are openings in the program or when a teacher-coordinator has reached his maximum enrollment.

POLICIES REGARDING PREREQUISITE COURSES

When there are prerequisite courses for entry into the cooperative program, will there be alternative ways in which students who did not have the course can qualify for admission? Certainly those who have had the prerequisite course would be given first consideration, but it may be possible to arrange an independent study or mini-course during the summer to qualify those who have not had the prerequisite course. In some programs these students enroll in the prerequisite course concurrently with the cooperative vocational education class.

POLICIES REGARDING CRITERIA

For some programs, criteria such as grade records, attendance, or performance on a particular competency test may be used. It is the teacher-coordinator's responsibility to justify that these criteria are a valid means for determining who should be enrolled. It is especially important that the criteria are evenly applied to all students being considered.

POLICIES REGARDING THE FINAL DECISION

Although it may seem the most democratic to take all who apply, and in the order of application, or to enroll those who have secured their own jobs, this does not insure that the program will serve those who can benefit from the instruction. The teacher-coordinator is likely to make the final decision; however, a representative committee consisting of a counselor, one or two employers, and one or two teachers could assist the teacher-coordinator in setting standards for selection and making decisions on difficult cases. When the methods and standards of selection have committee approval and support, the decisions of the teacher-coordinator are more likely to be considered fair and impartial.

This places a great responsibility on the teacher-coordinator, and he must try very hard to make decisions that are in the best interests of the students. These decisions may not seem fair in the eyes of others at times, and the teacher-coordinator, with the help of the representative committee, must conduct the selection process as objectively and fairly as possible.

The following criteria may be considered and given different weights depending on the objectives of the program:

1. Career objective matched to the program and available training;
2. Completion of prerequisite courses;
3. Potential for satisfaction in the training available;
4. Potential for employability and satisfactory performance;
5. Health and physical capability to work and complete school;
6. Willingness to give best effort to all phases of the program (classroom, youth organization, and on-the-job training);

7. Ability of the coordinator to provide instruction relevant to the student's interest and ability.

COORDINATOR-COUNSELOR RELATIONSHIP

The primary responsibility for gathering student information, screening applicants, and developing criteria for admission belongs to the teacher-coordinator who consults with the counselor and confirms his decisions on admission with a representative committee. Close working relationships with counselors can save a teacher-coordinator considerable time in the recruitment and guidance process. When counselors understand the purpose of a program and which types of students can benefit from instruction they can be more helpful to students and the teacher-coordinator. The success and the acceptability of the recruitment and guidance-admission policies depends to a great extent on how the teacher-coordinator has involved the guidance personnel in the school. Usually it is up to the teacher-coordinator to take the initiative in developing this relationship.

Concluding Statement

Recruiting and guiding students concerning entry into cooperative vocational education is one of the most challenging of the teacher-coordinator's tasks. The purpose of selecting students to participate in a program is to serve those who will benefit most from the instruction and training. The recruitment and guidance process is more likely to function well when (1) the purposes of a program are understood by all participating parties, (2) students are informed about occupations and their own needs, goals, interests, and capabilities, and (3) the teacher-coordinator has a well-defined set of policies and procedures for selecting the program participants.

REFERENCES

1. U.S. Department of Labor, Bureau of Employment Security. *Dictionary of Occupational Titles,* Vol. I and II. Washington, D.C.: U.S. Government Printing Office, 1965.
2. U.S. Department of Labor, Bureau of Labor Statistics. *Occupational Outlook Handbook.* Washington, D.C.: U. S. Government Printing Office. (published biennially)

ADDITIONAL REFERENCES

Boyd, Robert E. "Factors in Career Choice." *Illinois Teacher for Contemporary Roles* 16, No. 5 (May-June 1973): 323-33.

Buros, O. K., ed. *Mental Measurements Yearbook.* Highland Park, N.J.: Gryphon, 1972.

Krebs, Alfred H., and Jean E. Krebs. "Learning About the Individual Vocational Student." In Alfred Krebs, ed., *The Individual and His Education.* Washington, D.C.: American Vocational Association, 1972, pp. 106-18.

Patterson, Cecil H. "Counseling: Self-Clarification and the Helping Relationship." In Henry Borow, ed., *Man in a World of Work.* Boston: Houghton Mifflin, 1964, pp. 434-59.

Shartle, Carroll L. "Occupational Analysis, Worker Characteristics and Occupational Classification Systems." In Henry Borow, ed., *Man in a World of Work.* Boston: Houghton Mifflin, 1964, pp. 285-309.

Warmbrod, J. Robert. "Individual Goals and Vocational Education." In Alfred H. Krebs, ed., *The Individual and His Education.* Washington, D.C.: American Vocational Association, 1972, pp. 119-28.

SUGGESTED ACTIVITIES

1. Examine the occupational information in the *Dictionary of Occupational Titles* and the *Occupational Outlook Handbook* for several occupations in your vocational field. Describe what additional information a person who was considering these occupations as possible career choices would need to know.

2. List five sources, other than the DOT and the Handbook, which provide occupational information for students who wish to know more about occupations in your vocational field.

3. Prepare a list of questions you might use in a personal interview with a student who is applying for your cooperative vocational education program. Role-play the interview and discuss techniques of conducting personal interviews with prospective student-trainees.

4. Prepare a list of criteria that you feel should be considered in determining which students should be enrolled in a cooperative education program for your vocational field.

5. Prepare a five- to ten-minute talk or presentation you could use to inform students about occupations in your field and about your cooperative vocational education program.

Recruiting And Guiding Student-Trainees

6. Compose a letter or brochure which could be sent to parents of prospective student-trainees to inform them about your cooperative vocational education program.

7. Interview a teacher-coordinator or a counselor in a local school to find out what kinds of aptitude, interest, and achievement tests are given in the school and what information is entered in students' cumulative records. Determine which, if any, of this information would be helpful in deciding whether or not a student could benefit from cooperative training in your vocational field.

8. Prepare a list of the ways in which teacher-coordinators can apply their knowledge of career development when recruiting and guiding students regarding admission to a cooperative vocational education program.

9. Prepare a list of the ways in which teacher-coordinators can apply the theory of work adjustment when recruiting and guiding students regarding admission to a cooperative vocational education program.

Chapter 7   PLACING STUDENT-TRAINEES

This chapter deals with the placement of student-trainees in cooperative vocational education training agencies for on-the-job training. The importance of carefully planned placement is emphasized with specific guidelines for conducting placement surveys, selecting suitable training agencies, applying the principles of career development and work adjustment in the placement process, aligning students with the right employers and training positions, and preparing student-trainees for job applications.

The satisfaction of student-trainees with their training positions and the employers' satisfaction with the program hinge on the teacher-coordinator's being able to perform the placement function effectively. A careful study of this chapter should contribute to your ability to:

1. Value the importance of excellent placement practices;
2. Implement the principles associated with work adjustment when carrying out the placement function;
3. Facilitate the career development of students through the selection of appropriate training positions;
4. Plan and conduct an occupational survey;
5. Plan placements of student-trainees weighing such factors as the students' career goals, training environments, and the welfare of the vocational education program;
6. Evaluate potential training agencies in terms of predetermined standards;

7. Prepare student-trainees for job interviews by providing group and individual instruction;
8. Effectively align students with training agencies and positions;
9. Work with an advisory committee in facilitating the training of students with special needs;
10. Prepare a training agreement for a regular student-trainee;
11. Explain the types of information included in a training agreement for students with special needs.

Importance of Excellence in Placement

Experienced teacher-coordinators agree that careful placement of students is the key to the success of any educational plan that combines work and study. They also agree that in cooperative vocational education appropriate placement is crucial. The placement function takes on additional significance when one realizes that each placement of a student-trainee may affect positively or negatively, not only the career development of that student, but the training agency's acceptance of student-trainees in the future. It may also affect the image of the school itself in the employment community.

EFFECT ON THE STUDENT-TRAINEE

Program goodwill and tenure depend on continuous acceptance by students who participate in the program. Student-trainees use many criteria to evaluate a cooperative vocational education program, one of the most important being the satisfactions they receive from their occupational experience and on-the-job training which depend largely on excellence in placement.

It is a mistaken idea to think that all on-the-job experiences are helpful to students. Work experience may be helpful or harmful! If a student has a good experience, his on-the-job training will develop his occupational skills and lead to good work habits and attitudes. It will motivate him to learn an occupation and will encourage him to continue his education beyond high school, either as a full-time student or as a full-time worker enrolled in adult classes. A successful occupational experience provides a student with an excellent reference for permanent employment.

Conversely, a poor record in on-the-job training may jeopardize a student-trainee's subsequent opportunities with the cooperating employer and elsewhere. Whether a poor experience is the student's fault or whether it is caused by poor placement or supervision, the result usually is the same—the student's morale is low and his attitude toward work is poor. It is very important to keep in mind the consequences that good or bad placement may have on a student because the ill effects of an error in placement are difficult to overcome. In some cases, emotional problems and questionable moral standards have been traced to a student's initial employment experience.

EFFECT ON PROGRAM DEVELOPMENT

Although the welfare of the student-trainee being place in a training position is the teacher-coordinator's primary concern, he also must think about the long-range reputation of the total vocational education program. He must consider the possible effect of the current placement on future placements in the training agency being considered and on other present and potential employers of student-trainees. For example, usually it is better to place a "good" student in a new training station or agency in order to establish good rapport with the personnel and gain goodwill for future cooperation. This practice may pave the way for placement of less talented students.

A disgruntled student-trainee or a disappointed employer can damage severely the reputation of a cooperative vocational education program. The reputation of a program depends largely on whether the teacher-coordinator has carefully considered each student's abilities, interests, and aptitudes when placing him. Every effort must be made to place a student where he will be satisfactory to his employer and satisfied with his work and opportunities to learn an occupation.

EFFECT ON THE SCHOOL

Excellence in the placement of cooperative vocational education students promotes good public relations for the school. Always remember that the most essential element of a good public relations program is a good product. When student-trainees are placed on jobs in which they are interested and for which they are potentially qualified, the result is a highly motivated worker who is satisfactory as well as satisfied. When a training agency provides a good training environment and joins hands with the school in assisting its student-trainees to reach their highest potential, both institutions think highly of the other and the student feels that the school has done a good job.

Each time a teacher-coordinator places a student, he knows that the behavior of that student becomes an important factor to the employer and his employees in judging the quality of education provided by the school. Carefully placed, effective, efficient, and satisfied student-trainees can bring great credit to a school while poorly placed disinterested students can be a negative factor.

Career Development and Placement

The placement of student-trainees in positions with cooperating employers has a very important bearing on their career development. This relationship will be explained in part at this point by associating placement with several of the broad dimensions of career development identified in chapter 4. Further reference to this relationship will be revealed throughout the chapter.

Cooperative occupational experience may make career development easier or it may retard the student's progress toward his career goal. Good training environments enable student-trainees to study the occupational skill requirements and ways of life of persons employed in a variety of occupations and to formulate relatively accurate occupational images. On the other hand, questionable work experience settings may be the cause of false impressions of occupations and even of the industry as a whole.

OCCUPATIONAL AWARENESS AND SELF-CONCEPT DIMENSIONS

In cooperative vocational education, student-trainees not only have an opportunity to try out a variety of occupational skills while on the job to which they are assigned, but they have an opportunity to observe a good sample of the way of life of people engaged in the occupation represented in the training agency. Good training environments also enable students to improve the accuracy of their self-images. They have an opportunity to test their abilities and to obtain competent judgments concerning their achievements. For example, if a student has a career goal of becoming a nursing home supervisor, the experiences which he/she has as a student-trainee in a nursing home will either lead him/her one step nearer his/her career goal or it may so disenchant him/her that he/she will alter his/her career goal.

It is important to note that a student's disenchantment may not be caused by faulty placement, but by his faulty stereotype of the job or an inaccurate appraisal of his abilities and interests. When a student-trainee finds out what the distasteful aspects of an occupation are and realizes the amount and type of skill needed to master the essential competencies, he has an opportunity to decide whether or not he would be happy in that occupation.

WORK ETHIC AND EMPLOYABILITY DIMENSIONS

Even more important in a student's career development are the work habits and attitudes acquired while employed on his first job. Good supervision and co-workers who possess positive attitudes toward work expedite the development of competencies included under the work ethic and employability dimensions of career development.

Another factor of career development that depends largely on intelligent placement of student-trainees is the value of the type of experience in the eyes of potential employers. A given type of work experience may be judged by an employer to be negative or positive depending on its quality and whether or not it complements the tasks which an applicant is expected to perform. This factor relates to the work ethic and occupational preparation dimension of career development.

A student-trainee's experiences while at work have a lasting effect on his attitude toward an occupational field and a strong impact on his career development. Excellence in placement is the first of two aspects of obtaining maximum career development value from cooperative occupational experiences; the other is intelligent use of the training agency as a resource for this type of learning.

PLANNING AND OCCUPATIONAL PREPARATION DIMENSIONS

Students usually overgeneralize on single employment experiences. The outcomes of what happened to two student-trainees will illustrate this common phenomenon and accentuate the impact of placement on the planning and occupational preparation dimensions of career development.

Betty was employed as a cooperative student-trainee in the sportswear department of a department store. The manager of her department worked closely with the D.E. teacher-coordinator in developing a training plan for Betty. Her co-workers were friendly and helpful. The department manager told Betty about experiences on her buying trips and spoke highly of a distributive education adult course in which several salespeople in the store were enrolled. Other salespeople called her attention to new merchandise and frequently asked her to try on new garments. Several months before Betty graduated from high school the personnel manager of the store talked to her about permanent employment as an assistant buyer. Betty decided to become a full-time student of merchandising and management at a nearby community college with fashion merchandising as her career goal. As a result of her experience as a student-trainee, Betty felt that retailing in general and fashion merchandising in particular would offer an exciting, challenging, and enjoyable career.

Bob was employed part-time as a cooperative student-trainee in a supermarket. The manager had agreed that Bob's regular duty would be to bag groceries but that he also would have an opportunity to learn the duties of a stock clerk. Unfortunately, the manager was transferred to another city and the teacher-coordinator had difficulty in communicating with the new manager who always seemed "too busy to talk." Bob was told to stay at the check-out station and bag groceries. The checker-cashier with whom he worked complained bitterly about the boredom of her job. The manager frequently called unscheduled meetings after the store closed for the purpose of informing the personnel about decreasing sales. He informed them that "everyone's job is in jeopardy unless you get on the ball." Whenever Bob attempted to carry out the learning experiences on his training plan he was permitted to do so grudgingly if at all. The pay was good, so Bob stuck it out for that year. Although he had previously thought he would like to be a supermarket manager or join a wholesale food jobber where a former classmate was working, Bob decided that he would learn a trade instead. His experience at the supermarket convinced him that people employed in food distribution were disgruntled and unhappy. Although he had friends who were pleased with their cooperative experience in that field, he could see no future in food distribution for him. When his coordinator told him about a full-time job as a salesperson in a men's store and offered to recommend him for the job after graduation, Bob declined. To him, all retailers were alike.

Placement Surveys

It would be folly to start a cooperative vocational education program without any assurance that there would be enough jobs for graduates and a sufficient number of qualified training agencies for the student-trainees. Therefore, a careful study of relevant manpower needs and trends must be made long before a program is started. Program planners usually gather such information about a year in advance of the proposed starting date. Generally both secondary and primary sources of data are used. Although employment data are available through the Census of Business, the State Employment Service, and frequently through the local Chamber of Commerce, an occupational survey conducted by local vocational education personnel has been found to be necessary for sound program planning. Teacher-coordinators draw as much information as possible from existing sources and gather the needed additional data themselves. Occupational surveys and community surveys are conducted for a variety of purposes too numerous to be discussed here. Therefore, only placement surveys relating to cooperative vocational education will be considered.

PURPOSES OF PLACEMENT SURVEYS

The purposes of placement surveys vary according to the type and quality of information available from other sources; however, the most common purposes are:

1. To determine the number of business, industrial, and government employers of various types in the community to be served;
2. To determine the number of full-time and part-time employees in each occupation in each business, industry, or goverment unit;
3. To determine the number of high school students currently employed part-time by each employer;
4. To determine each employer's attitude toward preparing young people for careers through cooperative vocational education;
5. To introduce the teacher-coordinator to employers as a training specialist.

Survey questions sometimes included relate to employment qualifications of applicants for certain positions, peak and low employment periods, employment trends, type of equipment used, availability of company training, willingness of the employer to talk to the class, and special employment procedures. There are many others depending on how the information is collected, who collects it, and when the classes will start. Usually steering committee members counsel the teacher-coordinator concerning the placement survey purposes, content, and procedures.

PLACEMENT SURVEY PRACTICES

As mentioned above, placement survey purposes and content vary with the amount and quality of available information; placement survey procedures vary with the size of the community, the amount of financial and/or manpower resources, the number of vocational fields to be included in the survey, the experience of the personnel in survey work, and so on. It is not likely that the procedures will be the same in two communities.

Small Community Placement Surveys. In very small communities where there is only one section of cooperative vocational education, a placement survey is done by the teacher-coordinator alone with very little help from the guidance counselor, other staff members, or from students. For him, the school year generally starts in mid-August, or it may start earlier if the program is just being installed. The information is gathered informally but systematically via personal interviews. This gives a new coordinator an opportunity to meet the regular employers and training sponsors and to contact personally potential training agencies. It also affords him an opportunity to discuss the achievements of the previous year and to learn about job requirements first hand. Through such meetings he may gain an insight into the work environment.

Large Community Placement Surveys. While a small community teacher-coordinator can easily locate employment data and obtain a classified list of employers with relatively little effort, a teacher-coordinator in a large school system encounters all of the communication, protocol, and organizational problems associated with large-scale operations in general. Census data cannot be found which correspond to the geographical area served; it is more difficult to communicate with school administrative personnel; and it is more difficult to establish rapport with decision-making employers.

Usually there is a saving grace in a large school, namely that there are teacher-coordinators from other vocational fields who usually are very cooperative and willing to help a new teacher-coordinator. In addition, there may be a knowledgeable director of vocational education who has charge of all vocational education and whose duty it is to induct new vocational education personnel into the system. If cooperative vocational education has been operational for some time, placement survey procedures may be well established, an achievement which saves a new teacher-coordinator a great deal of time.

Cooperative planning among the teacher-coordinators representing the various vocational fields is essential if they expect to place student-trainees in the same community. This may be done in at least two ways. First, all of the coordinators from one vocational field may survey employers concerning jobs represented in their field only. For example, vocational office training (VOT) coordinators from four high schools in a city may join VOT coordinators from an adjoining county to survey employment trends, opportunities, and training needs in offices throughout the metropolitan area. Second, coordinators from all vocational fields in a school system may join in planning a comprehensive occupational, community, or placement survey of all business, industrial, and government enterprises in the community. Authorities seem to agree that a comprehensive occupational or community survey be undertaken periodically, but that surveys by each vocational field be conducted annually.

Any type of survey (community, occupational, or placement) should be undertaken systematically. A map of the various business and industrial areas should be divided into sections that can be surveyed in a week's time. A number of sections can then be allocated to each teacher-coordinator who will plan the number of visits he will make each day in order to complete his assignment.

Conducting the Survey. Regardless of the size of a community, a placement survey is axiomatic. It not only assures the school administration of placement, but helps the program to get started on the right foot in the employment community. Before conducting a survey, teacher-coordinators should publicize it and explain its purposes to interested parties. The superintendent of schools and the high school principals as well as the assistant principals and guidance counselors should be informed about the activity. It is also advantageous to keep business and civic organizations such as the local chamber of commerce and the junior chamber of commerce informed about the plans because, upon request, groups such as these will include a brief announcement about the survey in their newsletters.

Placement survey forms will vary according to whether the form is to be used for a single vocational field or for all vocational fields. The form is simply an interview schedule or guide to provide the teacher-coordinator with necessary information about training opportunities. The major questions should be based on the purposes of the survey described earlier.

The interview should be held with the manager, owner, or head of the establishment. Recall that the primary purpose of the placement survey is to ascertain the employer's capacity, capability, and willingness to train cooperative vocational student-trainees and this purpose can only be accomplished by discussing the cooperative program with a person who has the authority to speak for his organization.

Analyzing Survey Findings. After the information has been gathered, the data should be tabulated and analyzed. If a number of coordinators have participated in the survey, it is advantageous to meet with them to summarize the findings and interpret them. A report of the survey should be made available in attractive form to the superintendent of schools, the principal, state supervisors, and local advisory committee members. Without the identification of employers, the report is an excellent source of information for a news release.

UTILIZATION OF PLACEMENT SURVEY INFORMATION

When the placement survey has been completed and analyzed the teacher-coordinator possesses a relatively accurate knowledge of the number of student-trainees that could be accommodated if all of the training agencies were to be acceptable, which probably will not be the case. He/she also has reasonably accurate knowledge of the types of occupations for which on-the-job training can be provided. He/she is now in a position to start the very important process of planning the placements of students.

A teacher-coordinator who possesses the knowledge furnished by a good placement survey is not likely to be caught in the predicament of trying to locate a training position in an occupation where on-the-job training is not available. Unfortunately, neophyte coordinators too frequently do not consider placement opportunities carefully before admitting students to cooperative vocational education and consequently resort to questionable placement which may retard the students' career development and generate other serious problems for the students and all involved parties.

Planning Placement of Student-Trainees

When planning the placement of student-trainees, several factors must be considered: the students themselves, the training environment, and the welfare of the vocational education program in which the student is enrolled.

CONSIDERATIONS CONCERNING THE STUDENTS

It goes without saying that the career development of students is the most important factor to be considered when questions regarding placement are weighed. When determining suitable placements for student-trainees, teacher-coordinators should keep in mind the students' current occupational interests, their abilities, and long-range career goals.

Current Occupational Interests. At a very young age, some students have clearly defined career goals while other students have given little thought to what they want to achieve through a career. Every student enrolled in a cooperative vocational program should at least express an interest in a career field—one which becomes the focus of instruction. One of the values of effective on-the-job training is the clarification of career objectives that might have been vague before the student had this type of experience.

Long-Range Career Goals. Consideration should be given to the students' long-range career goals, even though they are tentative, so that appropriate placements may be obtained which will assist them in making their first steps toward these goals. It is important that the teacher-coordinator considers the amount and quality of the occupational planning the student has done. Does he have a career plan that includes the ways of preparing for this career? What are the parental aspirations for this student? How much instruction and guidance has he had in career planning? What does his counselor have to say about the realism of his career plans? Other important considerations regarding the students' career goals are the satisfactions students want from their jobs, their aptitudes and abilities, their attitudes toward work, their knowledge of the world of work, their concept of themselves in an occupational role, and their appreciation of the social value of work.

CONSIDERATIONS CONCERNING THE TRAINING ENVIRONMENT

There are four major factors concerning a training environment that should be carefully considered: (1) the potential of training agencies to help students develop technical competencies required in the occupation of their choice; (2) the potential of the training environment for cultivating career development competencies; (3) the potential of the training agencies' personnel to assist in the student's occupational adjustment; and (4) the previous record of the training agencies in training cooperative vocational education students and other beginning workers.

Technical Competencies. Technical competencies are the knowledges and understanding, skills, and attitudes required to perform the critical tasks of an occupation. Technical competencies include the specialized competencies required to enter and to advance in a career field and the special competencies required in a specific occupation within that field. For example, a student enrolled in cooperative industrial education may desire to be placed in an automobile repair shop as an automobile mechanic's assistant. The ability to learn and apply craft techniques, processes and principles, the ability to use independent judgment in planning a sequence of operation and in selecting proper tools and materials, and the ability to apply shop mathematics to practical problems are some of the technical competencies that should be developed. A student enrolled in horticulture may be placed in a nursery. On-the-job training should help him/her develop such technical competencies as the ability to plant seeds, seedlings, bulbs, etc., the ability to transplant flowers, the ability to plan the use of various fertilizers and chemicals, and the ability to cultivate plants.

A student enrolled in cooperative office education may be placed as

Placing Student-Trainees

a stenographer in a lawyer's office. While there he/she should be able to develop such technical competencies as the ability to understand the meaning and relationships of words and sentences, skill in taking and transcribing dictation, skill in typing, and ability to work with specialized terminology in the legal field.

A student enrolled in cooperative distributive education may be placed as a display helper and sign printer in a department store. The experience should help him/her develop such competencies as skill in arranging interior and window displays, skill in constructing backgrounds for displays, skill in using color, harmony, balance, and proportion in displays, and skill in developing copy for point-of-scale signs.

In the classroom, cooperative vocational education students are expected to obtain knowledges and understandings and, to a degree, some skills related to their entry jobs. In the preparation for some occupations the training agency has the major responsibility of increasing the students' understanding of the technical aspects of their jobs and of providing the experience that will develop the students' skills. When preparing for other occupations, much of this responsibility rests with the school. The capacity and the willingness of potential training agencies to develop identified technical competencies are of crucial importance when considering a training environment.

Career Development Competencies. Career development competencies are the knowledges and understandings, skills, and attitudes concerned with finding and maintaining a satisfying occupational role. The training agency should provide a climate in which a student can assess and analyze his needs, his interests, and his aspirations. The training sponsor and the student trainee's fellow workers should help him examine the potential opportunities and satisfactions of the occupational field and assist him in predicting his own chances of being successful and satisfied in that field. In this kind of atmosphere the student will be able to make better decisions and plans to achieve his goals.

Properly guided cooperative vocational education students test the theories of career development in the real-life situations where they are employed. The question to be answered is, Will the training agencies selected for on-the-job training of students provide the learning environment conducive to the development of identified career development competencies? (See chapter 4, for a list of career development tasks.) This is an important factor to consider if expected learning outcomes of cooperative training are to be realized.

Occupational Adjustment Competencies. Occupational adjustment competencies are the knowledges and understandings, skills and attitudes needed to succeed in a work environment. When planning the placements of student-trainees the question to consider is, Will the environment in this training agency be conducive for developing necessary occupational adjustment competencies?

It is essential for cooperative students to be placed where they are comfortable in "learning how to learn a job." Also, student-trainees need experience in participating as members and as leaders in worker groups, and they need guidance as they interact with co-workers, supervisors, and employers. They should be able to develop desirable work habits and attitudes by emulating their fellow-workers.

Managing work and leisure time is difficult for all workers and especially for cooperative student-trainees who have school work as well as employment to consider. This is another occupational adjustment competency that can be developed if the environment is suitable.

Record of Training Agencies. It has been said that "the best predictor of the future is a record of the past." This statement is relevant when considering the factors affecting a training environment for cooperative vocational education students. Some of the questions to consider are: What is the record of the proposed training agency in the training of cooperative vocational education students? in training other employees? What is the quality of training? How many former cooperative students are currently employed? Is the employer willing to train students with special needs? Will the current economic conditions in the industry affect adversely the retention of student-trainees? Are there unusual situations, such as strikes, that might affect cooperative training?

CONSIDERATIONS CONCERNING THE WELFARE OF THE PROGRAM

As mentioned earlier, student needs should have primary consideration in the selection of training agencies. When these considerations have been carefully considered, the next consideration should be the welfare of the vocational education program in which the student is enrolled.

Need for Occupational Diversity. There usually is an implicit need for representation among types of employers within an occupational field or fields for which students are being prepared. Generally speaking, both small and large firms should be included. For example, in a high school where there is only one distributive education section it is advantageous to have as training agencies a variety of retail eatablishments (eg., food, hardware, apparel, department stores) as well as wholesale firms and different types of service businesses (e.g., dry cleaning, office supply). This variety usually improves classroom instruction and at the same time increases community support for the program because of its broad base.

Experience has shown that there are training advantages in both small and large firms. A small firm usually provides an opportunity for the student to learn about the total business operation as well as to become skillful in his entry job. Also, there is a close personal relationship between the manager of a small firm and his employees that is not possible in a large firm. On the other hand, a large firm provides many advantages through the opportunities it provides for occupational specialization. A student-trainee in a large firm may have to obtain his training in a single department, but within that department he will be able to observe or experience every operation of the firm. He probably will receive the benefits of specialized training programs provided by the firm and he will be in contact with specially trained personnel, such as display directors, advertising specialists, and merchandising specialists. It usually is important to the welfare of the program, as well as to the students, to have both small and large firms as training agencies.

Effect of Economic Conditions. Ideally, in order to maintain community support for the program, training agencies should be rotated if more than enough training agencies are available and if employment is plentiful. However, if employment is scarce, the selection of training agencies necessarily will take into consideration the ability of the firm to provide regular employment for the cooperative student.

Selection of Training Agencies

The occupational survey report should provide a list of potential training agencies including the firms where cooperative students are employed. However, the teacher-coordinator must select the firms which will meet predetermined standards of training agencies if best results from on-the-job training are to be accomplished. In addition to the training environment previously discussed, the criteria for a training agency include standards relative to the following:

1. Employment opportunities;
2. Employer's policies for dealing with clientele and employees;
3. Management's attitude toward training;
4. Availability of suitable training sponsors;
5. Suitability of physical factors in relation to training;
6. Compliance with labor laws.

EMPLOYMENT OPPORTUNITIES

One standard of a training agency is that the firm can provide a job that is worthy of the student's learning time and efforts. The Vocational Amendments of 1968 specify that on-the-job training should be "related to existing career opportunities susceptible of promotion and advancement" and "does not displace other workers who perform such work" (Sec. 173[a]3). If the job in which the student is employed requires only a limited amount of training time, the training agency, to be qualified, should agree to rotate the student to other jobs within the firm or at least to provide some learning experiences on other jobs that lead to the student's career goal. There should be opportunities for increased responsibility as the student progresses in experience and training.

EMPLOYER'S POLICIES

Another standard concerns the employer's reputation in the community. It is essential that firms selected to train cooperative students have high ethical standards in dealing with their clientele and their employees. Some of the policies and practices to consider in selecting suitable training agencies are: (a) wage scales in relation to those paid for similar occupations in the community; (b) relationships with labor groups and other employers, and with customers and clients; (c) work standards and efficiency of operation; (d) hiring, promotion, and dismissal practices; (e) working conditions and employer concern for well-being of employees; (f) credit record and financial stability; and (g) support of community activities and welfare.

MANAGEMENT'S ATTITUDE TOWARD TRAINING

The attitude of management toward training is another important criterion for evaluating a training agency. One way of determining a potential employer's attitude toward training is to look at the training provided employees in that firm. Does it provide systematic training for regular as well as new employees? Does management encourage employees to participate in adult education offered by the various vocational education services? Do the managers take advantage of opportunities for further training?

Specifically, is the employer willing to provide training as well as employment to students? Is management willing to enter into a formal training agreement that will assure desired learning experiences on the job?

AVAILABILITY OF SUITABLE TRAINING SPONSORS

Closely related to management's attitude toward training is management's capacity for providing training on the job. Is the potential employer willing to designate a training sponsor for each student—a supervisor or an experienced employee who is capable and willing to give day-by-day instruction to the student-trainee?

It goes without saying that the training sponsors should have technical competence in the jobs to be taught. However, it is equally if not more important for them to have the willingness to allot sufficient time and effort to training. They should have the ability to adapt job instruction to the learning style and capabilities of the student. They should be skilled in human relations and be sensitive to the students' needs for recognition, guidance, and direction. The training sponsors' ethics and work habits should serve as models for the students to emulate.

The training sponsors should be willing to work with the teacher-coordinator in planning on-the-job learning experiences and related classroom instruction and in evaluating student progress.

PHYSICAL CONDITIONS

Since the student-trainee's job is functioning as a laboratory experience, the working conditions of the laboratory should be carefully evaluated. In general, the standards generally accepted for the occupation should provide the guidelines for evaluating the physical conditions of potential training agencies. Specifically, some of the factors to consider are:

1. Convenience of location with respect to students' being able to get there from school and home safely, and within a reasonable period of time;
2. Healthful and safe working conditions;
3. Hours of work which allow the student sufficient time to keep up with his school work, participate in some recreation, and get adequate rest;
4. Adequate equipment and facilities to practice the occupation for which training is planned;

5. Compliance with local, state, and federal labor regulations regarding wages, hours, working conditions, insurance, and hazardous occupations.

COMPLIANCE WITH LABOR LAWS

When placing student-trainees the teacher-coordinator must make certain that the employment is in compliance with local, state, and federal labor regulations. Any infringement of laws regulating employment is certain to give a cooperative vocational education program a poor image. Teacher-coordinators are expected to know the regulations which apply to student-trainees, the occupations, and the participating training agencies. This information is available from the regional office of the Wage and Hours and Public Contracts Division of the U.S. Department of Labor and from the corresponding state and local agencies which enforce local employment regulations. Problems of violations are best avoided by selecting training agencies that adhere to the regulations and by drawing up a written training agreement which specifies the conditions of employment—wages, hours, job duties, and responsibilities of the parties to the agreement. It is not the function of the teacher-coordinator to enforce the laws, but he is expected to inform participating employers when they are unknowingly violating regulations.

Wage Regulations. The laws providing for minimum wages and overtime standards apply to student-trainees who are employed by firms that are subject to the regulations. The teacher-coordinator should find out if the employment is covered by the Fair Labor Standards Act or subject only to state minimum-wage regulations. State standards may differ from federal laws, in which cases the higher standards must be observed. In discussing with the employer what wages to pay the student-trainee, the teacher-coordinator usually recommends that a student-trainee be paid the same wages as other employees in similar jobs, even though this may be more than the statutory minimum wage. Not every student-trainee in the class will receive the same wage rate due to differences in the nature of the training positions and the length of time it takes before the students become fully productive in their jobs.

Student-Learner Certificates. There are provisions for paying student-trainees less that the regulatory minimum wage; however, vocational educators and many participating employers have not found it necessary for most entry-level jobs. Neither the teacher-coordinator nor the employer wishes to be criticized for exploiting students by paying less than the minimum wages unless there is convincing evidence of higher training costs. Also, the difference between the required minimum wage and the lower rate has not been great enough to risk the effect on the attitude of the student from paying the lower rate. The provision, however, may make it possible to expand training opportunities and participation of employers in smaller firms, in rural communities where businesses would not ordinarily employ part-time students, and for highly technical jobs which require extensive training before a learner is capable of fully productive work. In order for a training position to qualify for the student-learner provisions it must meet the following criteria:

1. The occupation requires a sufficient degree of skill which necessitates a substantial learning period.
2. The student-learner is not replacing another worker.
3. Wage rates or working standards of experienced workers would not be depressed.
4. The occupational needs of the community and the industry warrant the training.
5. The employing firm has no serious outstanding violations of the Fair Labor Standards Act.
6. The number of students at certificate rates is only a small proportion of the establishment's working force.
7. The student-learner is at least sixteen years of age.
8. The student is enrolled in a bona fide vocational education program and a plan of instruction in school and on the job have been specified.
9. The hours of work permitted at certificate rates plus the hours of school instruction (not including study hall and non-credit activities) do not exceed forty hours a week. If school is not in session, such hours of employment do not exceed eight a day or forty a week.
10. The wages paid the student-learner are not less than seventy-five percent of the statutory minimum.
11. Records for each student paid the certificate rates and his occupation and rate of pay, along with the application are retained by the employer for three years.
12. An application for a student-learner certificate is filed with the regional or district office of the Wage and Hours and Public Contracts Division. It is signed jointly by the employer, a school official, and the student-learner (trainee). See appendix D for a sample copy of the "Application for a Certificate to Employ a Student-Learner."

Some states also have provisions for special minimum wages to be paid to cooperative vocational education students. When employment is not covered by federal regulations, an employer may wish to apply for an exception to the state minimum wage regulations.

Hazardous Occupations. There are also special provisions for sixteen- and seventeen-year-olds to be employed in certain hazardous occupations, provided they are enrolled in cooperative vocational education under supervision of the public schools. The requirements for exemption are described in detail in Child Labor Bulletin No. 101 available from the Wage and Hours and Public Contracts Division. The teacher-coordinator should verify that the conditions in the place of training meet these requirements. The exemption conditions and the regulations are relatively flexible which means that the teacher-coordinator and the employer must exercise considerable judgment in determining a student-trainee's ability to handle potentially hazardous job tasks. There are also state regulations and exemption provisions for vocational student-trainees which the teacher-coordinator should investigate before placement.

Aligning Students with Training Agencies and Positions

After the training agencies have been selected, the next important task is to align student-trainees with positions within these agencies. This entails a two-fold problem of satisfying the needs and wants of the cooperative vocational education students and of satisfying the needs and wants of the cooperating firm.

THE STUDENT-TRAINEE

Each student-trainee is seeking particular satisfactions from his occupational experience, and each brings to his job a different background. As nearly as possible, the student-trainee's abilities, interests, aptitudes, and personal traits should be matched with the requirements of the available positions in the training agencies. This is sometimes a very difficult task. Although achievement test scores, grades, and teacher evaluations provide information that is useful in measuring some of the student's abilities and traits, such factors as work motivation and social attitudes complicate the problem of aligning students with appropriate occupational experience. The student-trainee's career interest, his ultimate career goal, his previous occupational experience, his health, his emotional stability, his personality factors, and his character must be considered as well as his abilities and his aptitudes.

THE TRAINING AGENCY AND THE POSITION

In aligning student-trainees with positions, the needs and wants of the cooperating employer as well as the requirements of the available positions must be taken into account. It would be an ideal situation if in each community there were innumerable well-qualified training agencies whose managers were willing to designate certain positions within their firms as "training positions," and if the firm were primarily concerned with the learning outcomes of students placed in these jobs. Since these idealistic conditions seldom if ever exist, the teacher-coordinator must look carefully at the conditions that *actually* exist: How demanding is the training position in terms of physical endurance? How productive will the student-trainee be expected to be? What personality traits are ordinarily expected of an employee in this position? What is the personality of the training sponsor? What does the training agency expect of employees in terms of its image (appearance, speech, etc.)? What opportunities for advancement does the training agency provide?

These and other considerations concerning training agencies and positions within these cooperating firms must be weighed when teacher-coordinators are attempting to match students with training positions.

A SYSTEM FOR ALIGNING STUDENTS AND POSITIONS

There are several systems for aligning students and positions, no one of which is satisfactory for every cooperative education situation. The authors of this book believe that the best system is the one whereby the teacher-coordinator refers several students to an employer, who makes the final selection. However, under certain circumstances the system of assigning a student to a training agency or the system of the student's finding his own job may have merit.

Coordinator Selects Several Applicants. In the system in which the teacher-coordinator selects several students who apply for a position within a training agency, it is presumed that the coordinator carefully reviews the characteristics of the students and of the position before referring students for interviews. When applying the theory of work adjustment, "work personalities" are matched with "job environments" for optimal performance (see chapter 5). A selection of two or three students as applicants for each position is ideal because this gives the employer an opportunity to choose his student-trainee. The coordinator makes arrangements for the interviews with the employer and provides him/her with appropriate background information concerning the applicants.

The coordinator determines the ground rules for the interviews (e.g., the student should telephone the employment manager for an appointment; usually the student should be interviewed by the employment manager rather than by the department manager or foreman). After the interviews, the employer or the employment manager frequently calls the coordinator for further information or for the coordinator's recommendation if two or more students seem to be equally qualified. The final decision is the employer's. It should be communicated to the coordinator as soon after the interview as possible.

Ideally, the coordinator should visit the training agency to follow-up on the behavior of the rejected students during the interviews so that he will be better able to assist them in improving their interview techniques. Since time is of the essence during the period that placements are being made, a telephone conference sometimes has to take the place of a personal call. The employer sometimes gives his decision to the student he has selected and asks that the student report the decision to the coordinator. In this instance, the coordinator should verify this information with a telephone call that might use this approach: "Mr. Jones, this is Mary Brown, office education coordinator at Blackville High School. Johnny Sims told me his good news about getting the job in your bank. He is a lucky young man to have this opportunity. Before sending the other two students whom you interviewed for their next interview, could you tell me any ways in which either or both of them could improve in the way they present themselves?" Under the system of giving the employer a choice of two or three applicants for a position, there comes a time when there is only one applicant to send for an interview.

Coordinator Assigns Student to a Training Agency. There are situations in which a student has been rejected several times. Also, some disadvantaged students may not be able to compete for a position. Under either of these circumstances the coordinator may need to ask the cooperating firm to accept a student-trainee whom the coordinator has selected. The disadvantages of this procedure are that the latter type of student is deprived of the experience of competing for the position and that the employer is more inclined to be interested in an employee if he has made the selection. These disadvantages can be overcome to a large extent if the coordinator handles this type of placement carefully.

Usually the coordinator should provide the employer with complete information about the student and determine in advance if the

Placing Student-Trainees   171

employer feels he can employ the student. The coordinator should make the student understand that he must sell himself to the employer and that in the final analysis it is up to the student to get the job. The coordinator should assure the employer that even though only one student is sent for the interview he is under no obligation to provide on-the-job training for that student unless he feels that the student has potential for satisfactory performance in his firm.

Irregular Placement Situations. In almost any cooperative vocational education program there are instances where some students are already employed when they apply for cooperative training and other instances where, because of special needs, some students need unusual assistance in obtaining employment.

Students who are already employed may or may not have positions that qualify for on-the-job training. The position may be in a qualified training agency but may not be an occupation for which cooperative vocational education is offered. For example, a student employed as a bookkeeper in a hospital may apply for admission to a cooperative health occupations program. If the student career objective is accounting, he/she should be advised to apply for the vocational office training program. However, if the career goal is health occupations, the student should be advised of the possible positions related to health occupations within and outside of that firm to which he/she could be referred as a cooperative student. Another example is that of a student who says, "I've been a bagger at Joe's Supermarket for six months. I want to keep this job as a cooperative student because the pay is extra good." The teacher-coordinator must determine the student's career goal and see if there are opportunities for training beyond the duties of a bagger. If he approves this job, it might become repetitive and boring unless the scope of the occupational experience is broadened.

Countless illustrations could be cited to prove the importance of the coordinator's examining each situation wherein a student who is already employed applies for admission to a cooperative vocational education program. It is only after careful consideration of all the factors concerning the student and the training agency discussed earlier that the coordinator can decide whether or not the student's present job is suitable for his on-the-job training. If the coordinator does approve the student's present job, it is essential that both the student and the employer understand the difference between "work experience" and "on-the-job training" and that both are willing to accept the responsibilities of bona fide cooperative training.

Students with special needs may require unusual assistance in obtaining the opportunity for on-the-job training. Special needs may include such factors as lack of transportation, lack of suitable clothing, irregular attendance at school, emotional instability, immaturity, and a host of other things that might make an employer hesitate to employ an individual. Congress has recognized the fact that it is difficult to provide on-the-job training for individuals with special needs and through Part G of the Vocational Education Amendments of 1968 has provided incentives to encourage employment of these students. Each state is required to describe in its state plan the policies and procedures for the operation of a cooperative program for students with special needs. Some of the special provisions are that the employer may be reimbursed for added costs incurred in providing on-the-job training; that the cost of transportation or other unusual costs to the individual student may be paid; and that school systems may receive special financial assistance to provide personnel to coordinate such programs and provide instruction related to the students' occupational experience.

These provisions are made so that coordinators who are working with students with special needs may work with advisory committees and employers in providing training opportunities that may not otherwise be available. Advisory committee members may assist the teacher-coordinator in locating placements for students with special needs. They may also assist in individual counseling of these students, either by devoting some of their own time and talents or by encouraging other interested businessmen to counsel certain students. It is essential for an advisory committee to work with the teacher-coordinator in considering all the unusual factors affecting the placement of students with special needs, so that the students can be successful in their on-the-job training.

THE TRAINING AGREEMENT

It is highly desirable, and required in some state plans for vocational education, to have a written training agreement describing the training commitment to which each employer, the school, the student, and the parents have agreed. The training agreement sometimes includes a *training plan,* which is discussed in the following chapter. Although the training agreement is not a legal document, it serves as a "gentleman's agreement" which, except for just cause, should be honored by all the parties involved. The training agreement should be signed by each of the parties mentioned, and each should receive a copy of the agreement. The following topics usually are included:

1. The purpose of the training agreement;
2. The career goal of the student;
3. The duration of the training period;

4. The minimum and maximum hours of work;
5. Wage agreement;
6. Employer responsibilities;
7. School and teacher-coordinator responsibilities;
8. Student responsibilities.

A sample training agreement is shown in figure 7-1, p. 174. A training agreement may be used as a reminder of responsibilities for any of the parties who may become negligent. It was used to good advantage as evidence of a meeting of the minds in a case where a student was injured while on his cooperative education job.

Preparing Students for the Interview

The first impression that the employer has of the student-trainee is usually a lasting one. For this reason it is essential that students be trained either individually or in groups in techniques of applying for a job. The two factors that in large measure will affect the employer's impression of the applicant and which will influence his evaluation of the applicant's potential for success on the job are the application form and the job interview.

THE APPLICATION FORM

Although there are many variations in employment application forms, most of the information required is usually classified under one of the following categories: (a) personal data, (b) education, (c) experience, (d) hobbies, and (e) references.

Under the watchful eye of the teacher-coordinator, each student should have an opportunity to complete a sample application form. The teacher may discuss the fine points concerning the application form before the student begins to fill in the blanks or he may discuss it one section at a time and permit the student to complete that section before discussing the next one.

Some of the fine points which student-trainees should know may be listed as Do's and Don'ts, as shown in table 7-1, p. 175.

THE JOB INTERVIEW

Since the job interview is so crucial, every student-trainee should have an opportunity to role-play an interview. If the class is small, each

FIGURE 7-1

ARIZONA DEPARTMENT OF EDUCATION
DIVISION OF VOCATIONAL EDUCATION
T R A I N I N G   A G R E E M E N T

School _____ City _____ Date _____

The _____ will permit _____
         Training Agency   Student

to enter their establishment for the purpose of gaining knowledge and experience as (a) (an)

_____   _____
        Occupation   Beginning Wage

The course of training is designed to operate for a _____ month period with a minimum of fifteen hours per week. The training will be in accordance with the outline of training below, made and agreed upon by the employer and coordinator.

Training Plan
(FOR ALL OCCUPATIONS)

1. The school will make provision for the student to receive related instruction.
2. The status of the student while in training shall be that of student-learner.
3. The student while in training shall progress from job to job in order to gain experience in various operations.
4. The schedule of compensation shall be in accordance with existing local standards, labor laws, and policies.
5. The coordinator will assist with adjustment of any problems of the student.
6. The parent or guardian shall be responsible for the conduct of the student while in training.
7. The coordinator shall have authority to transfer or withdraw the student when he deems such action to be to the best interests of those concerned.
8. The student promises to abide by all implied and stated terms included in this training plan.
9. The student shall be subject to discharge at any time because of inefficiency or because of conditions within the industry or concern.
10. This training plan may be cancelled at any time provided due notice is given to all parties concerned.

(FOR HAZARDOUS OCCUPATIONS ONLY)

   A. The work of the student-learner in occupations declared hazardous shall be incidental to his training, shall be intermittent and for short periods of time, and shall be under the direct and close supervision of a qualified and experienced person.
   B. Safety instruction shall be given by the school and correlated by the employer with on-the-job training.

_____   _____   _____
        Employer   Title   Parent or Guardian

_____   _____
        Coordinator   Student

Original to Training Agency, Duplicate to Parent, and Triplicate to Coordinator

TABLE 7-1
Fine Points Concerning the Application Form

Do's	Don'ts
1. Bring a ballpoint pen and a pencil with you.	1. Don't ask unnecessary questions.
2. Follow directions.	2. Don't take too long to complete the form.
3. Either complete every space, put N.A. (not applicable), or draw a short line to show that you read the item.	3. Don't slouch in the chair; the secretary may be observing your behavior.
4. Write or print neatly.	4. Don't exaggerate.
5. Know the full names, addresses, and telephone numbers of your references. Be sure to ask their permission in advance.	5. Don't use friends or relatives as references.
6. Answer all questions honestly.	6. In answer to questions regarding type of job preferred, don't respond "anything." Specify jobs in which you are interested and for which you qualify.
7. Put "open" or "going rate" in the space regarding salary unless there is a special reason for not doing so.	
8. Have social security number to fill in appropriate space.	

student might role-play the interview before the entire class while other members of the class rate the interview. Either the teacher or a student who has had a successful interview experience may play the role of the employer. If the size of the class makes the above suggestion too time-consuming, the class may be divided into groups of six to eight persons. Each student in the several groups would then role-play the interview before his group while the others rated the interview.

Before students role-play the job interview they should be taught some of the preparations to be made before the interview takes place and some of the things they should and should not do during the interview.

Preparations Before the Interview. There are several things applicants should do before they are interviewed. To begin with, it is important for the student to do some research on the company so that he can ask and answer questions intelligently. It is a good idea for the student to have questions he wants to ask prepared before he is interviewed. He should find out the full name and correct pronunciation of the interviewer and the exact place and time of the interview.

Students always want to know what type clothes they should wear for the interview. The one rule that applies to all places of employment is that clothes should be neat and clean. Employers expect the applicants to wear clothes that are appropriate for the type of job the applicant is seeking, so no hard and fast rules can be given that would apply to all places of employment. The teacher-coordinator should discuss this problem with employment directors at the time he talks with managers about possible placements. As fashions change, standards of dress for work also change. For example, at one time it was considered mandatory for a girl to wear a hat and gloves when she appeared for the interview. When the wearing of hats became the exception rather than the rule of fashion, employment directors no longer expected the applicant to wear a hat. Also, local customs vary. What is expected of an applicant regarding appearance in a large city may be quite different from what is expected in a small community.

Things to Do During Interview. The twenty-seven items in the rating sheet used to evaluate contestants in the DECA "Job Application" competition suggest the behavior that employers expect of their applicants. Teacher-coordinators should explain the significance of each of the behaviors in the following list:

1. Promptly greeted interviewer and called him by name.
2. Introduced himself immediately.
3. Shook hands only after interviewer offered to do so.
4. Remained standing until invited to sit down.
5. When seated, sat comfortably and erect.
6. Did not place hands, elbows, hat, or papers on interviewer's desk.
7. Stated the purpose of his call.
8. Was polite and courteous, but did not over-do it.
9. Did not chew gum, smoke, or slouch in chair.
10. Supplied complete and accurate information to questions asked.
11. Answered questions briefly, clearly, and positively.
12. Answers to questions were well thought out.
13. Answered questions without hesitance.
14. Did not monopolize the interview.
15. Volunteered information not requested.
16. Asked pertinent questions.
17. Secured a clear answer in regard to wages.
18. Did not give impression he was interested in pay only.
19. Secured an answer as to whether he was to be employed or given further consideration.
20. Displayed calmness throughout the interview.
21. Used correct English.

22. Displayed self-confidence.
23. Was a good listener.
24. Was interested, alert, cheerful, and enthusiastic.
25. Was sincere.
26. Did not possess any annoying mannerisms.
27. Smiled frequently and at the proper time.

A Perspective on Placement

Now that you are aware of placement fundamentals, you probably will appreciate the fact that the tasks comprising this function of a teacher-coordinator's job are mastered only through consistent, conscientious effort. The complexity of the task varies widely from local program to local program. It coincides to some extent with the supply and demand for labor in the occupations for which the training is offered. In large measure, the success or failure of a cooperative education program depends on the quality of the student-trainees' experiences on their jobs which, in turn, depends largely on initial placement. What is the state of the "art" in placing cooperative education students? What are the trends?

THE PLACEMENT FUNCTION IN THE PAST

During the early years of cooperative education, when employers were still unaware of the long-range benefits of the cooperative plan, teacher-coordinators were highly concerned about relationships with employers, so high priority was placed on employer needs. In general, teacher-coordinators were quite sophisticated in the realm of job requirements and worker abilities, but usually they knew relatively little about the work-related needs of students. There was much anxiety about recruiting "good students," and counselors, where they existed, were chided about directing poor students into the several cooperative vocational education units. The void in knowledge of students' work-related needs seemed to be ignored both by employers and school personnel.

PLACEMENT TODAY

Employers' needs have not changed. Employers are as much concerned about worker productivity as ever, and coordinators are still sensitive to their dependence on cooperating employers for good on-the-job training. However, employers' attitudes toward youth have changed to some degree. Employers, in general, have learned that the younger generation has a different value system than most employers hold, and many youths possess a work ethic which is very different from that which prevailed a short generation ago. Many of them have become aware of the teacher-coordinator's problems in selecting and placing students because of their experiences in hiring workers from a variety of sources; hence, they are more open-minded about the type of student they will accept and more agreeable to participating actively in training of potential future employees.

Along the same vein of thought, contemporary teacher-coordinators usually perceive the complexity of the placement problem in greater depth. They realize that job satisfactions for the worker and the worker's satisfactoriness to his employer are interdependent. They sense that much more knowledge about the student and his needs is essential to cope with present-day placement demands. They feel the need for a more sophisticated placement procedure supported by valid, reliable instruments which measure a student's job-related needs and which assess the potential satisfactions (reinforcers) a student-trainee might receive from a given training position. They also realize a need for more knowledge about a student's attitude toward work and his work ethic. They appreciate the need for valid information concerning the competencies required to enter and advance toward a satisfying career. Some of the more progressive among them experiment with recently developed measuring instruments as supplements to their subjective judgments.

PLACEMENT IN THE FUTURE

Without doubt, community involvement in vocational education will continue to increase. Because of this accelerated community participation and the resulting expansion of cooperative education to new types of occupations and to new groups of students, many new problems will arise, and many latent needs will surface. These problems will continue to be researched, particularly those related to disadvantaged youth. An interesting fact is that most of the research on work adjustment done by the University of Minnesota Psychology Department was supported by rehabilitation funds. Ironically, we seem to have learned more about normal workers through research efforts intended to benefit handicapped workers than through efforts meant to help normal workers.

Conscientious readers will have reflected on the theory of work adjustment (1) discussed in chapter 5 while perusing this chapter on placement, associating the twenty dimensions of a worker's needs and job reinforcers with the several steps in the placement process. Certainly, the potential of the measuring instrument which identifies what a person wants in his ideal job, the MIQ (Minnesota Importance Questionnaire), will have been brought to mind during the discussion of the student-trainee's work-related needs. Likewise, the MSQ (Minnesota Satisfaction Questionnaire) may have been recalled during the treatment of the assessment of training agencies and positions. In a similar vein, the ORPs (Occupational Reinforcer Patterns) were likely to have been called to mind while reading about the alignment of jobs with students.

Concluding Statement

The conceptual framework for placement activities has been established, with a recommended application of a theory of work adjustment. The authors contend that in the near future most teacher-coordinators will, of necessity, become skilled in the various facets of cooperative education placement, particularly in the assessment of students' work-related needs. The rationale and mechanics of placement of student-trainees in training agencies and positions has been presented in this chapter. Your success as a teacher-coordinator will depend largely on how well you are able to apply this knowledge and build upon it in a dynamic world of work.

REFERENCES

1. Dawis, Rene V., George W. England, and Lloyd H. Lofquist. *A Theory of Work Adjustment.* Minneapolis: University of Minnesota, Industrial Relations Center, 1964.
2. Shotwell, H.D. "The D. E. Advisory Committee." *D.E. Today.* New York: Gregg Division of McGraw-Hill, 1972.
3. United States Office of Education. *Zero in on Cooperative Vocational Education—Training Agreements.* Division of Vocational and Technical Education, 1974, 32pp.

ADDITIONAL REFERENCES

Borow, Henry, ed. *Man in a World of Work.* Boston: Houghton-Mifflin, 1966.
Crawford, Lucy C., and Warren G. Meyer. *Organization and Administration of Distributive Education.* Columbus, Ohio: Charles E. Merrill, 1972, pp. 129-36; 158-66.

Mason, Ralph E., and Peter G. Haines. *Cooperative Occupational Education.* Danville, Illinois: Interstate, 1972, 535pp.

SUGGESTED ACTIVITIES

1. Check with the local office of the state employment service, the local chamber of commerce, or the public library to determine what information is available on (1) the number of local firms employing workers in the occupations you plan to teach; (2) the number of people employed locally in those occupations; (3) any anticipated changes in levels of employment; and (4) projected local needs for trained workers in those occupations.

2. Prepare a questionnaire or form which you could use to obtain or record placement survey information.

3. Select a business or place of employment in which student-trainees in your program might receive their on-the-job training and evaluate it as a training agency using the criteria discussed in this chapter.

4. Plan and role-play a situation in which the teacher-coordinator prepares a student-trainee for a job interview. Have observers critique the techniques used by the teacher-coordinator.

5. Prepare a list of ways in which teacher-coordinators can apply their knowledge of career development when placing student-trainees.

6. Prepare a list of ways in which teacher-coordinators can apply the theory of work adjustment when placing student-trainees.

Chapter 8 DEVELOPING THE OCCUPATIONAL EXPERIENCE LABORATORY

This chapter describes the way in which an effective teacher-coordinator guides the development of occupational experience laboratories in which student-trainees test on their jobs the principles and theories that they learn in the classroom. In the first section, the purpose and nature of the occupational experience laboratory are discussed; in the second section, various aspects of training sponsor development are described; in the third section, the five steps in training plan development are explained; and in the fourth section, illustrative training plans are presented for jobs in four different business or service categories.

As a result of studying this chapter you should be able to:

1. Explain the purpose of the occupational experience laboratory in relation to the central purpose of American education;
2. Describe the three general objectives of the occupational experience laboratory;
3. Describe the individualized nature of occupational experience learning;
4. Name the four major functions in the role of the training sponsor;
5. Describe the personal traits and the technical competencies required of an effective training sponsor;

6. Cite the major tasks and responsibilities of a training sponsor;
  7. Illustrate the need for individual and group instruction of training sponsors;
  8. Prepare a sponsor-development calendar;
  9. Describe each of the five steps in the development of training plans;
  10. Construct a training plan for a student-trainee on a specific job.

The entire training agency where a vocational cooperative student-trainee is employed is considered to be his occupational experience laboratory. However, unless his teacher-coordinator makes every effort to establish a training climate—both with management and with employees—the agency will remain just a place of employment rather than a training facility with a bona fide job, where planned educational experiences are used as media in teaching and learning.

Employers and employees who participate in training the student must understand the purpose of the occupational experience laboratory and their roles as educators. They must accept responsibility for the individualized nature of the learning that takes place on the cooperative student's job. Employers must appreciate the necessity of having a designated training sponsor for each cooperative student and the need for a training plan that incorporates the student's training in the classroom, on the job, in the community, and in the youth organization.

Purpose and Nature of the Occupational Experience Laboratory

PURPOSE

In order to fully comprehend the purpose of the occupational experience laboratory it is necessary to understand the purpose of education in America. The Educational Policies Commission has stated the central purpose of education in this way:

> The purpose which runs through and strengthens all other educational purposes—the common thread of education—is the development of the ability to think. This is the central purpose to which the school must be oriented if it is to accomplish either its traditional tasks or those newly accentuated by recent changes in the world. (1)

Practitioners of various cooperative vocational education programs seek to implement this purpose of developing the rational powers of individuals through guided decision-making experiences and by coordinating classroom learning with occupational experience. Through carefully designed on-the-job learning experiences the student-trainee learns to test the principles learned in the classroom and to apply these principles in real-life situations. The occupational experience laboratory provides a means whereby he or she may (a) acquire first-hand experience with job tasks, interpersonal relationships, equipment, and materials related to his/her career goal; (b) learn to use the scientific method of solving problems; and (c) develop skill in performing a wide variety of tasks and in handling human relations problems. The behavioral outcomes derived from these types of organized occupational experiences become the nucleus of the specific objectives of an occupational experience laboratory.

First-Hand Experience. Secondary school cooperative vocational education students study many things that are not familiar to them—technical job tasks, interpersonal worker relationships, certain equipment, and materials and products which cannot be properly used or simulated in a school environment. Some of the situations they encounter are rare and subtle, particularly those involving their fellow workers. Hopefully, they draw on their classroom experience, making practical applications of their learning. Without such on-the-job contacts with reality, classroom-learned principles and theory are apt to remain vague and incomplete, and important skills are not adequately developed. They may be forgotten before the student has an opportunity to put them into actual use. Good first-hand experience also motivates students to do more careful reading and studying in order that they may acquire the information needed to excel in performance of their jobs.

Occupational experience generates an objective search for knowledge—an outstanding characteristic of critical thinking. The discovery of truth through experience, rather than acceptance of authority, is essential to good thinking. The student soon learns that authorities in the school and in the business world do not always agree and that he must weigh the facts and make his own judgments. This affords him an excellent opportunity to develop skill in arriving at rational decisions.

Problem Solving. A large part of the casual unplanned type of work experience unfortunately gives the student little more than perceptual knowledge. Such knowledge may be useful, but the educational process is by no means complete with the mere acquisition of knowledge. The student needs to learn to use this knowledge when thinking and acting. The occupational experience laboratory provides the climate in which the student may learn to formulate and verify hypotheses in solving various types of problems. By solving problems in business and industry through methods similar to those used in research, widely applicable general principles are firmly established.

Acquiring Skill. The third objective of the occupational experience laboratory is to learn how to perform certain operations and to become skillful in executing them. The occupational experience laboratory is to be regarded *not* as just a place of accumulating experience, but as an educational laboratory where the student plans his activities under the guidance of his teacher-coordinator and training sponsor, tries out his ideas, acquires knowledge of procedures and operations by performing them, and develops skills through practice under supervision. He also learns how to be effective in human relations and improves his ability to make career plans.

INDIVIDUALIZED NATURE OF OCCUPATIONAL LABORATORY LEARNING

In order to implement the objectives of the occupational experience, all parties who participate in the training of students should recognize the individualized nature of the learning environment and the learning content required in the wide variety of cooperating training agencies usually utilized in a cooperative vocational education program. The role of the job in preparing the student for a career must be considered; individual interests, abilities, traits and attitudes of vocational cooperative students must be taken into account; and the possibilities for integrating the four sources of learning (school, job, community, and club) must be examined.

The Role of the Job. Generally speaking, the student's career goal should be his main incentive for learning. Maximum learning usually takes place to the extent that the student perceives the job on which he is training as a step toward his career goal. The job may not function in the same way for students with special needs whose goal is to acquire certain general work skills, habits, and attitudes before selecting a relatively specific career goal. Even in programs designed for students with homogeneous career goals, the degree of commitment to a career goal will vary among class members. Differences in the role of a job in the curriculum of a particular student must be taken into account constantly when planning and operating a cooperative vocational education program.

Individual Differences of Students. Cooperative vocational education students always vary in their abilities, interests, attitudes, and habits. Here again this calls for individualized planning of content and instruction. An occupational experience laboratory provides each student a unique opportunity to learn as an individual. No other student has a curriculum exactly like his. Through this he becomes a more resourceful

Developing The Occupational Experience Laboratory 185

and self-appraising learner. He develops the ability to learn by observation, by experimentation, and by practice, so that he becomes self-motivated. With help from his teacher-coordinator and training sponsor he can measure his individual progress toward his career goal.

Integration of Sources of Learning. A cooperative vocational education student has four sources of learning—the classroom, the job, the community, and the youth organization. The primary source of learning is the classroom because it is there that theories are proposed and essential principles and concepts are explained. The job and the youth organization supplement the classroom in that they provide media for applying the classroom learning. But the job and the youth organization also generate content much like a science laboratory does. Most of the instructional objectives are completed on the job. In similar manner, the youth organization provides a laboratory for the development of leadership skills and group participation skills, and other phases of the curriculum are enriched.

The integration of these four sources of learning requires great managerial skill on the part of the teacher-coordinator. Usually he has nearly as many teaching associates as there are students and sometimes more. He should capitalize on this enviable position which no other faculty member enjoys. He should take advantage of the fact that he and each training sponsor form a teaching team, and both the teacher-coordinator and the training sponsor have a very effective tool to utilize in planning for the individual's training. This tool is usually referred to as a training plan or sometimes as a schedule of experiences.

The remaining portion of this chapter is devoted to a discussion of the training sponsor and of the training plan. The training climate in the occupational experience laboratory depends in large measure on management's willingness to designate a suitable training sponsor for each cooperative vocational education student and to support each training sponsor in carrying out his responsibilities concerning the training of the student. The coordinator can then work with each training sponsor in developing a training plan which will provide appropriate on-the-job learning experiences and will help in establishing and maintaining a good working relationship between the school and the training agency.

The Training Sponsor

Although the concept of a training sponsor is old, it may be new to some vocational educators. Many business firms, particularly those employing a number of seasonal or part-time employees, appoint sponsors for new employees and thus delegate certain training responsibilities to those individuals who are asked to establish a close working relationship with the new employees who are assigned to them. In the same way, the cooperating employer designates a training sponsor for each cooperative education student. Let us look at the training sponsor's role, his qualities, his selection, and his preparation, and then consider the need for a sponsor's handbook and a developmental program for training sponsors.

THE ROLE OF THE TRAINING SPONSOR

The training sponsor performs a number of functions crucial to the success of the student-trainee. His major responsibilities are related to (1) the induction of student-trainees into the organization, (2) their training, (3) their evaluation, and (4) counseling them on matters relating to their work.

Induction. The training sponsor sets the stage among the employees for the acceptance of the cooperative student. He orients the student-trainee to his job and makes him feel welcome to the organization.

Training. The training sponsor participates in the construction and development of the training plan for the student-trainee under his supervision. He assists the student-trainee in carrying out classroom assignments related to his job and evaluates the learning experiences listed on the student's training plan.

Evaluation. The training sponsor evaluates the student's progress in learning his or her job and communicates to the teacher-coordinator the strengths and weaknesses of the student. He verifies the student's attendance and production reports.

Counseling. The sponsor counsels the student concerning his or her job performance and relationships with other employees. One manager who assumed the role of the training sponsor always referred to himself as a *coach*; another sponsor referred to himself as a *tutor*; another referred to himself as a *downtown teacher*. As these terms imply, a training sponsor takes the responsibility for preparing a student for a definite goal and gives him the individual attention necessary to attain that goal. He performs the role of teacher, supervisor, counselor, and friend.

QUALITIES OF THE TRAINING SPONSOR

An effective training sponsor possesses both the personal qualities and the technical competence that make him comfortable and happy in the very important assignment he undertakes.

Personal Qualities. A good training sponsor is one who has a sincere interest in young people. He knows and performs his job well and is loyal to the firm in which he is employed. He is willing to share his knowledge. He understands human relations and has good relationships with his fellow-workers. He has excellent character and has work habits which the student may emulate.

Technical Competencies. A training sponsor should be proficient in performing technical competencies which he teaches his student-trainee and capable of teaching the student various aspects of a particular job.

In addition to the qualities mentioned above, a training sponsor must have time enough to perform his tasks as a training sponsor.

SELECTION OF TRAINING SPONSORS

The selection of the training sponsor is the prerogative of the employer. However, the teacher-coordinator has the responsibility to provide the employer with the criteria of a good training sponsor and to discuss with the employer the functions that the sponsor will perform. Ideally, the employer discusses with the coordinator the individuals he considers potentially good sponsors and then the employer and the coordinator reach an agreement on the final selection.

In a small firm the training sponsor may be the manager himself. In a larger firm, a supervisor or an experienced employee is usually selected. The regular job title of the training sponsor varies. For example, a department head, an office manager, and a foreman may have comparable supervisory competencies that would qualify them as training sponsors. Experienced salespeople or other experienced employees identified as potential sponsors may lack the supervisory experience of department heads or foremen, but they may make very good training sponsors because of their other attributes and the amount of time they can allocate to the assignment. It is generally agreed that the job title of the training sponsor is not as important as the personal qualities and the technical competence of the individual who is selected to train the student on the job, and don't forget that time for training duties is mandatory.

PREPARATION OF THE TRAINING SPONSOR

The education and development of training sponsors is a continuous managerial activity, one that tests the true mettle of a teacher-coordinator. Both individual and group instruction are required in the preparation of training sponsors. Many of the competencies required of training sponsors are also highly desirable for their performance on their regular jobs, so they welcome the assistance and training that can be given to them through the vocational program. Since a training sponsor is really an instructor, a well-organized and clearly defined sponsor-development program will save the coordinator a considerable amount of time and energy and will result in more effective on-the-job training. When planning a sponsor-development program, it is advisable to consider all the problems of mutual concern to the coordinator and the training sponsors and then to determine which problems can best be handled through group instruction and which should be discussed in individual conferences with training sponsors.

Major Concerns. Some of the major concerns that need attention during the year are:

1. The sponsor's role
    a. His functions
    b. Reasons for his selection
2. The student's job
    a. Hours of work
    b. Rate of pay
    c. Student's specific and related job duties
3. The curriculum
    a. Major instructional objectives
    b. Curriculum content
    c. Relationship of the job to the class and to the youth organization
4. Learning experiences on the job
    a. Daily assignments
    b. The training plan
5. Production reports
    a. Purpose
    b. Sponsor's verification
6. Evaluation of student's progress
    a. Formal progress reports
    b. Informal progress reports
    c. Training profiles
7. Supervision of young workers
8. Career development
9. Work adjustment
10. On-the-job training
11. Sponsor's participation in youth organization and in the related class
12. Sharing of training materials
13. Preferred times for sponsor-coordinator conferences

14. Permanent employment for the student after graduation
15. The employer-employee banquet
16. Interpersonal relationships

Individual Instruction. Individual instruction for the training sponsor usually is done at the training agency during coordination visits. It may be planned and scheduled, or it may be spontaneous in response to a manifested need. The latter seldom is thought of as "instruction," but rather as a sharing of information. It usually is a pleasant task, one which affords an opportunity for a teacher-coordinator to build good will for his program and the school. Both types of individual instruction are very effective because the application of what is taught can be individualized and applied almost immediately.

Group Instruction. Group instruction of training sponsors may be provided in formal courses through one of the vocational education adult programs or it may take the form of seminars or clinics held periodically to discuss common problems.

Formal Courses. With increasing emphasis on accountability, management by objectives, and planning, programming and budgeting systems (PPBS), supervisory training is in demand, and training sponsors usually are very receptive to good training. Special classes for training sponsors may be organized, or when the size of enrollment does not warrant a special class the sponsors may be enrolled in regular formal adult supervisory training courses. Training within Industry (TWI) courses, which were introduced during World War II, are still popular in some sectors. A strong factor in the longevity of these packaged courses is that they were based on good research and field testing. Adaptations of the series—Job Instruction Training, Job Relations Training, and Job Methods Training—were made for use in distributive education. In some locations, vocational education personnel have revised the TWI courses, retaining the basic course structure.

Training sponsors also enroll in a variety of supervisory training courses taught by personnel from business and industry or by a teacher-coordinator. Teacher-coordinators often make good evening school teachers of subjects in this area because of their training in the psychology of learning, particularly in the supervision of young workers.

Seminars and Clinics. If it is not feasible for the teacher-coordinator to enroll the training sponsors in the formal courses, it generally is advisable to provide instruction through small group seminars or clinics held in close proximity to the training sponsors' places of employment. The advantage of giving the training through small groups rather than individual instruction is that the participants can exchange criticisms of their performances. In large communities, it may be difficult to persuade all the training sponsors to come to meetings in a central location, but it usually is relatively easy to get good attendance for small group meetings held for those in small geographic areas, for example, in shopping centers.

Experience has shown that at least one or two group meetings for training sponsors will enable the coordinator to go into more depth on certain topics than would be possible during individual visits. For example, presentations relating the training sponsor's role to the aims and objectives of the total vocational education program, the purposes of progress reports of various kinds, and the opportunities for training through vocational education adult courses make interesting group meetings. Any of these topics can be discussed individually, but the time consumed usually prevents a full discussion leading to a thorough understanding on the part of the training sponsors.

Value of Group Instruction. The contagious enthusiasm generated by dedicated training sponsors makes group meetings very worthwhile. The very fact that training sponsors have been invited to participate and that they are receiving recognition as individuals of special importance to the educational program makes them more sincere about responsibilities they are being asked to add onto their regular jobs. When experienced training sponsors, former cooperative vocational education students, and/or employers are invited to participate in selected class meetings, group training of sponsors can be very realistic as well as palatable and valuable.

A Sponsor's Handbook. It is highly desirable to provide each training sponsor with a handbook that includes an explanation of the various phases of cooperative vocational education. Many states have printed handbooks which, upon request, are made available to local teacher-coordinators. Sponsor handbooks are usually designed for specific occupational areas or clusters so that they can provide rather detailed information about the operation of a particular cooperative program. Topics usually included in a handbook are:

- Brief history, aims, objectives and scope of the program
- Benefits of the program to the employer, the student, and the school
- How the program operates
  - School and work schedules
  - Wages and other benefits
  - The instructional program
  - The youth organization
- The role of the training sponsor
- What the student-trainee should learn
- How to teach young workers

How to supervise student-trainees
How to evaluate student-trainee progress
Forms and procedures

A Sponsor Development Calendar. In order to space sponsor development activities properly throughout the year, the teacher-coordinator prepares a sponsor development calendar. As depicted in figure 8-1, both individual and group activities are scheduled.

FIGURE 8-1

CALENDAR OF SPONSOR DEVELOPMENT ACTIVITIES

June – July – August	Work with employers in obtaining appointment of training sponsors. Talk with sponsors about their roles. Identify sponsors who might be selected as guest speakers in class or as judges in competitive events.
September – October	Work with training sponsors in designing learning experiences to be included in the first part of each student's training plan. Conduct group meeting for training sponsors for purpose of discussing the philosophy of cooperative vocational education and the function of a training sponsor. Through individual conferences with training sponsors, determine strengths and weaknesses of student-trainees. Seek to enroll training sponsors in an adult vocational education course (e.g., "How to Train").
November – December	Ask sponsors' help in designing learning experiences for the second part of the students' training plans. Inform training sponsors and employers about the availability of high school students seeking seasonal employment.
January – February – March	Seek to enroll training sponsors in an adult vocational education course (e.g., "How to Supervise"). Conduct group meeting to discuss evaluation. Ask the sponsors' assistance in designing learning experiences for the third part of the students' training plans.
April – May	Recognize training sponsors at employer-employee banquet. Confer with training sponsors about permanent employment for senior cooperative students and about continuing employment and training for junior cooperative students. Make tentative arrangements for the placement of next year's cooperative students.

The Training Plan

A training plan is the key to effective instruction and learning at the training agency. It prevents any misunderstanding about what is to be learned and who is responsible for teaching it. It is an effective tool in making job and classroom experience more meaningful and relevant to student needs. A *training plan* is a written reminder, recording a meeting of the minds of the parties responsible for a series of on-the-job experiences which lead to the student's achievement of specified objectives. It should be articulated or combined with parallel accounts of classroom and youth organization experiences designed to achieve the same ends. It may be used as a part of a training agreement, shown in figure 7-1. Other terms used to describe documents similar to a training plan are Plan of Experiences, Plan of Increased Responsibilities, and Schedule of Processes.

In order to correlate classroom learning, on-the-job learning, and youth organization learning, it is essential that the training plan be designed so that it will serve as a guide to the student and the training sponsor. Although the teacher-coordinator takes the responsibility and the initiative in the process of developing a training plan and frequently provides a tentative check list of items to be included in the training plan, the coordinator, the training sponsor, and the student should agree on the specific competencies to be learned and the learning experiences to be provided on the job, and on the approximate date the broad categories of items can reasonably be expected to be completed. The training plan should afford an opportunity for both the student and the training sponsor to further develop and refine the training plan and to evaluate each element.

DEVELOPING THE TRAINING PLAN

The development of training plans for any cooperative vocational education student should focus on the student-trainee's stated career goal and interests. As he or she clarifies his or her interests and needs, it is assumed that realistic alterations in the training plan will be made. When developing the training plan, the coordinator and employer should discuss with the student those skills, attitudes, and aptitudes that are necessary for successful employment in the student-trainee's chosen occupational area. Broad competency areas for which training can be provided by the training agency during the student-trainee's period of employment should be identified together with the tentative dates for the completion of related study. Next, training for approximately one month should be detailed. The specific tasks that the student-trainee will perform during this month should be identified, and the analysis of those tasks together with a plan for mastering them becomes the responsibility of the student under the direction of the teacher-coordinator and the training sponsor. In-school instruction that needs to be provided to master the tasks should be identified.

Thus, effective training plan development is a continuous process which initially emerges as a global perspective of the year's on-the-job experiences and anticipated outcomes and then goes through a refining process. This slow but sure strategy precludes some frustrations that are likely to ensue if a completed plan is attempted at the outset.

Although the form and title of the training plan may vary from one state to another and may be different in various occupational clusters within a state, the steps in the development of a comprehensive training plan are the same. In order to prepare a systematic plan for the training of cooperative vocational education students, it is necessary to take the following steps: (a) identify the job tasks to be performed by the student-trainee; (b) specify major learning outcomes based on the competencies required to perform the tasks; (c) design learning experiences to develop these competencies; (d) specify those learning experiences to be obtained on the job and those which are job-related and are to be accomplished out of class; and (e) design a plan for evaluation of the student's progress and achievement.

Identifying the Job Tasks. The first step in preparing a training plan is the identification of the job tasks constituting the entry job leading to the student's career goal. In order to prepare himself for this step, the teacher-coordinator locates and studies published job descriptions and analyses and the training plans of former students whose training agencies and jobs were similar to that of the new student-trainee. If none are available, he is faced with the task of starting from scratch and making a job analysis. In either case, care should be taken to ensure the inclusion of related tasks as well as the specific tasks (see figure 8-2, p. 194).

A number of recent research studies provide lists of tasks for a wide variety of jobs and/or job clusters. Some of these are listed as references at the end of this chapter. Job analyses made by the training agency also may be excellent sources. They usually are available to vocational educators upon request. Last but not least among the sources of information about occupations is the *Dictionary of Occupational Titles*, Volume I, which provides over 35,000 job definitions containing job tasks.

These and other sources of information about job tasks make it possible for a teacher-coordinator to develop a tentative list of specific and related tasks for the position in which the student will be placed. The coordinator should verify the tasks with the training sponsor and/or authorities who know the field. Such experts may identify additional tasks or may suggest that certain ones be deleted.

Specifying the Desired Learning Outcomes. This portion of the training plan is sometimes deleted from the document that is ultimately given to the student-trainee and the training-sponsor, but specification of the major learning outcomes is an essential step in the development of a comprehensive training plan. The major learning outcomes are keyed to the student-trainee's career objective. They are derived from the compe-

FIGURE 8-2

Specific Job Tasks: Produce Clerk*

1. Unloads produce deliveries from supplier's or warehouse truck
2. Checks deliveries for proper quantities and weights
3. Checks deliveries for proper quality and freshness
4. Informs head produce clerk of improper quality, quantity or weight of merchandise
5. Opens boxes and containers for preparation of produce displays
6. Prepares produce for display by washing, trimming and separating of bulk produce
7. Packages produce items using treated film and trays
8. Bunches and bands select produce items in sizes and weights as directed by head produce clerk
9. Weighs and prices select produce items for display
10. Bags, weighs and prices select produce items using treated bags
11. Sets up dry and refrigerated produce racks according to layout assignment by head produce clerk
12. Checks produce items for spoilage and removes spoiled items for disposal or price reduction
13. Reduces price of distressed or spoiled produce and displays according to direction of head produce clerk
14. Reworks and trims unsold items for maximum freshness
15. Rotates all produce items for maximum freshness
16. Freshens wet produce by using water or ice
17. Places price cards or markers on produce racks as required
18. Paints and prepares special display signs
19. Decorates produce department with display materials
20. Assists customers in selecting and weighing produce
21. After weighing produce for customer, bags and price-marks it
22. Assists customers in finding items in other departments of the store
23. Explains and suggests uses of produce and possible cooking techniques to customers
24. Informs head produce clerk of movement and purchase requirements of produce items
25. Informs head produce clerk of distressed produce for his action
26. Cleans and maintains wrapping and weighing equipment
27. Cleans produce racks, salesfloor area, working area and coolers
28. Removes certain produce items from racks and places in coolers at end of the day
29. Disposes of trimmings and refuse

Related Job Duties—Display

1. Gathers products or merchandise from salesfloor or stockroom for displays
2. Sets up department displays of merchandise
3. Sets up department displays of sale items or specials
4. Sets up merchandise on shelves or floor attractively and neatly
5. Returns displays merchandise to stock
6. Coordinates displays of advertised and featured merchandise
7. Cuts cases for display
8. Puts shelf price tags in moldings

**Source:* Crawford, Lucy C., "Tasks and Major Learning Outcomes (Competencies)" taken from *A Competency Pattern Approach to Curriculum Construction in Distributive Teacher Education, Volume III*. Blacksburg: Virginia Polytechnic Institute and State University, 1967.

FIGURE 8-2, cont'd.

9. Makes, paints and puts up display signs
10. Puts up pre-made signs on displays
11. Attractively wraps and packages products for most effective displays
12. Stores display materials
13. Calls customer's attention to displays of specials
14. Locates displays in best traffic areas
15. Trims stock for better appearance

Related Job Duties—Stock

1. Tickets or marks stock
2. Checks selling floor shelves for depleted stock and fills in
3. Checks stockroom for depleted stock and fills in
4. Rearranges stock in department
5. Keeps stock in stockroom organized and accessible
6. Takes stock counts
7. Supervises stock counts
8. Reorders from stock counts
9. Takes physical stock inventory
10. Changes prices on stock
11. Checks on and inspects stock for damages, shortages, spoilage and breakage
12. Rotates stock on selling floor and in stockroom for best sales
13. Unloads trucks
14. Orders products or merchandise upon repeated customer requests
15. Checks in stock received and places in stockroom or on selling shelves
16. Cleans and dusts stock

Related Job Duties—Advertising

1. Supplies customers information on advertised items
2. Highlights advertised items on shelves in the department
3. Informs store employees about advertised merchandise
4. Keeps results on store ads
5. Reads own and competitor's newspaper ads
6. Posts current ads in heavy traffic areas in store

Related Job Duties—Customer Contacts

1. Gives customers directions
2. Adjusts customers' complaints and grievances
3. Gives demonstrations or cooking instructions
4. Supplies customer with information by telephone
5. Carries grocery bags to car for customers
6. Makes refunds

---

tencies needed to perform the specific and related tasks (see figures 8-2 and 8-3). They are not as easy to identify as tasks are because most practitioners in the occupation are not able to name the knowledges, skills, and attitudes needed to advance toward a career goal.

An analysis of each task is necessary to determine appropriate competencies. Since each task requires a number of different competencies and since many of these competencies relate to more than one task, it is ad-

FIGURE 8-3
Training Plan—Produce Clerk

Instructional Content	Major Learning Outcomes	On-the-Job Experience
SOCIAL COMPETENCIES A. Employee duties and responsibilities B. Appropriate grooming C. Employee relations D. Customer relations E. Career opportunities in the food distribution field	Knowledge of duties and responsibilities of cooperative part-time job Understand that customer loyalty can be built with friendly service Ability to analyze careers	Using the check list provided you, determine the duties you will be expected to perform. Add any not listed. Make a list of customers' names that you know who come to your department during a one-week period. Did you speak to them by name? Interview your sponsor regarding career opportunities in the food distribution field and major requirements for success in your chosen career.

SELLING
A. Stock Display
  1. Importance of display in self-service stores
  2. Stock displays as "silent salesmen"
B. Suggestion Selling
C. Stock Care
	Knowledge of ways of displaying merchandise to create interest and desire in customers
	
	Knowledge of how to display related items or pre-package larger quantities to increase sales
	
	Knowledge of department and merchandise locations throughout the store
	
	Knowledge of housekeeping duties that must be performed
		Describe five different types of display used in the produce department of your store
		
		With sponsor's permission, study the effect on sales of pre-packaging produce in a variety of sizes and units. Keep a record for one week.
		
		Draw a lay-out of your store showing location of merchandise in all departments.
		
		Using your check list of job duties, note the stock keeping duties that are performed (1) daily, (2) weekly, (3) occasionally. Use (1), (2), (3) as codes.

visable to analyze the job tasks in terms of the organizational system used in the appropriate curriculum or in terms of the major functions performed in the employment situation. For example, in distributive education the occupational competencies may be organized around the marketing functions of advertising, display, merchandising, operations, and selling and around the product and service technology, basic skills of communications and mathematics, and the social skills.

The major learning outcomes listed on the training plan are the competencies identified in the various competency areas. In many instances, the competency and the learning outcome are identical; in other instances several competencies are combined into one learning outcome.

Designing Learning Experiences. Learning experiences are those activities designed to assist the student-trainee in reaching his career goal. They include classroom, on-the-job, and club activities. Although the training plan ordinarily lists only the on-the-job activities in reference to an outline of classroom instruction, a complete training plan should include learning experiences for the classroom and, where appropriate, learning experiences that will be developed through the youth organization.

Common learning experiences that assist the student to acquire knowledges and understandings needed in his career include reading of selected material, observations and interviews, listening to tapes, viewing slides, film strips, or single concept films, and listening to lectures and discussions. Role-playing and demonstrations may be utilized to begin the development of a skill or build an attitude. Most of the latter type of experiences take place in the classroom in preparation for on-the-job experience and for facilitating career development. However, learning experiences on the job and in the youth organization are needed to provide an opportunity to practice in real-life situations. Learning experiences to develop attitudes might also include the analysis of cases and situations and the evaluation of critical incidents related to interpersonal relations.

Designate the On-the-Job Experiences. The crucial part of a training plan is the description of learning experiences to be obtained on the job. Obviously, the specific tasks of the student's part-time job are important learning experiences and should be detailed on the training plan. However, if the student is to obtain experiences in related job tasks and in experiences that will prepare him for advancement, it is necessary to design experiences that both the sponsor and the student feel are appropriate and feasible. Some of these experiences may involve observation on the job, interviews with the manager or other employees, and consultation with the training sponsor to obtain information. Writing the report of such observations and interviews may be done at home or, at times, in the classroom, but the activity should be specified as "on-the-job" because the job or the training agency is the source of the information.

Formulating a Plan of Evaluation. Plans for evaluation of learning experiences may vary according to the type of experience, but all plans have this in common: both the sponsor and the student evaluate the experience. In many instances, the means of evaluation are stated in the experiences. One way of handling other evaluations is to provide evaluation forms on which the sponsor and the student can indicate not only the quality of the performance but the value to the student in reaching his learning objective. Evaluation is in itself a learning experience and should not become so complex and burdensome that it detracts from the experience for which it was designed.

ILLUSTRATIVE TRAINING PLANS

There are many different patterns of training plans which have been found to be helpful to the students, the sponsor, and the teacher-coordinator. The teacher-coordinator should select the pattern that best serves the needs in his particular situation or he should design his own. After he has a model training plan for a particular job, the coordinator, the student and the training sponsor can work from that model in tailoring a plan to meet the needs of an individual student.

Child Care Aid. An example of a training plan for a Child Care Aide is given in figure 8-4, pp. 200-201. The authors utilized research findings of a job analysis reported by Martin (see footnote, figure 8-4) to develop this plan. By examining the tasks and the major learning outcomes, it was possible to design relevant on-the-job experiences. If a teacher-coordinator of occupational home economics decided to use this model he/she would discuss the plan with each student to be employed as a Child Care Aide and with each training sponsor in order to select the learning experiences most appropriate to each student's placement. He/she would decide what portion of the training plan to include in the plan to be given the student and the sponsor, and might add a column in which to check completion dates. Evaluation is built into the learning experiences.

Produce Clerk. Specific and related tasks used to develop a training plan for a produce clerk were presented in figure 8-2. Figure 8-3 shows the training plan per se. In the Crawford research on which this plan is based, job analyses were conducted in terms of tasks that were regularly performed by a worker in each job title and in terms of tasks related to all other aspects of store operation. The competencies identified in the Crawford research are included in the training plan as major learning outcomes, and on-the-job experiences designed to develop the compe-

Developing The Occupational Experience Laboratory 199

tencies are specified. The distributive education teacher-coordinator should examine this model to determine what type of plan would be most suitable for his students who will receive on-the-job training as produce clerks. He may decide to discuss the specific and related tasks with each student and sponsor and as a result prepare a training plan including only the tasks to be performed. He may want to discuss the suggested learning experiences with the sponsor to determine whether or not they are feasible. After this discussion he may decide to include agreed-upon on-the-job learning experiences as a part of the plan.

Bank Teller. The example of a training plan for a bank teller in figure 8-5 (p. 202) is based on the identification of broad areas in which training could be given during a student's cooperative experience to develop the skills and attitudes necessary for successful employment in the student's chosen occupational area.

Dental Mechanic. Figure 8-6 (pp. 203-4) provides a schedule of experiences on the job for a student whose career interest is dental mechanic. Since the job of the dental mechanic requires a highly developed skill, the student will need to acquire a skill in each process before learning the next process. This example typifies training plans that require a "schedule of processes" needed to develop psychomotor skills.

Detailing Tasks a Month in Advance. It is suggested that detailed tasks be identified and written on the training plan for a period of approximately one month's training in advance of the date that the training is to take place. In-school instruction and reference materials should be identified by the teacher-coordinator, the training sponsor, and possibly the employer for the month. At the end of the month the student's performance on the tasks should be evaluated and additional and/or remedial training should be planned accordingly. The broad areas which were identified at the start of the cooperative experience and which are commensurate with the students' career interests and capabilities always provide the basis for developing further training.

Concluding Statement

The key to developing an occupational experience laboratory is the establishment of a training climate that makes it possible for the teacher-coordinator and the training sponsor to work together as a team in assisting the student to reach his career objective.

The preparation of the training sponsor to assume his role is vital to the success of any cooperative vocational program. It is not fair to the sponsor or to the training agency to expect the sponsor to carry out the

FIGURE 8-4

Training Plan—Child Care Aide (Partial List)

Student-Trainee _____   Teacher-Coordinator _____
Firm _____
Training Sponsor _____

TASKS PERFORMED AS DETERMINED BY JOB ANALYSIS	INSTRUCTIONAL CONTENT	MAJOR LEARNING OUTCOMES — The Student-Trainee will:	ON-THE-JOB EXPERIENCES
Becomes oriented to the child care center Learns what is required of a child care aide Observes policies of center concerning work schedules, absences, and health regulations	UNIT I—What Is a Child Care Aide	Become aware of tasks, competencies and opportunities involved in working as a child care aide Recognize employment opportunities in child care service	Using the check-list provided you, determine the duties you will be expected to perform. Interview your employer. Determine the number of people employed in different jobs in your child care center.
Works cooperatively with staff and accepts instruction and guidance from director Participates in staff planning and evaluating sessions concerned with center policies and program Helps to evaluate own progress in meeting responsibilities in the center Follows regularly assigned schedule of responsibilities and assumes other responsibilities as needed	UNIT II—Child Care Aide: A Member of the Team	Recognize factors which contribute to successful working relationships with others Assess own personal qualities in relation to job requirements Evaluates self periodically Identify factors involved in planning a satisfactory schedule for preschool children	Make a list of the personal qualities you observe in your fellow workers. List under desirable and undesirable. Check yourself against the list of personal qualities you observed at work. Rate yourself from 1-5 with one being the highest rating. Obtain a copy of the schedule for preschool children in the place where you work.

200

Unit	Learning Outcomes	Tasks
UNIT III—The Child and His Family	Recognize the basic needs of young children	Make a list of the characteristics of children age 2-5
	Describe characteristics of children from two to five	Identify the areas of development of children in your place of employment.
	Comprehend the principles and areas of development of children	Ask your training sponsor to name the four most important influences of the family on the children with whom you work.
	Analyze the influence of the family on the growth and development of children	
UNIT IV—The Child in a Child Care Center		
UNIT V—Children's Food and Eating Habits		
UNIT VI—Children's Play—A Learning Experience		
UNIT VIII—Toys and Games for Children		
UNIT IX—Health and Safety		
UNIT X—Nature and Science Experiences		
UNIT XI—The Exceptional Child		

Source: Tasks, instructional content and major learning outcomes taken from Doretha Martin's "Proposed Course of Study Outline for Child Care Aide Based on Findings of Job Analysis," *Illinois Teacher*, March-April 1972. Reprinted by permission.

FIGURE 8-5

Training Plan—Bank Teller (Partial List)

The _____ will permit _____ from _____ High School to enter their establishment as an employee under the supervision of _____ for the purpose of gaining knowledge and experience in the occupational area of 04.04 Finance and Credit so that the student may prepare for a career as a(n) Bank Teller (all purpose.)

Approximate Time	Learning Activities	OJT	In School	Evaluation	Individual Study Assignment
All Year	Customer Relations				
	1. Greet all customers	X			
	2. Direct customers to proper services departments		X		
	3. Practice proper human relations				
6 Weeks at Drive-in Window	Negotiable Instruments				
	1. Handle money	X	X		
12 Weeks in Bank	a. Counting				
	b. Packaging				
	c. Identify fraudulent money and or practices				
	2. Read Endorsements	X			
	3. Handle checks	X	X		
	a. Travelers		X		
	b. Personal				
	c. Company				
	d. Cashier				
	e. Certified				
	f. Dividend				
	g. Fraudulent				

Source: Richard L. Lynch and Thomas R. White. *Distributive Education Training Plans* (Bloomington: Indiana University, 1971). Reprinted by permission.

FIGURE 8-6

Schedule Of Experiences

Job Title _____Dental Mechanic_____   Name of Trainee _____
On-the-Job Trainer _____   Training Period _____

Possible Experiences:

FULL DENTURE CONSTRUCTION

_____ 1. Handle impressions and cast instructions
_____ 2. Pour a separate plaster cast
_____ 3. Make a shellac base plate impression tray
_____ 4. Box an impression and apply separating medium
_____ 5. Pour a separate artificial stone cast

TRIAL BASEPLATE AND BITE BLOCK

_____ 1. Make a trial baseplate
_____ 2. Make a wax baseplate

ARTICULATION TECHNIQUE

_____ 1. Adjust a Gysi Simplex Articulator
_____ 2. Mount casts on the Gysi Simplex Articulator

LEARN THE CHARACTERISTICS OF ARTIFICIAL TEETH

_____ 1. Learn the names of all the teeth
_____ 2. Learn the surfaces and about their cusp formation
_____ 3. Learn the sequence in each quadrant
_____ 4. Identify teeth
_____ 5. Learn to attach artificial teeth to the denture base

SELECTION OF ARTIFICIAL TEETH

_____ 1. Use flexible millimeter ruler
_____ 2. Determine the length of the upper anterior teeth
_____ 3. Determine the width of the upper anterior teeth
_____ 4. Select posterior teeth

ARRANGEMENT OF ARTIFICIAL TEETH

_____ 1. Set up teeth for edentulous dentures
_____ 2. Make a cardboard template
_____ 3. Seal biteplate to casts
_____ 4. Remove biteplate wax from cuspid to cuspid
_____ 5. Make roll of wax on the baseplate and seal labially and lingually
_____ 6. Arrange upper anterior teeth
_____ 7. Arrange lower anterior teeth
_____ 8. Arrange upper and lower posterior teeth (note sequence of arrangement)

_____ A. Set up one side at a time
_____ B. Seal baseplate to cast
_____ C. Note sequence of arrangement
_____ D. Check lateral occlusion and protusive occlusion

_____ 9. Make a chart showing the buccal, labial and proximal inclination of each tooth

DENTAL WAXING AND CARVING

_____ 1. Shape and contour baseplate wax
_____ 2. Know the parts of tooth to be covered with wax before flasking
_____ 3. Restore the lingual anatomy

FIGURE 8-6 cont'd.

RELIEVING DENTURE BEARING AREAS

_____1. Remove the palatial portion of the baseplate
_____2. Apply foil relief metal
_____3. Learn areas requiring relief

DENTURE FLASKING TECHNIQUE

_____1. Remove the cast and trial denture from the articulator
_____2. Prepare the cast for investment
_____3. Invest a cast and trial denture in a flask

APPLYING TIN FOIL

_____1. Cut tin foil
_____2. Apply to a full upper denture
_____3. Apply to a full lower denture

FLAX SEPARATION AND WAX ELIMINATION

_____1. Open a poured flask after it is placed in boiling water bath for 5 minutes
_____2. Remove wax and shellac baseplate
_____3. Wash flask again
_____4. Remove remaining debris with tweezers (carefully)

DENTURE PACKING TECHNIQUE

_____1. Prepare and pack acrylic resin in powder and liquid form
_____2. Prepare and pack acrylic resin gel
_____3. Apply tin foil to the cast
_____4. Complete final closure of the flask

PROCESSING OF THE ACRYLIC RESIN

_____1. Cure the acrylic resin

DEFLASKING AND REMOVING OF DENTURES FROM THE MOLD

_____1. Remove the mold from the flask
_____2. Remove the upper denture from the mold
_____3. Remove the lower denture from the mold
_____4. Strip away the tin foil

Source: Virginia State Department of Education, Virginia Polytechnic Institute and Virginia State College. *Suggested Work Experiences in Selected I. C. T. Occupations,* 1970.

responsibilities of this important role unless both individual and group instruction are provided. The result is that the individual selected for this role will not only be a more effective training sponsor, but a more effective employee of the firm.

As the sponsor works with the coordinator and the student in developing a training plan he is able to perceive his firm as an occupational experience laboratory in which the student can practice in a real-life situation the theories he has learned in the classroom. He can then take pride that he is a partner in the cooperative vocational program.

It is in this climate that the cooperative vocational education student can be effectively trained.

REFERENCES

1. "The Central Purpose of American Education." Washington, D.C.: NEA, 1961, p. 1.

ADDITIONAL REFERENCES

Crawford, Lucy C. *A Competency Pattern Approach to Curriculum Construction for Distributive Teacher Education*, Vols. I-IV. Blacksburg, Virginia: Virginia Polytechnic Institute, 1967.

Ertel, Kenneth. *Identification of Major Tasks Performed by Merchandising Employees Working in Three Standard Industrial Classifications of Retail Establishments*. Moscow: University of Idaho, 1966.

Lanham, Frank W., et al. *Developing of Performance Goals for a New Office and Business Education Learnings System (NOBELS)*. Columbus, Ohio: The Ohio State University, 1970.

Maley, Donald. *An Investigation and Development of the Cluster Concept as a Program in Vocational Education*. College Park, Maryland: University of Maryland, 1966.

Samson, Harland E. *Characteristics of Middle Management Employees*. Madison, Wisconsin: The University of Wisconsin, 1969.

University of Illinois. *The Illinois Teacher*. Urbana, Illinois: University of Illinois, 1972. Selected issues provide analysis of jobs requiring knowledges and skills in one or more areas of home economics.

SUGGESTED ACTIVITIES

1. Prepare a training plan for a cooperative student who might be enrolled in your program.

2. Prepare a sponsor-development program for a school in which you might become a teacher-coordinator.

3. Write a letter to a cooperating employer explaining the need to appoint a training sponsor.

4. Prepare a list of ways in which teacher-coordinators can apply their knowledge of career development when planning and operating an occupational experience laboratory.

5. Prepare a list of ways in which the theory of work adjustment can be applied to planning and operating an occupational experience laboratory.

Chapter 9 ORGANIZING AND ARTICULATING INSTRUCTION

Cooperative vocational education is a vocational instructional program which capitalizes on many learning sources. *Instruction* takes place in the classroom and the teacher-coordinator's office, also on the student-trainee's job, wherever the youth-group organization activities take place, and in many other places throughout the community. The primary unit in this multilateral instructional system is the school—the classroom and the teacher-coordinator's office of the school. The school is where a major portion of critical career guidance and careful instructional planning should take place. In the classroom and the teacher-coordinator's office the teacher-coordinator and his student-trainees plan activities that help the student's progress toward his career goal. Certainly, the teacher-coordinator and the student-trainee meet with the training sponsor to assess the student-trainee's job progress and to plan numerous job-related activities, but the focal point of the instructional system is the school. This chapter will deal with the selection, organization, and articulation of in-school instruction. It complements the preceding chapter which deals with the occupational experience laboratory.

As a reward for your efforts in studying this chapter you should be able to:

1. Demonstrate a desire to provide student-trainees with instructional content and methods that are relevant to their vocational needs;
2. Formulate an instructional planning system that will facilitate articulation and coordination of instruction offered in the classroom, on the job, in the community, and through the youth group organization;
3. Apply your knowledge of the three competency areas (technical, occupational adjustment, and career development competencies) when planning the individual and group study plans of student-trainees;
4. Achieve articulation of instruction through selection of viable teaching methods and learning activities;
5. Explain the need for special facilities and equipment for cooperative vocational education programs and recall their functions.

Readers of this book will recall that there was some discussion of the teacher-coordinator's teaching-learning tasks in the third section of chapter 3 which served as a precursor to the theory underlying cooperative vocational education, but only a cursory account of the instructional planning and classroom activities that should take place in the school was presented there. A brief review of that material is recommended to the reader at this time. The concepts associated with the unique characteristics of student-trainees, their learning resources, the types of content material they use, and the factors considered when selecting learning activities are germane to the discussion that follows.

Concern for Relevant Content and Instruction

Even though cooperative vocational education contains elements that foster built-in curriculum relevance, a program characteristic that was alluded to in chapter 1, a viable curriculum does not necessarily materialize unless the teacher-coordinator in charge (program manager) utilizes those elements when making decisions pertaining to curriculum and instruction. It is easy for a new teacher-coordinator to drift inadvertently toward an academic, deductive type of teaching that is relatively independent of the student's occupational experience, particularly so for one who has been teaching noncooperative-type classes for some time. Frequently the school environment is academically oriented, and he finds it expedient and acceptable to pursue a traditional style. (It is much easier to plan and prepare a unit of instruction in which all students use a textbook and respond in a similar way than it is to plan one in which the individual needs of students are analyzed and multiple media are employed in arriving at desired outcomes.) This phenomenon is not confined to vocational instruction. The tendency for educational institutions to lose their orientation toward their clients was epitomized by Tyler in the following statement:

> . . . we now see that schools and colleges, like other institutions, become program-centered, losing their orientation toward their clients. Most institutions begin as responses to the need of certain clients for services. As the years go by, programs are developed that are reasonably acceptable to the clients they have been serving. Then the institution is likely to believe that its program is its raison d'être rather than the need for its services. When this program-worship stage is reached, the institution seeks to find clients who like the program and can get along with it, and to deny admission to others. After a time, the terminology develops that those not admitted are "poor students," "not intelligent," not of "college calibre." In many cases, as in the founding of Land-Grant Colleges, new institutions have to be established to serve the clients rejected by the older ones. (4)

Although cooperative vocational education students are in close contact with reality while they are on their jobs and their instructional needs are apparent, it is possible to neglect this aspect of the program when planning and executing classroom instruction. Those teacher-coordinators who are not far removed from their own occupational experience in the content field, or are concurrently employed in it themselves, are likely to be job-minded and to capitalize on the students' occupational experience if they are trained to do so. Likewise, teacher-coordinators who maintain close working relationships with their training sponsors are inclined to utilize sources outside of the classroom. However, unless there is a functional instructional planning system that articulates the inputs of the several types of learning sources (school, training agency, community and youth organization), a sporadic and sometimes conflicting flow of instructional inputs is likely to occur. When this happens, the result usually is confused learners and ultimately graduates with poorly balanced competency patterns.

An Instructional Planning System

Fortunately, the formulation and maintenance of a system of instructional articulation and coordination is not difficult if the concept of the teacher-coordinator's being a manager of instruction is fully accepted. If a teacher-coordinator really believes that a student-trainee's job is a crucial forward step in the student's career development, that a student's training plan is a critical element in the successful completion of that step, and that the training sponsor is an effective extension of the school faculty, he will not be comfortable until he achieves a system of articulation and coordination that fits his situation. When a well-articulated and coordinated program of instruction exists, the curriculum becomes interrelated to a high degree. There is important interaction among and between the four main sources of learning—school, job, community, and club. As the teacher-coordinator improves his managerial skills, the cyclical flow of planning, instructional execution, and evaluative feedback from each learning source accelerates and learning productivity increases.

When a teacher-coordinator's system of articulation and coordination of instruction approaches an interrelated stage, the role of the youth organization and the community in the development of a satisfied and satisfactory worker becomes clear. When this stage is achieved, it becomes apparent that student-trainees must have experiences which transcend their jobs and classroom work. More appropriate, meaningful, and frequent uses are made of the total training environment, including the community and the youth group organization, in providing activities that contribute to the development of competencies associated with personal development and occupational advancement.

THE INSTRUCTIONAL FUNCTIONS

An instructional flow chart (figure 9-1) shows one way of organizing the members of the instructional staff of a cooperative vocational education program. It takes into account a large portion of Sullivan's component functions 12, Conduct Related Class (chapter 3, figure 3-1), 14, Coordinate, and 15, Evaluate Student Progress, all of which are instructional functions (3). A brief explanation of the role of each of the faculty members in the four main learning sources follows.

Instruction in the School. The coordinator's office (1A on the flow chart), which should be close to the cooperative education classroom, is the location of initial planning of instruction. (It should be large enough to accommodate the teacher-coordinator and a student or two.) Here the individual-student and group needs are analyzed and learning strategies may be generated. Also, individual instruction and confidential counseling take place here.

The classroom (1B on the flow chart) is the location of some individual instruction, a considerable amount of small group instruction, and nearly all of the total class instruction. It is also the setting for

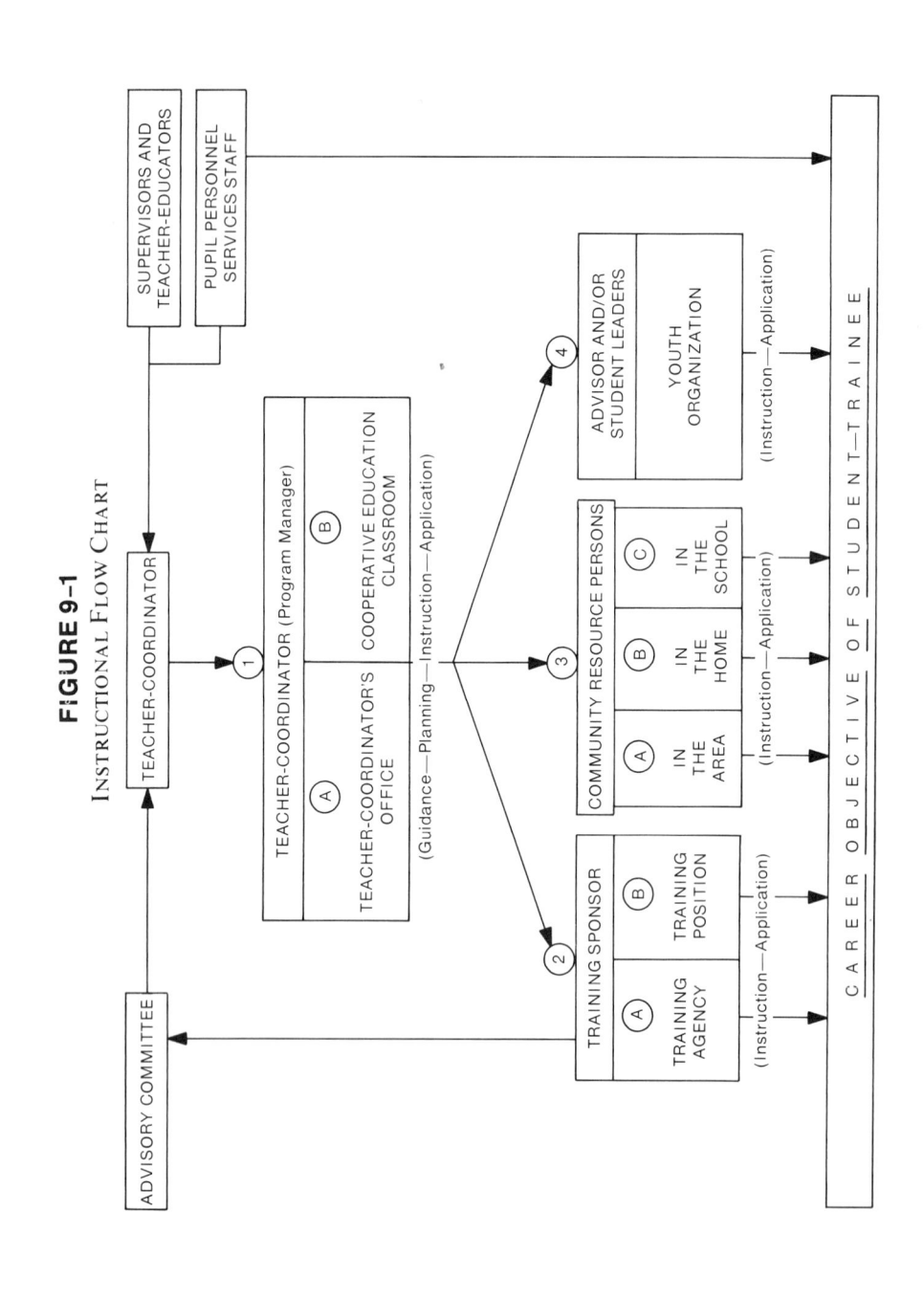

FIGURE 9-1
Instructional Flow Chart

Organizing And Articulating Instruction

teacher-pupil planning of certain aspects of content and learning activities. Many of the social competencies and capabilities that are best learned through peer group instruction should be learned in the classroom. The classroom setting also is needed to develop minimum proficiencies in competencies entailing a high degree of risk before they are applied on their jobs. In many cases, employers cannot allow student-trainees to practice their skills and experiment with performance methods while they are on the job. Also, theory and principles are very difficult to learn on the job alone because of the time needed to teach them and the limitations of the training sponsors in organizing this type of instruction. Classroom instruction must be articulated with job instruction and knowledge gleaned from experiences in the youth organization and in the community.

Instruction While at Work. Instruction while at work may be considered in two parts: instruction that is independent of the job for which the student-trainee was hired, and that which he receives on his job from his training sponsor and co-workers. Both are important in a student's career development.

Nearly all training agencies (2A in the flow chart) offer opportunities for learning beyond the immediate job—how the organization functions, opportunities for advancement, career opportunities, first-hand information about the way of life and value systems of workers in other departments, and so on. Whether or not a student-trainee takes advantage of such opportunities rests largely with his teacher-coordinator. Most youngsters remain ignorant of such learnings unless they are assigned to exploit them. Adding information gleaned from the training agency broadens a student-trainee's experience, moving his curriculum a step above job training only.

Instruction in the Community. Student-trainees get around the school and the community relatively freely, therefore they are able to use the resources of the community with little extra effort. Also, part of the function of bridging the gap between school and community is to teach them to use sources of information that will be readily available to them after completing the program. Such sources may be divided into three categories: those in the vicinity or area, those in the home, and those in the school.

Student-trainees may be given assignments relative to their career goals which draw on information obtained from community resources in the area (3A in the flow chart). For example, they may use the public library as a source of information, also the Better Business Bureau, the Chamber of Commerce, the telephone company, City Hall, real consumers, shoppers, customers, competing businesses, workers in other occupations, and other resources. In effect, all cooperating training agencies where the student trainees are placed contribute indirectly to the development of each student-trainee through class discussions in which all the establishments are mentioned. During class discussions the various practices and procedures of the cooperating training agencies may be compared. Such discussions lead to the discovery of underlying principles governing those practices. Thus student-trainees gain transferable understandings rather than narrow job skills, moving their curricula another step above job training only.

The home (3B in the flow chart) may be an excellent resource when students are taught to use it properly for that purpose. Parents, brothers and sisters, other relatives, and friends can provide opinions and information, particularly about competencies in the realm of occupational adjustment. In addition, a teacher-coordinator who visits a student's home can glean valuable information about the student-trainee's needs, values, and habits which facilitate the teacher-pupil planning process.

There are many neglected learning resources within the school system itself (3C in the flow chart) which may be considered community resources in a broad sense because they are not part of the regular instructional staff of the program. Teachers, clerical staff, and maintenance personnel are workers, too, subject to many of the problems of the co-workers of the student-trainees, and when properly approached may make excellent resource persons. Students frequently are equally good resources and, for certain types of problems, guidance counselors and school administrators can be very helpful. Of course, each faculty member is an expert in his teaching field, a resource we sometimes tend to overlook. Again, these resources within the school, and others, may be ignored unless the program manager brings them to the attention of his "faculty" and students.

Instruction through the Vocational Youth Organizations. A vocational youth organization is a vehicle for helping future personnel develop group membership and leadership competencies which prepare them for satisfying and satisfactory roles as adult citizen workers. Some of the most effective learning takes place when the students assume the major responsibility for planning and conducting their own activities. However, guidance by the advisor is needed if the group members are to select activities that further the development of competencies needed in a work environment.

Articulation of Instructional Functions. The teacher-coordinator, as a manager of instruction, must assume the responsibility of coordinating the inputs emanating from the school, the training agency, the community, and the vocational youth group organization. The process of instructional coordination starts with the student's career goal. At the outset, the student is placed in a training agency on a job which will help him progress toward that career goal. The training sponsor is conscious of that goal and works with the teacher-coordinator in planning relevant learning experiences on the job and elsewhere. He is constantly aware of what is being taught in school and, within limits, assigns to the student-trainee work that articulates with it.

Being in charge of the learning that takes place in the school, the teacher-coordinator is able to make assignments and plan activities that dovetail into the student's schedule for learning his job. This usually is done cooperatively with the student-trainee—and sometimes with the help of others. It is not always easy to agree on activities that match the learning style of a particular student.

ANCILLARY PERSONNEL

Like his counterparts who manage private and public enterprises in the community, a teacher-coordinator needs the advice and counsel of ancillary personnel. Therefore he obtains help with his instructional problems from three other sources, in particular: the advisory committee, local and state supervisors, and teacher-educators, and from guidance counselors and other pupil personnel services workers. He usually consults fellow teachers and neighboring teacher-coordinators also. Figure 9-1 illustrates the relationship between the teacher-coordinator and those who support his program.

Vocational Competency Areas

For many years, vocational educators have concentrated on teaching the technical skills and knowledges with less concern for the nontechnical competencies relating to the worker's career development and work adjustment. Although some vocational education leaders had recognized the need for expanding the scope of instruction to include work-related personal-social competencies, little progress toward that end was made until the early 1960s. At that time the matter of unemployment, particularly that of unemployed youth and nonwhites, received national attention. The new definition of vocational education in the 1963 and 1968 vocational education acts and the extension of vocational education services to additional clients and occupational groups helped promote a broader concept of vocational education. Individuals included in the category of "areas of high youth unemployment and school dropout" need many of these nontechnical competencies in order to hold a job. Youth dissatisfactions on the part of scholastically able students, as well as the social and economically handicapped persons, suggest a trio of competency areas which transcends all occupations.

It seems to the authors that dividing vocational competencies into three interdependent areas will help in planning the development of well-rounded young workers who may move up the occupational ladder as far as their abilities and interests permit. These areas are (1) *technical competencies*—skills and knowledges; (2) *occupational adjustment competencies*—those needed by all workers regardless of occupation; and (3) *career development competencies*—those relating to self-understanding and occupational awareness. The writers believe that these areas of competency should be developed simultaneously at any level because of their interdependence and for motivational reasons. However, the ratio of time devoted to each competency area should vary widely depending on the educational level and the vocational maturity of the particular group being served.

Figure 9-2 is a graphic portrayal of the three broad competency areas. These competency areas also include capabilities. "Capability" is used here to encompass a broader spectrum of human behavior than "competency." Here capabilities relate to potential behavior, the ability to act in a situation even though the individual has not been confronted with it, as well as the performance of the competencies normally required by an occupation or position. Capabilities relating to potential behaviors may occur in any of the three areas, but they are more prevalent in the career development and occupational adjustment areas than in the technical area.

Note the double arrow lines that intersect the competency areas. They are meant to show the interdependency among the three areas. For example, a student without a career goal (area 1) will not likely put forth his best effort to master the skills and knowledge required in an occupation (area 2), nor is he likely to be highly concerned about making a satisfying occupational adjustment (area 3). Likewise, a student-trainee who is weak in the technical competency realm (area 2) probably will have more difficulty with occupational adjustment (area 3) and will be less likely to persist in the occupation for which he is preparing (area 1).

CAREER DEVELOPMENT COMPETENCY NEEDS

Career development competencies and capabilities are placed at the base of the triangle portraying the three competency areas. This does not mean that they are considered more important than the others; the main reason for placing them in this position is their catalytic function.

FIGURE 9-2
VOCATIONAL COMPETENCY AREAS

Mastery of occupational duties and responsibilities

TECHNICAL COMPETENCIES
Skills, knowledges and attitudes

OCCUPATIONAL ADJUSTMENT COMPETENCIES
Personal adjustment to work environment

Personal adjustment to superiors, co-workers, and work conditions

CAREER DEVELOPMENT COMPETENCIES
Continuous testing and adjusting to career goals

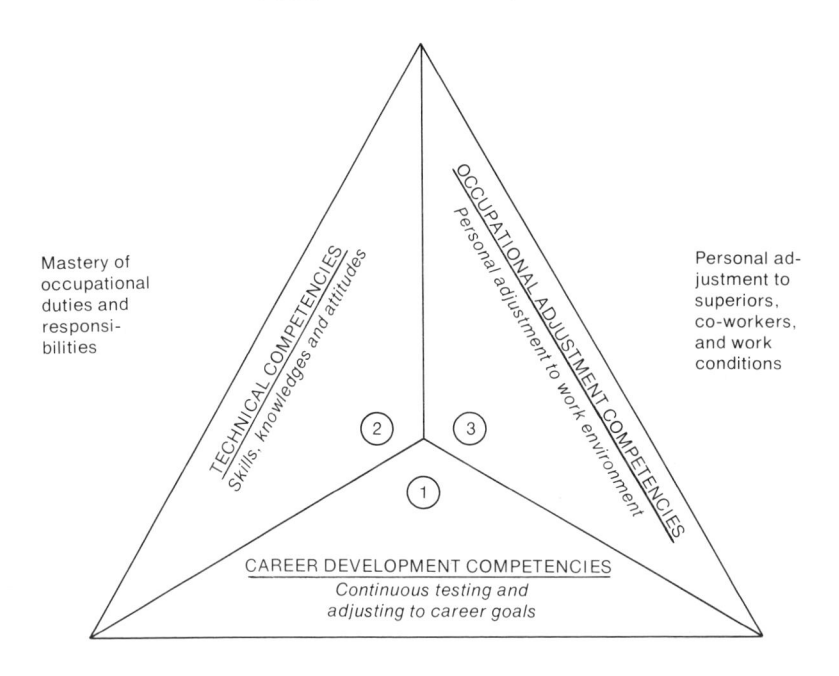

Understanding himself and his relationships to his occupational field

In most cooperative vocational education programs they are a strong motivational factor. Secondary school students tend to appraise instruction in terms of their personal goals; and students without career goals of any kind, however tentative, are not likely to gain a great deal from vocational instruction. Thus, the teacher-coordinator should continuously provide opportunities for vocational self-appraisal and occupational exploration.

Chapter 4, which treats career development, provides a list of developmental tasks related to careers and two highly condensed lists of desired outcomes covering the entire gamut of career development. Looking exclusively at tasks or competencies that might be included in a list of responsibilities assumed by a teacher-coordinator, the following entries were suggested: helping the student-trainee to

A. Understand the occupational cluster of his choice;
B. Find out what duties and responsibilities are carried out by persons employed in those occupations;

C. Determine the nature of selected occupations drawn from occupational cluster of his choice;
D. Estimate his own potential for success in those occupations;
E. Predict whether or not he would like the occupations selected for the study;
F. Select tentative career goals;
G. Determine the course of action leading to the tentative career goals;
H. Learn how to apply for a position;
I. Learn the techniques of changing jobs.

TECHNICAL COMPETENCY NEEDS

The technical competencies to be considered by the teacher-coordinator, the employer and training sponsor, and by each student-trainee are more specific than those in the career development or occupational adjustment categories. They can be readily identified through a task analysis of the particular occupation being pursued by the student-trainee. They usually make up a major portion of the student-trainee's training plan.

OCCUPATIONAL ADJUSTMENT COMPETENCY NEEDS

The occupational adjustment competencies (area 3 in figure 9-2) are equally essential to well-balanced vocational development of secondary and post-secondary school students. Student-trainees who get along well with their employers, supervisors, and co-workers, who perceive and are appreciative of their work environment, and know how to go about learning their jobs tend to form positive attitudes toward their chosen career fields. They usually are satisfied with their jobs, and they are willing to expend the necessary effort to master the essential skills and technical information.

Chapter 5 of this book provides an explanation of the theory of work adjustment and explains some of the basic problems in this capability area. The state of the art in relation to work adjustment is still in its initial stages, but a good start has been made in exploring this aspect of cooperative vocational education. Readers are encouraged to review chapter 5 at this time in order to obtain a better understanding of the scope of the competencies to be included in a balanced program of cooperative vocational education instruction.

An initial attempt to identify some of the important competencies and capabilities included in this area at the University of Minnesota (5) revealed four clusters of occupational adjustment competencies based on social behavior and nine major competencies in learning how to

TABLE 9-1
Occupational Adjustment Competency Clusters Based On Social Behavior

Competencies Related to Work Personality	Competencies Related to Work Mastery	Competencies Related to Supervisory Relations	Competencies Related to Co-worker Relations
1. Participates in individual and group activities both inside and outside of the work environment which will aid his vocational development or enhance a work-related skill.	6. Analyzes his own behavior in a work situation with regard to why he does or does not do more than the minimum required.	11. Demonstrates through his own dress and manner an awareness that the position one achieves in work world is closely related to the personal impression he creates.	17. Performs in a given work situation in a manner which indicates that he understands that success or failure depends not alone on technical proficiency but on quality of interpersonal relations as well.
2. Demonstrates sensitivity to the needs of co-workers and perceives himself as a significant person in the satisfaction of these needs.	7. Expresses vocational maturity through a personal involvement in the work task and situation, responding positively to problems.	12. Copes with authority exercised by others in the work environment in ways which lead to realization of his own personal goals.	18. Demonstrates the ability to depend on others and to be depended upon in the work environment.
3. Analyzes the motivations of supervisors and co-workers in the work environment who may hold conflicting expectations regarding his present work performance.	8. Demonstrates effective work habits by planning and scheduling work tasks and assignments.	13. Elicits and considers suggestions and evaluations of supervisor and co-workers regarding work performance.	19. Shows a genuine concern for his fellow workers and expresses a shared responsibility for success or failure of the work group.
4. Contributes positively to group effort and group goals in a work situation by demonstrating ability to both compromise and exercise influence in the achievement of group goals.	9. Demonstrates an ability to budget his time effectively by managing his leisure, work and home affairs in ways that enable him to achieve individual goals.	14. Demonstrates ability to use constructively success or failure in a work situation.	20. Displays an awareness of the dynamics of group behavior by successfully functioning as a contributing member of a task-oriented group.
5. Perceives himself to be successful in coping with new social and work roles.	10. Uses communication skills when giving or evaluating instructions.	15. Demonstrates ability to evaluate and cope with a variety of expectations so that he may satisfactorily perform in a given work situation.	21. Handles own position of authority in work environment in ways which lead to effective realization of personal goals and development of others.
		16. Identifies appropriate content in the work environment which must be communicated to others.	

learn a job. The social type occupational adjustment competencies were divided into categories related to (1) work personality, (2) work mastery, (3) supervisory relations, and (4) co-worker relations (see table 9-1). The occupational adjustment competencies relating to "how to learn a job" are named in figure 9-3. Enabling objectives are listed for each competency.

INDIVIDUALIZED CURRICULUM PLANNING IN SCHOOL

In any well-managed cooperative vocational education program no two student-trainees pursue exactly the same curriculum, even in specialized programs where all students have similar career goals and the technical competencies learned in school are the same. For example, employers' performance procedures and standards in the application of technical competencies vary from one training agency to another; each training environment is different from any other with wide differences in social climate, operating policies, working conditions and so on; importantly, each student-trainee differs from his classmates in terms of his needs in the three competency areas discussed above. These differences in individual needs and training environments imply the need for individualized curriculum and instructional planning with each student bearing a responsible role in the process. There are several good reasons why the school should be the central location for planning curricula that meet the individual needs of students and why the student-trainee should be the prime person in the planning process.

School-Based Individual Curriculum Planning. Although the school is by no means the sole source of information for individualizing a student-trainee's curriculum, it is the best place for collating the information gathered about needed competencies. First, there usually is little time for in-depth planning for individual needs while the student is at work. Second, competent assistance from the teacher coordinator, counselors, and other staff members is readily available. Third, there usually is an element of objectivity and freedom from bias in the school environment that may not exist in the work situation.

The job is the place where many needs become manifest and latent talents frequently are discovered. Classroom planned try-out experiences and coordination follow-up calls bring out the student-trainee's weaknesses and strengths. Youth group organization experiences and community contacts may serve the same purpose. Irrespective of the source, the information and data should be used in organizing a plan of study and experience that will synchronize with the competencies needed for satisfactorily achieving the student-trainee's goal at the end of his

FIGURE 9-3
"Systems" Approach To Learning A Job

Broad Instructional Goal: Through work-relevant behavior develops an ability to learn, adjust, and advance in his chosen occupation.

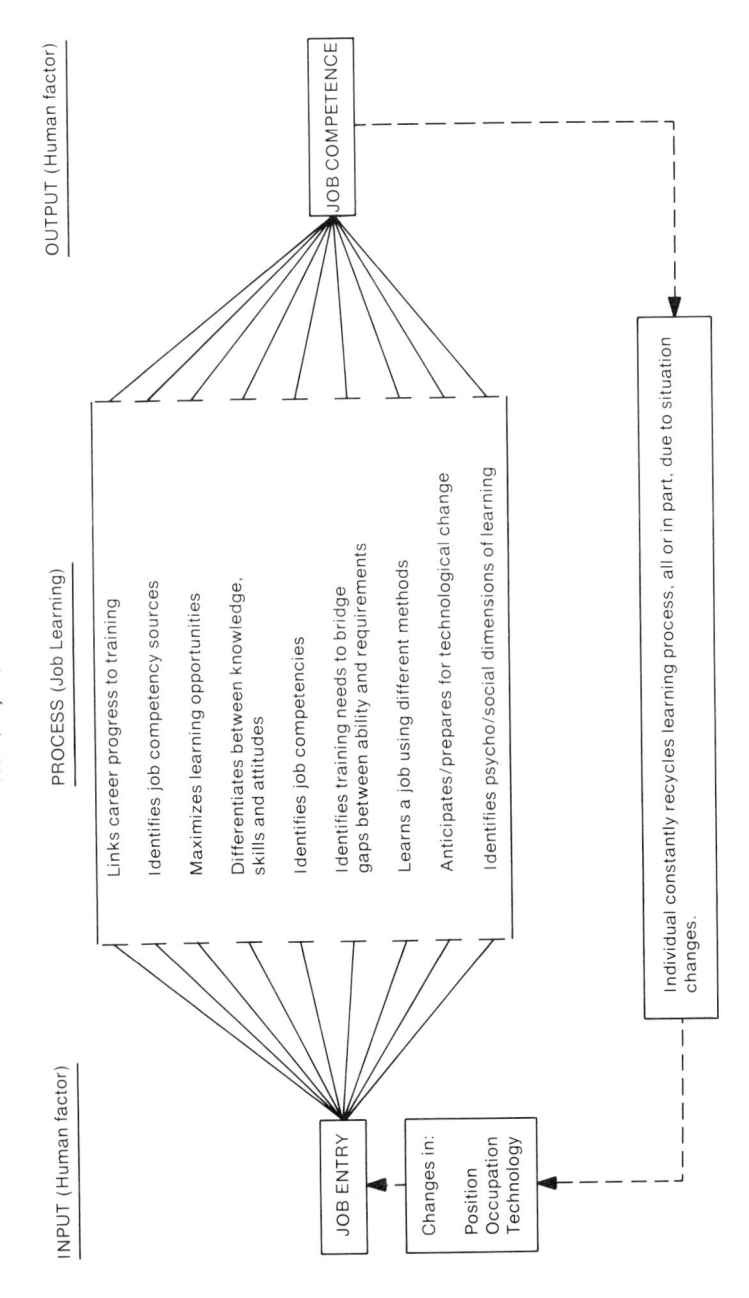

INPUT (Human factor)

PROCESS (Job Learning)

- Links career progress to training
- Identifies job competency sources
- Maximizes learning opportunities
- Differentiates between knowledge, skills and attitudes
- Identifies job competencies
- Identifies training needs to bridge gaps between ability and requirements
- Learns a job using different methods
- Anticipates/prepares for technological change
- Identifies psycho/social dimensions of learning

OUTPUT (Human factor)

JOB COMPETENCE

JOB ENTRY

Changes in:
Position
Occupation
Technology

Individual constantly recycles learning process, all or in part, due to situation changes.

219

tenure in cooperative vocational education. His plan of study and experience should be flexible enough to be altered as new needs and opportunities are revealed.

Student Involvement in Individual Curriculum Planning. Direct student involvement in planning the individual curricula of class members and in planning the activities to be used in achieving their career goals (for the period of time that they engage in cooperative vocational education) cannot be stressed enough. A high degree of competency in career planning and decision making is one of the most valuable assets a young person may possess. The student's feelings and knowledge about his needs and wants are critical elements in planning a program of study and experience. Without such participation it is very difficult for a teacher-coordinator to stimulate intrinsic motivation. If a student does not appreciate the need for an important competency or does not condone the learning activities selected to achieve it, it is not likely that he will put forth his best effort to learn it. Finally, participation in planning an individual program of work and study for himself provides an excellent opportunity for making a student more responsible for his learning and helps to initiate the skill of combining work and study which hopefully will persist after he leaves the cooperative vocational education program.

Flexibility in Individual Curricula. Student-trainees usually change more rapidly than their counterparts who follow the regular curricula largely because they spend a great deal of time in an adult work environment. When properly guided they learn a great deal about themselves in a short period of time, some of which may result in the need for curriculum modification. Discovery of new talents elicits the cultivation of those talents, and experiencing failure may suggest a modification of a student-trainee's curriculum, but not necessarily so. There are many reasons for keeping a student-trainee's curriculum quite flexible.

The high probability of changing curriculum needs mandates periodic checkups on the individual student-trainee's development through his job, his club activities, and classroom-generated learning. Following up students on their jobs and other measures of learning progress will be discussed in chapter 10. Whether the need for individual curriculum modification is discovered on the job, in the community, or through the youth organization, regular re-examination of curriculum content and learning methods is imperative and the school is the place to plan the change.

Articulation of Instruction

Although this is not a book on teaching methods, there is so much interdependence between teaching methods and coordination activities that some pertinent things must be said about methods of instruction and direction of learning activities.

Most teacher-coordinators are aware of the fact that occasionally a student-trainee's behavior in the classroom is affected by what has happened to him at home, on his job, during a youth organization activity, or in the community. They hope that classroom behaviors and attitudes will carry over to the students' jobs and into their youth group meetings. Perceptive teacher-coordinators realize that there is constant important interaction among these environments and exploit this phenomenon through carefully articulated learning activities. They understand the need for appropriate ratios of inputs from each learning source. In light of this need, the question arises, How does a proficient teacher-coordinator manage to articulate the learning that takes place in the classroom, at the training station, in the community, and in youth group organization activities? Obviously, this is not a unilateral task.

ACTIVITIES THAT HELP UNIFY LEARNING EXPERIENCES

Some cooperative vocational education classrooms are full of excitement with vocationally meaningful subject matter and highly motivated students; others may be dull and obviously boring. The difference does not rest as much with the caliber of the students or the personality of the teacher as with what the teacher teaches and the teaching methods and learning activities he uses. The secret of a stimulating classroom or school laboratory is to use genuinely meaningful subject matter and to select teaching methods that will achieve the students' goals. How is this done?

Interdependence Between Content and Methods. Meaningful subject matter evolves from the use of teaching methods and learning activities that provide a vehicle for generating meaningful subject matter and produce mutually acceptable goals. However, no type of instruction will produce meaningful subject matter and motivate students unless the teacher is capable of directing it toward the vocational needs of his student-trainees. For example, the conference method is an excellent way to focus on mutually acceptable goals and to maintain student motivation, but the conference leader must know enough about the subject to be investigated and about the backgrounds of the participants to help them define their problem and select appropriate discussion topics. The principle of interaction between subject matter and methods operates in several other teaching methods which draw on real-life experiences outside of the classroom.

Typical Teaching Methods. As suggested above, the conference method (borrowed from adult education) is a popular method of instruction in cooperative vocational education classes because students can draw on their job, community, and youth group organization experiences and fit them into meaningful patterns of behavior that advance them toward their career goals. There are other methods which serve this purpose such as the *field interview* (interviews with employers, training sponsors, co-workers, other business personnel, parents, teachers, and others) and the *field observation* (structured observations outside the classroom at the training agency and in the community). Active problem-solving methods are favorites of successful teacher-coordinators who apply them to everyday problems encountered in the work world. *Role-playing* and its corollaries *reverse role-playing* and *team role-playing* prove particularly effective in learning attitudes as well as in problem solving. *Buzz sessions* and *brainstorming* are frequently used to develop creative thinking. *Case problems* drawn from experiences of former and sometimes present student-trainees usually provide relevant instruction. Traditional teaching methods such as informal discussion, debate, and round table discussion have a place when used discretely.

INDIVIDUAL ACTIVITIES

Individual job competencies, alluded to in chapter 3, are an integral part of the student-trainee's curriculum. They should be identified and recorded in his related study plan along with the competencies for the single occupation being studied. They enable the learner to compare the policies and practices of his training agency with those of similar establishments. Attention to these types of competencies enables the student-trainee to make unique contributions to discussions that lead to important generalizations and principles. Student study time must be devoted to individualized occupational competency materials such as *job manuals, job study guides, programmed instruction, special purpose learning packages, manufacturers' literature,* and *trade magazines*. During follow-up coordination calls, a perceptive teacher-coordinator discovers many individual student needs pertaining to each of the three vocational competency areas, particularly in the occupational adjustment area. Such needs are quickly served through planned learning activities which frequently incorporate all four of the learning sources.

Most teacher-coordinators become aware of certain individual student's competency needs during youth group organization activities, particularly those in the area of personal-social competencies, but few of them think of the club as a medium for competency development when helping student-trainees prepare their individual learning plans. Up to the present time the youth group organization has not been utilized fully in carrying out in a systematic way the objectives of the distributive education program.

MEDIA ARTICULATION

Edgar Dale's cone of experiences is a useful tool when planning how to teach vocational education subject matter. Dr. Dale (1) has arranged broad categories of learning experiences into a continuum that ranges from direct purposeful experiences at the base of the cone to verbal symbols at its peak. This cone should be appropriate for use by most teacher-coordinators because the continuum of activities seems to correspond roughly to the relative effectiveness of the educational media used in cooperative vocational education. For this reason, an adaptation of the cone was prepared by Meyer and Ashmun (2) for use in distributive education. Figure 9-4 relates media of the field on the left half of the cone to methods on the right. Adaptations to other fields of vocational education can be made easily.

The cone of experiences can be used by instructors and students alike to stimulate ideas for learning activities. Usually, teacher-coordinators who elicit student participation in the selection of learning activities not only provide more productive instructional units but teach useful learning techniques that likely will persist in the years ahead. Participation in the selection of media and learning activities by student-trainees may pay other dividends. Student-trainees may let their training sponsors and other personnel know about the school's need for instructional materials, thereby obtaining such things as samples, literature, exhibits, and the use of relevant audio-visual materials.

Facilities and Equipment

Facilities and equipment have a great deal to do with the articulation of learning from the several sources in cooperative vocational education (school, training agency, job, home, community and youth group organization) and consequently with the relevance

FIGURE 9-4

A Distributive Educator's Concept Of Dale's Cone Of Experiences

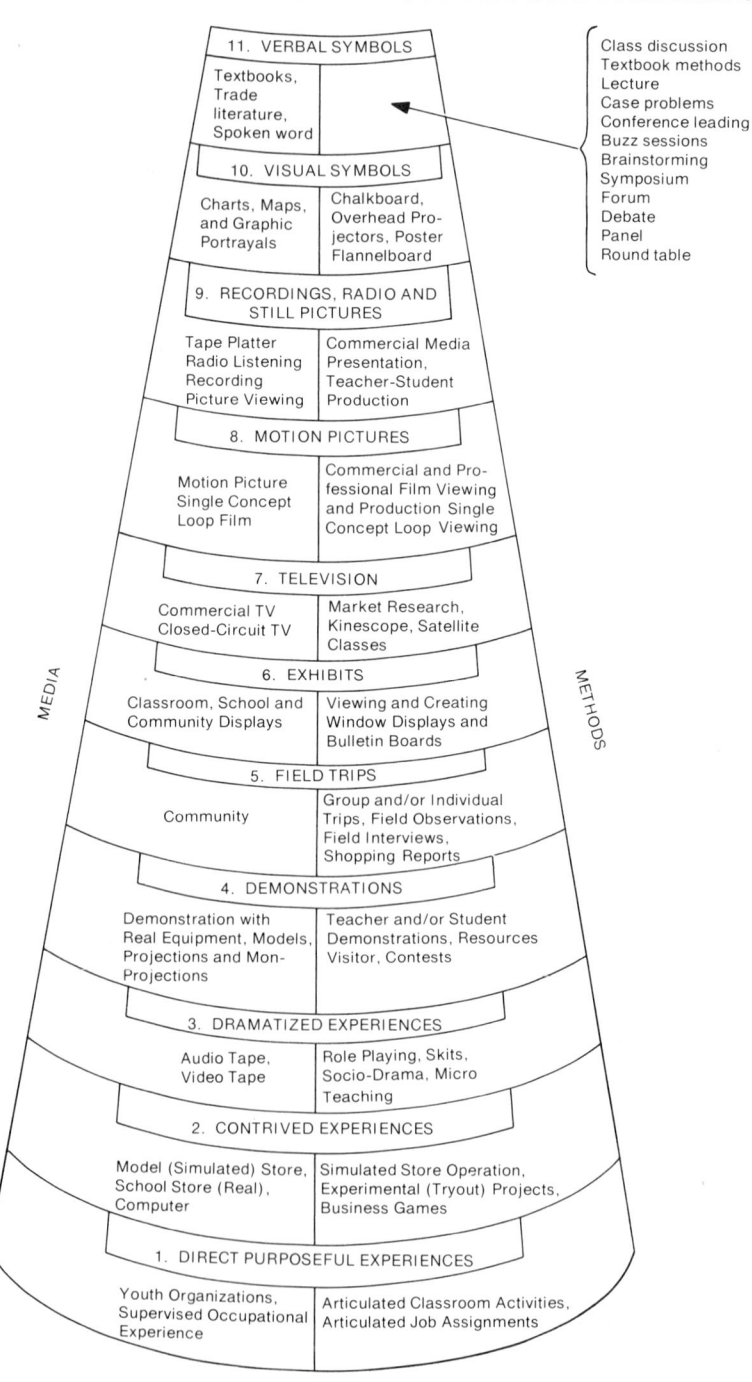

11. VERBAL SYMBOLS
- Textbooks, Trade literature, Spoken word

10. VISUAL SYMBOLS
- Charts, Maps, and Graphic Portrayals
- Chalkboard, Overhead Projectors, Poster Flannelboard

Class discussion
Textbook methods
Lecture
Case problems
Conference leading
Buzz sessions
Brainstorming
Symposium
Forum
Debate
Panel
Round table

9. RECORDINGS, RADIO AND STILL PICTURES
- Tape Platter, Radio Listening, Recording Picture Viewing
- Commercial Media Presentation, Teacher-Student Production

8. MOTION PICTURES
- Motion Picture Single Concept Loop Film
- Commercial and Professional Film Viewing and Production Single Concept Loop Viewing

7. TELEVISION
- Commercial TV, Closed-Circuit TV
- Market Research, Kinescope, Satellite Classes

6. EXHIBITS
- Classroom, School and Community Displays
- Viewing and Creating Window Displays and Bulletin Boards

5. FIELD TRIPS
- Community
- Group and/or Individual Trips, Field Observations, Field Interviews, Shopping Reports

4. DEMONSTRATIONS
- Demonstration with Real Equipment, Models, Projections and Non-Projections
- Teacher and/or Student Demonstrations, Resources Visitor, Contests

3. DRAMATIZED EXPERIENCES
- Audio Tape, Video Tape
- Role Playing, Skits, Socio-Drama, Micro Teaching

2. CONTRIVED EXPERIENCES
- Model (Simulated) Store, School Store (Real), Computer
- Simulated Store Operation, Experimental (Tryout) Projects, Business Games

1. DIRECT PURPOSEFUL EXPERIENCES
- Youth Organizations, Supervised Occupational Experience
- Articulated Classroom Activities, Articulated Job Assignments

MEDIA — METHODS

and permanency of what is taught in the classroom. As much or more attention should be given to locating, planning, and equipping a cooperative vocational education physical facility as to planning any other vocational classroom, laboratory, or shop. Unless the school facility permits and invites the teaching and learning of the occupational competencies chosen for the program, those goals are not likely to be given much attention there. For example, it is very easy for a general related instruction class to degenerate into a general education class covering subjects that have little relationship to vocational competencies if the classroom makes it difficult to use the methods suited to teaching those competencies or if the teacher-coordinator has no place to confer with student-trainees in private.

NEED FOR SPECIAL FACILITIES AND EQUIPMENT

If all the student-trainee's required vocational competencies could be learned effectively and efficiently on the job, a classroom facility would not be needed, but this is not the case. Employers do not have the time, the economic resources, or the expertise to provide all the instruction. The training sponsor should be able to guide the learner in mastering the individual job competencies, help him to develop the competencies needed in his occupation, supervise his performance of occupational cluster competencies, and *evaluate* his general occupational competencies. He very seldom has the preparation necessary to teach the general employability skills or the time to teach the occupational cluster competencies. Even if he did, there is grave doubt about the advisability of his doing so.

Although the general characteristics of a cooperative vocational education facility may be similar for all vocational programs, the type of equipment and supplies required varies a great deal among the fields. For example, the extent of the dependence on real-life experience to learn occupational cluster competencies varies widely—a young person can master typewriting skills in the classroom laboratory alone, but salesmanship skills usually must be taught in conjunction with occupational experience in order to be mastered. Hence, the role of cooperative vocational education in the development of occupational cluster competencies differs among occupational fields as well as among student groups to be served.

The need for special facilities and equipment for cooperative vocational education programs may be grouped into two categories: programmatic reasons and methodological reasons.

Programmatic Needs. A large majority of student-trainees are employed in the private sector of our economy, many of them in highly competitive businesses where employee productivity is a critical element in their success. Their employers, unless they are reimbursed under Part G of the Vocational Education Act of 1968, do not condone student experimentation on the job when high risks are involved. For example, in distributive education even a promising beginner cannot be expected to sell "big-ticket" items; he must do his practicing in the classroom first and probably demonstrate his ability by selling lower-priced items on his job. This suggests the need to have classroom facilities and equipment which approach a realistic work environment in the area of training. Many competencies needed for a single occupation and for an occupational cluster should be initiated in the school setting before a student-trainee practices them on his cooperative education job.

Other programmatic reasons for having special equipment in a classroom laboratory are the public relations and publicity value of an attractive room that clearly identifies the program, not only from the standpoint of attracting prospective students, but from the viewpoint of program image among adults who are associated with the program as classroom resource persons, adult education students, advisory committee members or employers who visit the school for various reasons. Also, a properly equipped cooperative vocational education classroom laboratory usually provides an excellent facility for adult vocational education classes and in some situations has been used as a meeting room for selected school committees.

Methodological Needs. The methodological needs for a specially designed and equipped cooperative vocational education instructional unit are at least as important as the programmatic needs because a program that does not deliver students with general employability skills may not survive very long. Regardless of the occupational goals of student trainees, certain facilities and equipment are needed to maximize instructional outcomes in the realm of general vocational competencies. Personal-social behaviors that are so essential to occupational adjustment and advancement cannot be effectively taught in a physical setting that inhibits social learning activities such as discussion, role-playing, use of resource visitors, and the use of audio-visual materials.

The general vocational competencies alluded to above are integral components of all cooperative vocational education curricula, therefore the type of equipment required applies to all cooperative education programs, but in a large percentage of cooperative education programs students prepare for a single occupation or an occupational cluster. Preparation of students in such programs requires special individualized instructional materials and equipment for the storage and use of such materials. Students pursuing career goals within an occupational cluster frequently need small- and large-group instruction relating to their occupational cluster which also calls for certain modifications in the classroom setup. In light of the varied purposes and goals of cooperative vocational education programs, it seems logical that facility and equipment should be carefully planned in relation to curricular needs.

FACILITY AND EQUIPMENT PLANNING

Obviously, it is only feasible to describe briefly the general facility and equipment requirements for cooperative vocational education programs. The following facets of facility and equipment planning will be discussed: (a) location of the facility, and (b) equipment requirements.

Location of the Facility. One factor to be considered when selecting a location for a cooperative vocational education facility in a school is its proximity to the parent department, an important consideration from the standpoint of interpersonal relations among staff members and faculty support. The location and visibility of the classroom has some impact on the program image in the eyes of students and faculty. Other factors, such as the amount of available space, noise level, and traffic pattern, should be considered. In some school systems the facility is located in the business and/or industrial community.

Proximity to one of the school entrances usually is an important criterion for reasons of easy access to outsiders who are involved with the program, and also from the viewpoint of minimizing student-trainee traffic at irregular hours.

Equipment Requirements. General equipment requirements relate largely to the facilitation of interpersonal communication among class members, to provisions for individualized study and instruction, to guidance and counseling activities and to the need for flexibility in the arrangement and use of equipment.

Facilitating Interpersonal Communication. The very common need for the development of personal-social occupational competencies holds high priority. It calls for careful planning of office and classroom equipment and layout that not only facilitates teacher-pupil communication but that enables student-trainees to profit from the help of their peers. In many schools, the teacher-coordinator's office is located adjacent to the related vocational education classroom with easy vision of regular student activities from that private office. It is essential that the teacher-coordinator's office has a door to the corridor so that it may be entered without disturbing the classroom activities. Audio and video-tape recording equipment is readily available and furniture is arranged to facilitate comfortable exchange of experiences and ideas.

Individualized Study and Instruction. Individualized study and instruction calls for a system of materials procurement, handling, and storage on which the success of this aspect of the program depends. Learning packages and/or job study guides must be available at the time needed by student-trainees and easily stored and retrieved so that time will be conserved and motivation retained. Planners should keep in mind that individual study materials include literature relating to the development of occupational adjustment and career development competencies as well as the technical competencies.

Facilitating Guidance and Counseling. Cooperative vocational education is based on the concept of individualized curricula that implement the vocational needs of student-trainees. If this concept is accepted, provision should be made for privacy when counseling activities take place. Each teacher-coordinator should have an office with easy access to the corridor and a telephone that has a direct connection to outside lines. Individual student files should be maintained. Furniture should be arranged so that both parties are comfortable during interviews and consultations. Selected guidance literature should be readily available.

Need for Flexibility. Because of the variety of purposes served by a cooperative vocational education facility, it is very important that careful attention be given to making such flexibility possible. Insofar as possible, all equipment should be movable, preferably on rollers or casters. Folding doors and/or movable partitions may be used to secure special equipment. Chairs and trapezoid tables provide much more flexibility in arrangement than rectangular ones. And, above all, plenty of storage space should be provided. Nothing seems to cause as much confusion as inadequate storage space unless it is the poor use of such space.

If students are expected to complete projects or independent study assignments in the facility at times when the classroom laboratory is in use, it is necessary to have work rooms, conference rooms to accommodate small groups, and a reference room for storage of materials.

PROCUREMENT OF EQUIPMENT

Perhaps you have noticed that in many school systems some departments enjoy the best space and are very well equipped while others appear to be in dire straits. There are reasons for this common phenomenon, most of which can be traced to the performance of the department head. There are techniques that usually produce equipment that is coordinated with the vocational needs of class members. Teacher-coordinators are in a unique position to obtain such equipment.

When to Get Space and Equipment. The best time to obtain the proper kind and amount of space and equipment is during the initial planning phase of the program. The later the date after that, the more likely it is that hard competition for school funds will arise. Once the program has begun, each day that it operates without the proper environmental conditions is a testimonial to the fact that the teacher-coordinator can get along without it. When changes in equipment or new equipment are required after the program is under way, the best time is well in advance of the deadline for budget requests for obvious reasons.

Where and How to Get Equipment. The first and sometimes only source that is called to mind is a supply house, but there are other ways of acquiring equipment such as through donations, loans, purchasing used equipment, and letting the students make it or possibly earn the money for it. When purchasing equipment through regular channels is the most desirable way of obtaining it, there are several ways of increasing the probability of one's requisition being approved:

1. Know exactly what you want.
2. Make it easy to order—brand, size, color, source or sources and approximate cost.
3. Show why you need it in terms of *student* learning benefits.
4. Get the proper backing for your request—advisory committee, knowledgeable employers, experts.
5. Show order of priority.

When other factors are equal, the request that is most easily understood and easiest to fill usually gets the attention of the administrator and the person who prepares purchase orders.

When school budgets are tight or when supply houses are unable to provide equipment that articulates properly with occupational training needs, used equipment from regular dealers or from used equipment dealers may suffice or even serve your purposes better. In some situations, the equipment may be restored to excellent condition by students who learn some transferable competencies in the process.

Other sources of equipment are donations and loans. Employers may have surplus equipment which can be purchased at a reasonable price or which they may donate to the school if the program's needs are known. In addition to the sources alluded to above, there are situations in which students are allowed to earn money for the purchase of special equipment. Such projects can produce salutary results.

MAINTAINING AN ARTICULATED INSTRUCTIONAL FACILITY

The best way to maintain equipment and adequate supplies is to use them properly. Nothing is as disconcerting to administrators as unused equipment, and few things are more pleasing than money well spent to enhance the learning.

The secret to maintaining up-to-date equipment and appropriate and adequate supplies rests in the budget. Justifiable depreciation schedules and specific budget allocations for equipment and supplies should be provided in the regular budget of the department or the school. Rising prices and differences in materials needed by vocational fields and types of programs make it difficult to state an estimate, but during 1975 an allotment of $10 to $15 per student-trainee for the first year of the program and $8 to $10 per student during subsequent years is reasonable.

Concluding Statement

Organizing and articulating instruction in a multi-learning-source cooperative vocational education program is without doubt one of a teacher-coordinator's most professional responsibilities. The tasks included in carrying out this assignment call for deep understanding of each student's needs, for keen awareness of his wants, and for consistent focus on those needs. Providing for a student-trainee's needs and wants necessitates a working knowledge of the several sources to which he looks for help in learning the competencies required in the occupation he hopes to master. If these sources were simple and consistent in what they communicated to a youngster, the matter of guiding his learning would not be difficult, but they are dynamic and sometimes erratic. Without the teacher-coordinator's help in planning and carrying out an educational program, little learning takes place. As a case in point, think of how much more valuable your occupational experience would be to you were you to repeat it today knowing what you do now.

In this chapter you were given a model for an instructional planning system which took into account the several learning sources. You were informed about vocational competency areas as vehicles for arriving at a balance of types of instructional inputs needed to maintain motivation and produce a well-rounded worker. In order to learn the desired competencies, various instructional methods and general guidelines were called to mind, and facilities and equipment that aid articulation of instruction were discussed.

Now that you have been exposed to the meaning and purpose of classroom instruction, you are obligated to pursue further the study of organization and articulation of instruction through formal and informal educational means.

REFERENCES

1. Dale, Edgar. *Audio-Visual Methods in Teaching,* 3d ed. New York: Holt, Rinehart and Winston, 1969, p. 107.

2. Meyer, Warren G., and Richard D. Ashmun. "Media in Distributive Education." *Audiovisual Instruction* 15 (April 1970): 33-36.
3. Sullivan, James A. "Managing Cooperative Vocational Education Programs." Southern Illinois University at Carbondale: *Occupational Education Quarterly* 4, No. 3: 1-2.
4. Tyler, Ralph W. "Changing Concepts of Educational Evaluation." AERA Monograph Series, 1. *Perspectives of Curriculum Evaluation.* Chicago: Rand McNally, 1967, p. 41.
5. Wenschlag, Roger E. "Study to Identify the Occupational Adjustment Competencies to be Included in the Distributive Education Curriculum." Mimeographed report, Distributive Education Department, College of Education, University of Minnesota, Minneapolis, 1970, 25pp.

ADDITIONAL REFERENCES

Drawbaugh, Charles C. and William L. Hull. *Agricultural Education: Approaches to Learning and Teaching.* Columbus: Charles E. Merrill, 1971, 324 pp.

Harms, Harm, B. W. Stehr, and E. Edward Harris. *Methods of Teaching Business and Distributive Education.* Cincinnati: South-Western, 1972, 552 pp.

Larson, Milton E. *Teaching Related Subjects in Trade and Industrial and Technical Education.* Columbus: Charles E. Merrill, 1972, 366 pp.

McMahon, Gordon G. *Curriculum Development in Trade and Industrial and Technical Education.* Columbus: Charles E. Merrill, 1972, 134 pp.

SUGGESTED ACTIVITIES

1. Identify two competencies to be developed in each of the four sources of learning used in cooperative vocational education—classroom, job, community, and youth organization.

2. Identify two competencies for each of the three competency areas and briefly describe a good method of teaching each competency to student-trainees in a cooperative education program in your vocational field.

3. Review the "Cone of Experiences" in figure 9-4 and identify which methods are most effective and stimulating when you are the recipient of instruction.

4. Draw a scale model of the classroom facility which would be appropriate for a cooperative education program in your vocational field. Include an office, storage space, and other essential features mentioned in this chapter.

5. Prepare a list of the ways in which teacher-coordinators can apply their knowledge of career development when organizing and articulating instruction.

6. Prepare a list of the ways in which the theory of work adjustment can be applied when organizing and articulating instruction.

Chapter 10 FOLLOWING UP STUDENT-TRAINEES AT WORK

In chapter 8 you learned about the purposes and characteristics of a functional occupational experience laboratory located in the training agency, and in chapter 9 you gained insight into the responsibilities of a teacher-coordinator when helping a student-trainee plan his individual curriculum and how to implement it. The latter chapter also included a discussion of classroom experiences that facilitate the development of capabilities not easily acquired in a work environment alone. Fortified with this background, you now are prepared to investigate the tasks included in following up a student-trainee at work.

You will recall the concept of the teacher-coordinator's being a program manager which was introduced in chapter 3. It is during coordination follow-up calls in the employment community that a teacher-coordinator exercises some of his most critical administrative responsibilities. Unless he accepts responsibility for the learning productivity of each training agency and has the skill to supervise harmoniously his staff of training sponsors, desired student behavioral outcomes will be sporadic at best.

Careful planning and skillful execution of coordination follow-up activities is crucial to the successful operation of all cooperative vocational education programs. This chapter explains the purposes and techniques

Following Up Student-Trainees At Work

of following up student-trainees at work. Specifically, the aim is to help the reader learn the following competencies:

1. Explain the purposes of coordination follow-up calls at the training agency;
2. Prepare a checklist of teacher-coordinator tasks, monthly time schedule, weekly time schedule, and log;
3. Set up systems for the coordinator's notebook and his files;
4. Prepare for, execute, and detect the need for a coordination follow-up call;
5. Direct the formulation of a plan for evaluating an occupational experience laboratory;
6. Direct the construction of a performance rating form.

Purposes of Follow-Up Calls

The central purpose of follow-up calls on employers, training sponsors, student-trainees while they are at work, and other training-agency personnel is to maintain and improve learning opportunities for student-trainees. Some of the calls are informative and instructional in character, some preventative, and some are remedial. They are prompted by a wide variety of situations. Some of them are planned regular visits to check on a student's job progress; others are not anticipated, being caused by some emergency affecting the student or a special problem that has arisen at the training agency. Some are initiated by the teacher-coordinator, others are requested by employers, training sponsors or by the student-trainee. Most of them are scheduled and take place during the teacher-coordinator's regularly assigned coordination periods, but they may occur at almost any time of day or even at night.

Coordination follow-up calls can be classified in a number of logical ways. However in this discussion, they will be grouped by purpose into four categories, each of which requires a somewhat different approach. The broad purposes are: (1) to improve the student-trainee's instruction and learning while at work, (2) to aid the learner in making work adjustments, (3) to glean information and gather instructional materials, and (4) to take care of miscellaneous matters relating to the program.

IMPROVEMENT OF INSTRUCTION

Improvement of the learning that takes place at the training agency is the dominant reason why well-established teacher-coordinators make follow-up calls. Such calls are made to: (1) help articulate job instruction with that from other sources such as the classroom, (2) plan individual instruction for a student-trainee, (3) evaluate a student-trainee's progress, and (4) help the training sponsor improve his instruction.

Articulation of Instruction. Articulation of instruction is placed first in this discussion of improving learning on the job because of its importance. Articulation and coordination of learning activities are key tasks in program management. Articulation of instruction is by no means confined to desk work. Teacher-coordinators send their training sponsors memos and/or newsletters containing unit outlines of classroom work and other pertinent information about what transpires at school, but this is not enough. They believe that articulation is a two-way street and that direct input from the training agency is a critical requirement. They feel that personal face-to-face contact is the best way to do this. Telephone calls and communications on paper are not adequate for the task.

Planning Learning Activities. A closely related reason for the teacher-coordinator's calls on training agency personnel is the joint planning of learning activities for individual student-trainees. The student-trainee may be included in many of the conferences between the training sponsor and the teacher-coordinator. The training sponsor sees the student-trainee from a different perspective than that of the teacher-coordinator. He is in a position to observe certain behaviors that would not occur in the peer environment of the classroom and can detect strengths and weaknesses that might affect the student-trainee's progress toward a career goal.

The input of the training sponsor into planning individual learning activities for student-trainees under his direction is potentially high. This adjunct faculty member is not only aware of the feasibility of certain learning activities to be carried out in the training agency as proposed by the teacher-coordinator and/or the student-trainee, but he may have original ideas for learning activities based on past experiences as a supervisor or learner.

Evaluation of Student's Progress. Perhaps the most common reason for coordination follow-up calls on training agency personnel is to evaluate student progress and achievement. As valuable as this task can be, it is not the dominant reason for follow-up calls in well-established programs. Overemphasis on this type of call may indicate a contradiction of the managerial concept of the teacher-coordinator's job in that a sufficient amount of time may not have been devoted to the planning, organizing, coordinating, and controlling functions of management. A small percentage of calls devoted to other follow-up tasks reinforces the idea that the training agency independently specifies, controls, and evaluates the learning that takes place on the job.

There are many facets to evaluating a student-trainee's performance on his cooperative education job. The ways of evaluating the learning that takes place in the occupational environment frequently control the type of experiences and instruction that the student-trainee receives during the time he spends at his training agency. This intriguing topic will be treated in detail later in this chapter.

Helping the Training Sponsor with Instruction. Conscientious training sponsors almost invariably welcome tactful suggestions on how to teach and supervise young workers; they also appreciate selected teaching materials. Nevertheless, they may be reticent about asking for help from the teacher-coordinator unless a very free working relationship exists. Therefore, the teacher-coordinator should tactfully inquire on a regular basis whether or not he can be of service in the realm of teaching and learning materials.

Sometimes student-trainees report inadequate or poor instruction on their jobs. When this challenging situation exists, the teacher-coordinator carefully investigates the problem and if the training sponsor needs help, diplomatically offers his services. He usually works with the student-trainee independently to teach him how to elicit good instruction. For more information on sponsor development refer to chapter 8.

ASSISTING WITH WORK ADJUSTMENTS

Work adjustment during a student's tenure in cooperative vocational education is largely a matter of maintaining compatibility between his work-related needs and the requirements of his particular job assignment. When students have career goals within the parameters of the program and are carefully placed in training-agency positions, problems of work adjustment are minimal, but even then may arise. Obviously, the behavior of some adolescents is difficult to predict, and work environments that appear to be stable at placement time may change. Thus, all teacher-coordinators engage in follow-up calls relating to work adjustment.

Assisting with work adjustments covers a wide spectrum of tasks and responsibilities. Most of the activities in this sphere can be grouped into three categories: assistance with learning the technical competencies, helping make occupational adjustments, and facilitating career development on the job.

Assistance with Technical Competency Learning. Occupational clusters vary a great deal in their dependence on the employers' facilities, equipment, and work environment. For example, it is much easier to duplicate the equipment of a modern office and to replicate an office work climate than it is to provide a classroom environment in distributive occupations where the essential elements are merchandise, bona fide customers, co-workers, and equipment. The people-oriented skills are very difficult to teach in the classroom alone. Comparable situations exist in the health occupations and home economics-related occupational clusters. In these people-oriented occupations the teacher-coordinator relies on the employer to supply the unique equipment and technical expertise that are essential to learning many of the required competencies. For this reason, teacher-coordinators in such occupational areas spend more time becoming acquainted with the technical competencies required of student-trainees so they can help them with their learning problems. Many times student-trainees have problems in learning the required technical competencies that cannot be diagnosed by the training sponsor and which call for first-hand observation by the teacher-coordinator. In light of the coordinator's not being the sole authority on instructional content, it is important that he spend a reasonable amount of time dealing with technical job problems of his clients as has been done in the agricultural education farm management program.

Unfortunately, technical competency mastery has been played down or discounted by general education-minded counselors and administrators, particularly those with interests in the special needs area. These individuals do not realize the importance of the interdependency among the technical, occupational adjustment, and career development competency areas. They fail to see that a student who does poorly in performing technical competencies nearly always finds it difficult to cultivate acceptable occupational adjustment competencies and extremely difficult to establish career development competencies. This situation provides another reason for the teacher-coordinator to spend time at the training agency making certain that each student-trainee is progressing in technical competency.

Helping with Occupational Adjustments. The importance of occupational adjustment, particularly as it relates to matters such as relationships with supervisors and co-workers and progress on the job, has been stressed throughout this book. Cooperative vocational education is recognized for its achievements in this competency area. It seems safe to say that more unscheduled training agency visits are made for reasons related to occupational adjustment than for any other reason. Established teacher-coordinators make a point of checking on a student-trainee's performance in this realm on nearly every call. Their motive is to identify small annoyances before they become grievances.

Even though student-trainees study human relations in the classroom and apply the principles during youth group organization activities and in their homes, they occasionally encounter problems at work that require the counsel and/or intervention of the teacher-coordinator. Sometimes they need help in gaining the acceptance of their co-workers, or the subgroup structure of the work group changes in such a way that the student-trainee is affected adversely. In some cases personal conflicts occur between the student-trainee and his training sponsor or between the student-trainee and another employee. There seems to be no limit to the number of possibilities for human relations problems. Many of the student-trainees' occupational adjustment problems may not be enjoyable experiences at the time they are encountered, but they offer fruitful opportunities for personal growth on the part of the student-trainees and sometimes for the teacher-coordinator also.

Facilitating Career Development. More and more attention is being given to the teaching of career development competencies. Teacher-coordinators are just beginning to realize the value of such capabilities in the preparation of young workers and in their job and occupational tenure when they enter the labor force. It is highly probable that career education will augment this interest, so an increasing percentage of visits to training agencies may be attributed to this objective.

Career development calls on employers and training sponsors usually relate to the creation of opportunities for the student-trainee to investigate work roles, life styles, and value systems of employees in positions associated with the student's career goal. The training agency provides a veritable opportunity for the student-trainee to obtain first-hand knowledge of occupational information. Career development calls may also relate to broadening the scope of the student-trainee's job assignments to include career exploration experiences. Many student-trainees have discovered latent capabilities and talents through try-out experiences while on their cooperative education jobs.

ELICITING INFORMATION, INSTRUCTIONAL MATERIALS, AND ASSISTANCE

Teacher-coordinators who enjoy good working relationships with their training agencies obtain much help from them in the form of information about new developments in an occupational field, understanding of the policies, procedures and practices they follow in performing their functions, and in actual participation in instructional activities.

Keeping Abreast of the Content Field. It is virtually impossible for a teacher-coordinator to keep up to date on all developments in the occupational field(s) he represents. Fortunately, he has an advantage over his colleagues in other vocational educational programs in that in most instances he has ready access to current information from experts in the employment community. Also he has inputs from advisory committee members and from personnel in cooperating training agencies. Usually he can be invited to trade association and other interest group meetings where new developments are explained. Coordination calls relating to professional development in the content field usually are highly condoned.

Understanding Training Agency Policies and Practices. Visits to training agencies to obtain information about their policies and practices that are not confidential are welcomed by employers. They usually find it very difficult to teach new employees the rationale for their policies and welcome help with this task. Unless a teacher-coordinator is informed about certain rules and regulations of cooperating training agencies and the rationale for the policies and practices they follow, he cannot do justice to class discussions concerning the principles on which they are based. Teacher-coordinators are encouraged to allot time in their schedules for study of operating policies and practices in cooperating training agencies.

Obtaining Help with Classroom and Youth Organization Activities. Up to a point, involvement of training agency personnel in educational activities outside of their places of employment enhances the value of instruction and builds good will. Established teacher-coordinators use good judgment in eliciting assistance from cooperating training agency personnel in that they make reasonably certain that their contributions will be mutually beneficial and that opportunities to do so are distributed appropriately among them. When training agencies are carefully selected, very few cooperating employers will refuse *timely* invitations to participate in appropriate program activities. A teacher-coordinator might request personnel from cooperating training agencies to participate in the program as classroom resource visitors, employer-employee banquet speakers, youth organization competitive event judges, interviewees on career information in their fields, consultants on student projects, and public relations advisors.

Miscellaneous Purposes for Visits to Training Agencies. There are numerous miscellaneous reasons for visiting personnel members of a training agency which do not belong to categories discussed above. Space does not permit discussing them, but some of them deserve being mentioned in order to provide an overview for persons entering the field of cooperative vocational education. In alphabetical order they are:

Absenteeism from school and/or work	Student-learner permits
	Stealing money or property
Conflicts with co-workers	Training plan modification

Dishonest acts
Immoral conduct
Indifference to school and/or job
Lethargy in general
Safety regulations
Sponsor development
Violation of training agreement
Union rules and regulations
Wage and hours law problems
Work schedule adjustments
Youth organization matters

Planning a Coordination Schedule

Unless a teacher-coordinator knows what his duties and responsibilities are and has made a task-analysis of his job from the standpoint of time management he will not be able to fulfill his obligations even when his per-pupil-load is reasonable. Scheduling one's time and adhering to a schedule is one of the most difficult tasks of most managers, and particularly so for a teacher-coordinator. Established teacher-coordinators report that it takes from one to three years before they are able to plan and adhere to a time schedule, but that it is the only way that they can operate effectively.

COORDINATION TIME ALLOTMENT AND SCHEDULE

It has been customary for cooperative vocational education program planners to calculate coordination time on the basis of one-half hour per student per week. Although this rule of thumb is a carry-over from the early days of cooperative education, it seems to suffice for the average high school or post-secondary education program. It is built on the assumption of average traveling distance and normal ability student-trainees. Any deviation from standard would have to be taken into consideration.

Checklist of Teacher-Coordinator Tasks. A good place to start when making a task-analysis for a particular job as a teacher-coordinator is with Cotrell's Performance Requirements for Teacher-Coordinators which is reproduced in appendix C. A common procedure is to check and record the elements that apply to the job being studied, then to add those tasks that do not appear on the list. Tasks that recur each month can be entered immediately into the monthly schedules and those that occur irregularly and infrequently can be recorded in a separate list by months for the time period included in the teacher-coordinator's contract.

Monthly Time Schedule. After completing the checklist of continuing and monthly coordination tasks the teacher-coordinator is ready to prepare a monthly schedule of activities. The next step is to procure lists of the dates of other events and activities which affect his time schedule such as the school calendar; school faculty and committee meetings; district, state, regional and national youth group organization meetings; professional organization meetings and convention dates; meetings of civic, business, and industrial organizations that relate to his content area(s); state department conferences; and any other affairs that affect his time-planning schedule. Monthly time schedule booklets may be purchased or prepared similar to that shown in figure 10-1. After entering the items from the two sources above on the proper dates, the teacher-coordinator's next step is to enter the items from the lists of monthly and continuing activities, carefully considering the program objectives.

Obviously, unless a teacher-coordinator has a time schedule to help him plan ahead, the probability of neglecting important tasks will be high. New teacher-coordinators in particular need to review frequently their monthly calendars.

Weekly Time Schedule and Log. Every coordinator should carry a weekly date book at all times. The next week's activities should be planned during the previous week in response to needs as they become manifest. Time should be allotted for preparation for coordination calls as well as for lesson planning and emergencies that are bound to occur.

Experienced teacher-coordinators usually keep a daily log of their activities with notations on their achievements and problems encountered. This memory aid proves to be very useful when problems arise and when they need to refresh their memories during the preparation of reports. It also has proved to be valuable evidence in justifying their use of coordination time.

THE COORDINATOR'S NOTEBOOK

The coordinator's notebook, which he takes with him on coordination calls, contains a digest of essential information about the program and each student-trainee. It saves time and energy. For example, there are many times when information about a student is needed during a visit to a training agency, and if the information is not close at hand, much time may be wasted in procuring it and communicating it back to the employer or training sponsor, and by then it may not be as useful as it would have been.

Patterson (1) has prepared an excellent procedure for the preparation of a coordinator's notebook which could be useful to coordinators in all vocational fields. Soon after a new term is begun, she has each student prepare a loose-leaf binder sheet giving the name of his or her training agency; name, telephone number, and location of the training sponsor;

FIGURE 10-1

OCTOBER

SUNDAY	MONDAY	TUESDAY	WEDNESDAY	THURSDAY	FRIDAY	SATURDAY
A good month to submit State and National Membership information and dues.				1	2	3
4	5 3 pm Faculty Mtg	6	7	8	9 10 am DECA Mtg.	10 Monthly Reports due.
11	12	13	14	15	16	17
18	19	20 1 pm Advisory Mtg.	21	22 State Vocational Assn. Mtg. (Thursday and	23 DECA, Inc. Annual Meeting. Friday, all day)	24
25	26	27	28	29	30	31

essential information about the employer; name, address, telephone number, and social security number of the student; names of parents or guardians, their places of employment; and the student's home room, schedule of classes, lunch periods, beginning hourly wages, and work schedule. On the bottom of the page she notes special information about the student and dates of events that are important to the student. The back of the sheet is used to note coordination visits, special information that will be helpful to the coordinator when reviewing the job progress record, and training information or job duties. Information from this notebook can be used for correspondence, compiling records, making reports, making training plans, and in many other ways.

THE COORDINATOR'S FILING SYSTEM

Very few irregularities can disrupt a teacher-coordinator's time schedule more or cause a greater number of problems than a poor filing system. There just are too many materials to keep track of to be without an orderly filing system, and more than a few well-meaning persons have failed because of the lack of one. Teacher-coordinators who think that they do not have time to build a filing system may never have calculated how much time they spend looking for things. It is not prudent to wait for new file drawers and filing materials when temporary substitutes are easily acquired. Even a cardboard carton with used file folders turned inside out looks neater than a stack of loose papers, and it will help to organize the papers.

Janie Sullivan (2) has researched the problems associated with planning and implementing a teacher-coordinator's filing system and has made recommendations of value to personnel from all vocational education fields. Even though good filing guides are available (2), it is evident that a standard filing system will not work for everyone. Nevertheless, there are certain procedures that lead to the development of a system that will meet the needs of an individual teacher-coordinator.

Filing Supplies. A popular plan is to begin with two drawers—one for an alphabetical file, the other a subject file. Procure a set of alphabetical file dividers for the first drawer and a set of dividers designed for inserting name tabs for the subject drawers. When selecting supplies you will need to decide on the positions for the divider guides and the position for the tabs on the file folders. School supply catalogs will show the choices available. File dividers usually are available with guides staggered across their width or in the left position. File folders are available in square-cut, half-cut, third-cut, fifth-cut and two-fifths-cut. Left-position guides on dividers with right-tab half-cut or two-fifths-cut file folders enable the teacher-coordinator to turn the left-hand group inside out if all right-hand tabs are desired using all of the folders in a box. Folders with tabs in the same position are easier to find and the drawer is more uniform; also more flexible. Staggered tabs are easily seen, but if a folder is added the sequence is interrupted, and you must look back and forth on the folders which is confusing and time-consuming. The same principle applies to the position of the guides on dividers.

The next step is to decide what subject divisions you will need which will be discussed in the following section. Assuming this is done, let's think ahead about the use of the files. When the material becomes too voluminous for a standard folder, you may substitute an expanding wallet folder with bellows-type sides, or you may wish to create sub-classifications for the material. When subheadings are needed within a division, you may wish to index the tab arrangement using three tab positions; the main division, the subhead, and the folder title.

It may be a good practice to have a separate place for files that will be used only by you and those to which the students may have access.

Designating the Subject File Divisions. A filing system for the distributive education program at Killeen (Texas) High School (2), developed over a period of years, has proved adaptable to growth. It may be used as an example, but not as a model, for choice of subject file divisions. Since a good filing system plays such an important part in long-range program development the major headings will be given below. The specific folder topics that are used in Killeen are listed merely to clarify the major headings. It is not suggested that anyone set up a file including these particular minor divisions.

Coordinator's Files. Drawers containing material that is not used by the students may be tagged in red to provide a bright "stop light" to students.

   I. Alphabetical File—for miscellaneous materials that do not fit into any of the special topics provided elsewhere. Letters of the alphabet are used on the dividers.
  II. Subject File—dividers are labeled as follows:
      A. Administration—may include folders on Adult Classes, Advisory Committee, Coordinator's Handbook, Coordination Visits, Program Standards, Public Relations, Publicity, and Student Enlistment.
      B. Audiovisual—may need subdividers for film catalogs, bulletin board ideas, and illustrations. Other folders may be Film Program Material, List of Charts and Posters, and Film Requisitions and Invoices.
      C. Guidance—grew from a single folder, which was in the alphabetical file drawer. It now has been subdivided into

Careers, College, Miscellaneous, and Testing.
D. Professional Organizations—may include AVA, CTA, DECA Advisory, NADET, TADET, TSTA, and TVTA.
E. Publications and Supplies—includes all catalogs, etc.
F. School Records and Reports—may include Employer Rating Forms, Equipment Guarantees and Instructions, Memos to Teachers, Occupational Survey, Requisitions, School Calendar, Schedule, Senior Handbook, Student Handbook, and Teacher Handbook.
G. State and Area Reports—may include Closing Reports, Daily Schedule Report, Dates Due Schedule, Follow-up of Graduates, Occupational Enrollment Summary, Organization Report, Training Plans, Training Plan Samples, Travel Reports, and Travel Regulations.
H. Student Records—includes an individual folder for each student with his application, grade record, training plan, employer rating forms, etc. Current ones kept in a file drawer. Transferred each year to inactive file.
I. Teaching Aids, DE I—subdivided as follows:
  1. Current Plans—folder for each six weeks
  2. School and Business Relationships
  3. Basic Selling
  4. Communications for Distribution
  5. Mathematics for Distribution
  6. Basic Organization of Distribution
J. Teaching Aids, DE II—subdivided as follows:
  1. Current Plans—folder for each six weeks
  2. Advanced Selling
  3. Sales Promotion
  4. Merchandising
  5. Retail Credit
  6. Marketing in Our Economy
K. Teaching Aids, General—for all those things you "may use someday." It includes mainly product and business information that is needed for writing individual lessons but is not yet ready for student use. This material is often made available to students by the coordinator but always with suggestions for its use.

Coordinator-Student Files. These drawers are tagged in green to give the "go" signal.

I. Distributive Education Clubs of America—a combination of the alphabetical and subject file. Material is filed in alpha-

betical order in single folders at the front of the drawer. Behind that are topics that need to be further subdivided. They include:
   A. Banquet
   B. Contests
   C. Fund Raising
   D. Officers
II. Individual Lesson Materials—holds the individual lesson manuals and references as well as lessons that have been locally written. Material is filed in expanding wallets.

Scheduling Calls on Training Agencies

The importance of being in the right place at the right time when calling upon training agency personnel cannot be overemphasized. Timing of a follow-up call to assess the progress of a student-trainee can make a great deal of difference in that student's career development. Teacher-coordinators without recent occupational experience in their vocational teaching field may benefit from a discussion of protocol and techniques in this critical area; those who have may appreciate a refresher treatment.

FREQUENCY OF FOLLOW-UP CALLS

Time intervals between follow-up calls on training agencies to check on a student-trainee's progress in his vocational development is subject to so many variables that no general rule can be applied except to say, "often enough to ensure optimal student-trainee progress on his job and to make certain that annoyances do not grow into grievances." Much depends on the needs of the student, the characteristics of the training agency and the training position, the time of the year, and the size and characteristics of the community.

Time of the Year. Regardless of the type of student served or any other factor, the teacher-coordinator will make follow-up calls more frequently during the beginning of the school year than he will later on in the year when student-trainees are well established in their training positions. Another factor related to the frequency of calls is the seasonal nature of some types of business and industry in which student-trainees are employed. Adjustments in the frequency of visits to training agencies during their busy seasons should be considered also.

Needs of Student-Trainees. Obviously, vocationally mature students require less frequent attention than many of those with special needs related to their attitudes and values. Even within a homogeneous class of cooperative vocational education students, in which the members are carefully selected on the basis of their motivation from a realistic career objective, there will be some student-trainees requiring more attention than others. Good academic students may find adjustment to a work environment more difficult than many of their less academically talented classmates. For reasons such as these, all teacher-coordinators should set up a schedule of follow-up visitations to training agencies.

Other Factors Affecting the Frequency of Follow-up Calls. Some occupations seem to demand more follow-up service than others. For example, a student-trainee placed in a retail sales position where the occupational environment contains many variables and productivity standards are not well established may need more frequent attention than an occupation in an industrial setting with specific standards and a less complex occupational environment. Another factor to consider when scheduling follow-up coordination calls is the nature of the supervision provided a student-trainee on the job. For example, a student-trainee who works alone part of the time in a business office may need more contacts with the teacher-coordinator while at work than one who is under constant high quality supervision. The size and characteristics of the community may also bear on the frequency of follow-up coordination calls, and obviously, so will the size of the class. Each teacher-coordinator needs to assess the past practices but not allow them to interfere with doing what he conscientiously feels is the right thing to do.

TIMING FOLLOW-UP CALLS

Other factors being equal, there is a "best" time of the month, week, and day to make follow-up calls in most every training agency. Appropriate timing of follow-up calls usually helps bring about fruitful results, whereas a poorly timed call might be a complete waste of the time of the person on whom you call as well as your own time. The need to consider busy and slack seasons has been mentioned. What other factors should be considered when preparing a coordination follow-up schedule?

Identifying Appropriate Meeting Times. Days of the month, days of the week, and times of the day are important considerations in arriving at productive contacts with training sponsors and other training agency personnel. Even within the same training agency, appropriate calling times vary among units or departments of the organization. For example, some units of an establishment may be busy near the end of the month while others find this to be a slack time. Mondays may be a busy time in some types of retail distribution, while Wednesday is rushed in others. Generally speaking, shortly after opening hours or before closing time are poor times for good rapport with training agency personnel.

In light of all these variables, the logical procedure is to inquire into the most appropriate time to make follow-up calls at the time the student-trainee is placed in his or her training position. Sometimes there is a conflict between your schedule and that of the person contacted and the meeting time is negotiated. In some situations, lunch time may be the only time you can get together. Incidentally, this can be a very favorable time when in the usual meeting place the training sponsor is plagued with interruptions.

Advisability of Making Appointments. Appointments are still in good taste and afford certain advantages, even in situations where there is a good working relationship with training agency personnel. In the first place, an appointment is an act of courtesy and a gesture of respect for the person contacted. In effect you are saying that you realize that his time is valuable and that yours is too. Second, your time is a scarce resource and you don't want to waste time waiting to see someone. Third, an appointment usually gives you more control over the situation. In most cases the person contacted feels that inasmuch as he or she has granted the "interview" it is courteous to let you control it. Other reasons for making appointments for follow-up calls could be cited.

MAINTAINING THE SCHEDULE

Once the schedule has been completed and the appointments have been made well in advance, the teacher-coordinator has a moral commitment to follow the plan. Unless he does so, his student-trainees will suffer the consequences. There always will be potential interruptions which must not be permitted to happen, and there will be legitimate emergencies which cannot be avoided. The extent to which a teacher-coordinator allows school activities to interfere with coordination duties is an index of the priority he places on the coordination aspects of the job. In a sense it indicates whether he is primarily a program manager or a classroom teacher.

Preparing for a Follow-Up Call

A very successful American management consultant relates how, as a boy in Baghdad, he was confined to his bed because of an extended illness. He would watch the lamplighter at twilight carefully prepare the street lamp outside his window for lighting. The lamplighter would meticulously trim the wick, clean the chimney, and proceed through a lengthy preparation leading up to the actual act of lighting the lamp. He would then methodically put each tool back in its proper place, dispose of the waste, and continue on his way to the next light.

It occurred to the management consultant that in the retinue of the lamplighter lies the secret to success in most any occupation. It seems that everyone wants to be a "doer"; that's where the action is; that's the fun part of the job. But the success of doing rests on the adequacy of the "get ready" procedures, which only those who have discovered the secret take seriously. The "put-away" phase of the task that follows the doing phase is equally important because on it the adequacy of the "get-ready" phase of the next task depends. Like the lamplighter, the secret of success in coordination follow-up calls rests in the "get-ready" phase of the task.

STUDYING AVAILABLE INFORMATION AND DATA

It stands to reason that the more a teacher-coordinator knows about the student at the time he meets with the student-trainee's training sponsor and/or employer, the more productive his call is apt to be. Thus, the information in the coordinator's notebook described earlier is a starting point. Other sources of information include the training plan described in chapter 8, the student-trainee's weekly work report, the training profiles, recent job progress reports, student's work diary and any other pertinent information.

A review of information provided by the sources above may suggest that the student-trainee's interest, aptitude, and/or achievement test scores be reviewed before making the follow-up call. For example, if the teacher-coordinator knows that the student-trainee is experiencing some difficulty in adjusting to his work at the training agency, he may see fit to examine the student's *Minnesota Importance Questionnaire* (MIQ) which was discussed in chapter 5.

After reviewing a student-trainee's records, established teacher-coordinators usually hold a brief conference with student-trainees to let them know that they will meet with training agency personnel and to assess their opinions and attitudes concerning their work. Teacher-coordinators usually ask whether or not there is anything students would like to have mentioned or anything to inquire about. This step in preparing for the follow-up call is important because it conveys the impression that the teacher-coordinator is a liaison person whose goal is to facilitate learning rather than check on students.

Another timesaver may be for the teacher-coordinator to telephone the training sponsor or employer to check on his appointment and to determine whether there is something he should bring with him for the meeting. Such forethought may eliminate extra trips.

PLANNING THE MEETING

Having clearly in mind the purpose of the call and having a plan for achieving the objectives of the meeting helps to ensure a productive session. Follow-up calls may assume a variety of purposes, each of which may require a slightly different plan and strategy, so the first step in planning is to decide on tentative purposes. Some examples are:

> Check student's progress in learning his job and his satisfactoriness to his employer.
> Establish a desirable relationship between the school and the training agency.
> Obtain information about working conditions at the training agency.
> Provide the training sponsor with useful information and materials.
> Obtain advice from the employer or training sponsor on materials for the student-trainee to use in class.
> Elicit advice regarding the operation of the program.
> Plan a modification of the training plan.
> Increase the variety of occupational experiences.
> Settle differences between student-trainee and a supervisor or coworker.
> Ensure that the employer is meeting his responsibilities.

Protocol varies among training agencies and sometimes within an organization. Also it may be advisable to plan a strategy, particularly if an issue is involved. In some situations it may be advisable to dress for the occasion, and it is always necessary to be in the proper mood for a call.

Executing the Follow-Up Call

Although different follow-up calls require diverse procedures and strategies, there are some general suggestions concerning protocol and behavior that may serve as reminders for beginners and those who need a refresher.

PROCEDURAL TIPS

There are many rules governing personal contacts with individuals that apply to general situations as well as to coordination follow-up calls. A few of them that seem particularly appropriate to the teacher-coordinator's role as a manager of a program are mentioned here mainly to generate the addition of others:

Be on time for your appointment.
Respect the chain of command (e.g., if you are contacting a student-trainee, obtain the supervisor's permission).
Make the purpose of your call manifest at the beginning of the contact.
Come to the point; don't waste time.
Be objective; don't oversell or undersell the student.
Show empathy for the employer's problems.
Don't tell the employer how to run his business.
Avoid favoritism.
Avoid controversial topics.
Don't overstay your welcome.
Thank the person for his or her time.

BEHAVIORAL SUGGESTIONS

Neophyte teacher-coordinators sometimes find it difficult to assume the appropriate role in a given situation, and many of them act too formal or too familiar to elicit the right kind of reception. In most instances it is better to be conservative and let the person being contacted take the initiative.

Another role-finding problem of the beginner is that of establishing his social relationship with an employer. Some coordinators are likely to be condescending and give the impression that the employer is doing them and the school a favor when they accept student-trainees. This places the coordinator in an awkward position when it becomes necessary to suggest changes relative to the employer's responsibilities concerning the program. Conversely, a few new teacher-coordinators assume the attitude of officials, which is even more objectionable. Every teacher-coordinator, including those serving the "disadvantaged," should be convinced in his own mind that cooperative education is of mutual benefit to both the school and the employer. Equality must prevail if a program is to survive over an extended period of time.

Detecting the Need for a Follow-Up Call

Following up student-trainees on their jobs according to a well-planned schedule is the mark of a good teacher-coordinator, but sensitivity to the need for intermediate calls or improvements in regular training agency visits is even more important. This ability demonstrates an interest in student welfare and a zest for program improvement. Whether a signal emanates from the student, from the employer, or from any other person, established teacher-coordinators are constantly alert for subtle signs and hints that suggest a need for improving the occupational experience aspect of their programs. Sometimes such signals may be prompted just by reading a professional journal article. Expressions of satisfaction with a student-trainee, and also of dissatisfaction with one, trigger an inquiry into the situation to see what can be done to capitalize on a student's talent or correct a weak point.

These expert teacher-coordinators keep good records on their student-trainees, and from these records they often are able to detect a need for individual conferences or for a follow-up call to training agency personnel. They pay close attention to absence and tardiness records, students' work hours, wages paid, irregularities in the students' progress on the training plan, youth group organization participation, observable interpersonal relations with fellow class members, and many more. Three of the devices that are especially designed to aid and improve on-the-job learning and instruction are the weekly work record, the training profile, and the rating of job performance and vocational growth.

WEEKLY WORK RECORD REPORT

The weekly work record report is a simple, widely used report that provides the teacher-coordinator with a brief description of what took place on the student-trainee's job during the preceding week. Content and administrative procedure regarding the form vary somewhat from community to community, but the forms have common content similar to that in figure 10-2: a report of job tasks performed, related vocational study in class (usually of an independent or individualized nature), weekly time and earnings summary, and supervisor's comments and signature. Additional items used in some communities are: What did you learn through instruction or experience on the job this week? From whom? To whom were you responsible for your work? What fa-

FIGURE 10-2

PART-TIME OCCUPATIONAL TRAINING PROGRAM

WEEKLY REPORT

Trainee _____ Home Room _____
Firm Name _____ Business Phone ____
What have you done on the job this week? _____

_____
_____
_____
_____
_____
_____
_____
_____

Related assignments in classroom: (Indicate subject studied, topic considered, and how related to job.)

_____
_____
_____
_____
_____
_____
_____
_____
_____

Following Up Student-Trainees At Work

Weekly Time and Earning Summary			Supervisor's Comments		
Date	Start Work	Stop Work	Time Worked		
^	^	^	Hours	Minutes	^
		Total			

Time Worked _____ **X Hourly Rate** _____ =
Weekly Earnings _____   Signature

DUE EACH _____ MORNING AT BEGINNING OF OCCUPATIONAL RELATIONS CLASS PERIOD.

vorable opinion was expressed about your work this week? By whom? Has there been any change in your salary or in your job during the past week? Sometimes the teacher-coordinator's comments are added to the report.

From this report a teacher-coordinator spots problems and achievements that signal the need for attention. The form also calls the training sponsor's attention to what the student is doing both on the job and in school and the student's reaction to what he has done. It provides a visual record of hours worked for all three parties. It may also help the teacher-coordinator enrich class discussions if he recalls the student's activities and calls on him during the discussion. The same advantage applies to making assignments.

THE TRAINING PROFILE

A training profile is a more sophisticated document that serves much the same purpose but usually does not include a time and earnings summary (see figure 10-3). It is administered at longer intervals, frequently at the end of each grading period. The main purpose of the training profile is to improve communication regarding the training and experience a student-trainee receives on a job. It is an operating procedure to use in assuring that instruction takes place on the job and to help make the student-trainee more responsible for seeing to it that he is properly trained. It indicates clearly to the employer that he has certain responsibilities in the total instructional program.

Many teacher-coordinators have the training sponsor fill in the form independently and compare the profiles of both parties. This not only helps improve the reliability of the measures but creates a better work environment due to clarification of the responsibilities of the parties involved. Discrepancies between the two profiles may indicate the inability of a student-trainee to recognize the training he has received, or it can signal a real deficiency in training.

Evaluating Occupational Experience Laboratory Achievement

Periodic evaluation of a student-trainee's occupational experience laboratory performance serves many purposes: it is used as a measure of achievement and progress, as an important component in arriving at a grade for one or more units of school credit, as a motivational device (artificial), and when properly planned it can be an excellent diagnostic tool to indicate areas of need for further training. In cooperative vocational education, the latter is of primary importance because goal-oriented students and conscientious teacher-coordinators are highly concerned about identifying the learner's strengths and weaknesses so that something can be done about them at an early opportunity.

The state of the art in the realm of evaluating the performance of student-trainees at their training agencies is still in an early developmental stage for a number of reasons, the first being the complexity of the task. It is difficult to develop a system of measurement that will deal adequately with the wide array of competencies required in the occupations for which student-trainees are preparing, even in a program serving students with similar career goals. Consequently, emphasis has been placed on general worker traits, while critical technical competencies

FIGURE 10-3

Sample Of A Distributive Education Profile

Measuring Degree of Training

Training Station _____ Student's Name _____

Job Assignment _____

Student's Career Objective _____

PROCEDURE: *For each statement circle number*

1. *if he has had NO training*
2. *if he has had VERY LITTLE training*
3. *if he has had ADEQUATE training*
4. *if he has had a GREAT AMOUNT of training*
5. *if activity does not apply*

I. REQUIRED KNOWLEDGE

1 2 3 4 5 1. Store system
1 2 3 4 5 2. Merchandise return and exchange procedures.
1 2 3 4 5 3. Where to find and how to use reference materials.
1 2 3 4 5 4. Federal excise tax schedule and state tax schedule.
1 2 3 4 5 5. Store regulations
1 2 3 4 5 6. Who should answer questions other than those relating to special department or counter problems.
1 2 3 4 5 7. Pricing policy and code systems.
1 2 3 4 5 8. Store organization and how the trainee fits into store personnel.
1 2 3 4 5 9. Opportunities to see buying problems and sources.
1 2 3 4 5 10. Stock turnover, its importance and how it is handled.
1 2 3 4 5 11. Credit policy and procedure.
1 2 3 4 5 12. Delivery policy and schedule.

II. BASIC AND REGULAR CYCLE OF DUTIES AND RESPONSIBILITIES

1 2 3 4 5 1. Covering and uncovering merchandise.
1 2 3 4 5 2. Housekeeping.
1 2 3 4 5 3. Arranging stock.
1 2 3 4 5 4. Checking price tags.
1 2 3 4 5 5. Filling in items from stock.
1 2 3 4 5 6. Operating cash register and making change.
1 2 3 4 5 7. Tallying sales and counting change at end of day.
1 2 3 4 5 8. Filling out regular stock orders.
1 2 3 4 5 9. Studying literature for product information.
1 2 3 4 5 10. Helping maintain stock control records.
1 2 3 4 5 11. Replenishing wrapping and packing supplies.

FIGURE 10-3 CONT'D.

III. PREPARING MERCHANDISE FOR SALE

1 2 3 4 5   1. Checking merchandise in.
1 2 3 4 5   2. Inspecting merchandise.
1 2 3 4 5   3. Ticketing or marking new merchandise.
1 2 3 4 5   4. Setting type on marking machines and printing tickets.
1 2 3 4 5   5. Replacing soiled price tickets.
1 2 3 4 5   6. Changing prices when directed.
1 2 3 4 5   7. Figuring prices from invoice.

IV. SELLING AND SERVICE TO CUSTOMERS

1 2 3 4 5   1. Selling merchandise.
1 2 3 4 5   2. Suggestion selling.
1 2 3 4 5   3. Holding customers for other experienced salespeople.
1 2 3 4 5   4. Calling supervisor for a double check on unusually large multiple unit sales.
1 2 3 4 5   5. Gift wrapping packages.
1 2 3 4 5   6. Wrapping take-with merchandise.
1 2 3 4 5   7. Handling returns.
1 2 3 4 5   8. Handling complaints.
1 2 3 4 5   9. Filling mail and telephone orders.
1 2 3 4 5   10. Calling customers on telephone.
1 2 3 4 5   11. Making sales on the telephone.
1 2 3 4 5   12. Directing customers.

V. SALES PROMOTION

1 2 3 4 5   1. Preparing and arranging price tickets and show cards.
1 2 3 4 5   2. Arranging counter displays.
1 2 3 4 5   3. Arranging show cases and wall cases.
1 2 3 4 5   4. Placing merchandise on mannequins.
1 2 3 4 5   5. Arranging window displays.
1 2 3 4 5   6. Checking store advertisements.
1 2 3 4 5   7. Suggesting tie-in sales.
1 2 3 4 5   8. Planning special sales promotion features.

VI. PERIODIC AND INCIDENTAL DUTIES

1 2 3 4 5   1. Assisting in taking annual and spot inventories.
1 2 3 4 5   2. Participating in store-wide contests and activities.
1 2 3 4 5   3. Reporting shoplifting and store accidents.
1 2 3 4 5   4. Reporting significant comments made by customers about merchandise and services.
1 2 3 4 5   5. Attending store meetings and training sessions.
1 2 3 4 5   6. Doing comparison shopping.

VII. ADDITIONAL

1 2 3 4 5   1. Opportunities to discuss advancement in the business firm.
1 2 3 4 5   2. Opportunities to discuss progress on the job.
1 2 3 4 5   3.
1 2 3 4 5   4.

have been treated in a very general way. Some other reasons are that program purposes and objectives vary so much that it is difficult to find common ground for the development of an appropriate system, the amount of sophistication among potential evaluators and even teacher-coordinators in the area of tests and measurement is frequently limited, and research conducted by business and industry has been concerned mostly with worker satisfactoriness up to the present time. Also, there are teacher-coordinators who see little value in a *common* evaluation system.

When developing a system for the evaluation of student-trainee achievement at a training agency, some teacher-coordinators have found the materials produced by the Minnesota Work Adjustment Project to be very helpful. The concept of work adjustment, the instrument used to measure the satisfaction a worker receives from the job on which he is employed (MSQ), and a worker's satisfactoriness to an employer (MSS) can supply useful information on the evaluation of some important learning outcomes of the occupational experience laboratory (see chapter 5).

BENEFITS DERIVED FROM A GOOD SYSTEM

Many teacher-coordinators believe that the identification of benefits derived from a good system for the evaluation of learning outcomes of training agency experiences is a helpful first step in the formulation of such a system. Thinking in terms of benefits to the groups of individuals using the report seems to stimulate constructive thinking about the essential criteria to be evaluated and the sources of information needed to assess those criteria. A partial list follows.

Benefits for Student-Trainees
    Identification of strengths and weaknesses
    Provision of helpful suggestions from training sponsor and other raters
    Knowledge of what the employer is looking for
    Preclusion of becoming a forgotten employee
    Realization that all behavior on the job is a matter of record
    Establishment of a permanent record of employment

Benefits for the Training Agency
    Communication with the school
    Stimulation of student-trainee productivity
    Development of a prospective employee
    Maintenance of supervisor's interest in training
    Experience in personnel and training tasks for training sponsors
    Useful record for the student-trainee's file

Benefits for Parents
    Authoritative information
    Help to see the need for home cooperation
    Basis for discussion of the personal habits and problems of their children
    Improved communication with the school

Benefits for the Teacher-Coordinator
    Information about student-trainees that can be used for counseling, preparing individualized instruction, modifying training plans, making class discussions more relevant, and eliciting teaching assistance from other staff members
    Facilitation of communication with training sponsors, parents and students
    Motivation of student-trainees
    Evidence of learning for administrators, supervisors, parents, and others
    Support for the student-trainees' grades
    Information for program evaluation more accessible

BUILDING A SYSTEM

As indicated above, adopting another program's system of evaluating occupational experience laboratory achievements will not result in equitable treatment of student-trainees. If a teacher-coordinator is to be fair to all students, he must employ a custom-designed system that will be flexible enough to accommodate most of the differences that exist among training positions. This cannot be adequately done by a teacher-coordinator alone. Earlier, it was mentioned that a teacher-coordinator is constrained by his own background of occupational experience and professional preparation. Therefore he needs inputs from other sources to counterbalance his stereotype of occupations represented in the goals of his students.

Evaluation System Committee. One plausible answer to the need for assistance is an Evaluation System Committee composed of members who can provide the necessary inputs and, of course, guidance by the program advisory committee. The composition of an Evaluation System Committee might include representatives of participating employees (program graduates when possible), the advisory committee, related-subject area faculty members, school administration, counseling services, and expert practitioners in the occupational content field(s) being considered.

Following Up Student-Trainees At Work

Sources of Inputs on Learning Outcomes. Obviously, a single rating form, no matter how comprehensive it may be, will not do justice to all student-trainees in a program; other sources need to be tapped. Potential inputs from the following list may be weighed:

- Performance rating scales completed by employer or training sponsor
- Regular company employee rating forms
- Weekly work reports
- Training plan progress record
- Training profiles
- Quality of work on job-related assignments
- Responses to questions about his or her job
- Shopper's reports
- Co-worker ratings and/or opinions
- Work attendance records
- Production reports on job tasks
- Quality of "my job" manual
- Standardized tests of occupational proficiency

Other sources can be added. The students themselves may be creative in recommending ways to evaluate their proficiencies.

Selection of Evaluative Criteria and Standards of Performance. Choosing the evaluative criteria to be used in assessing student-trainee achievements during the occupational experience component of their curriculum begins with a review of the purposes and objectives of the program and of the outcomes desired from experiences at their training agencies. It takes into account the student's vocational goals as well as the job and occupational requirements of the position held. In most regular cooperative vocational education programs, the criterion measure or standard for each criterion evaluated is the performance of the average producer who works at the same task, rather than that of other students of the same age, other part-time help, or former student-trainees. In other words, does the student-trainee perform as well as, better, or not as well as a regular full-time employee? Some programs that serve students with special needs may employ different standards, depending on the characteristics of the students and the purpose of the program.

The criteria measured or appraised in cooperative vocational education usually are expressed as competencies—classified as either technical competencies, occupational adjustment competencies, or career development competencies—described in chapter 9. Since the occupational experience laboratory offers excellent opportunities for first-hand experience with work adjustment and career development, as well as for the technical competencies, one might expect good representation of all three types of competencies in a student-trainee's evaluative criteria.

Performance Rating Forms

Rating forms that are filled in by employers and/or training sponsors are the most common type of evaluative device for collecting information about student-trainee achievement on their jobs in training agencies. Once a form has been prepared, it is a very convenient instrument for gathering information; almost too convenient because it tends to replace other methods of assessing student-trainee achievement. Then too, it may become the "tail that wags the dog." That is, it may influence the direction of instruction rather than be dependent upon it. This pitfall can be avoided in part by careful preparation of the form.

PREPARING THE FORM

Preparing a good rating form is a challenging task, which on the surface seems simple, but unless the decision makers proceed systematically and cautiously, the final product will not serve its purpose.

Determining the Evaluative Criteria to be Assessed. Usually the Evaluation System Committee first selects the evaluative criteria to be used in measuring the desired outcomes from the entire occupational experience laboratory. As suggested earlier, this should include competencies in all three competency areas. For example, knowledge of the life style of workers in a given occupation might be a desired outcome, but one that may not lend itself to a rating form. It would then be allocated to one of the other sources mentioned earlier. Only those outcomes that the intended raters would be competent to evaluate would be included in the rating form. The proposed raters should feel that each criterion they rate is important and that they are competent to rate it. Therefore, if a form is to be filled in by raters who cannot qualify to judge an item, provision should be made to indicate that he is not, e.g., N.A. (not applicable).

Selecting the Type of Response. The utility of a response depends on how the question is asked. Rating form builders must decide whether to use a checklist, a checkoff system, an annotated checklist, or another type of response to elicit the opinion of the rater. The type of response used should cause the rater to consider each item carefully, and space should be provided for constructive criticism pertaining to each criterion rated. Specific questions such as, "What could be done to improve this

Following Up Student-Trainees At Work 261

competency?" would elicit more helpful responses than merely a space marked "Comments." The form should be easy to complete. Provision should be made to indicate if there was no opportunity to observe the competency. Figure 10-4, pp. 262-63 illustrates some of these features.

Other Suggestions. Some other things to do when preparing a rating form are:

    Include an introductory statement that elicits cooperation
    Provide for an overall rating
    Make good use of space
    Submit the form to the advisory committee for opinions
    Obtain the approval of the appropriate school administrator
    Don't ask an employer to make an educator's decisions

PUTTING THE FORM TO GOOD USE

Herein lies the secret to an effective, efficient rating system. The raters must be competent and well motivated. This is achieved through selecting the proper persons to do the rating and through educating them to do the task well.

Selecting the Raters. Who should do the rating? How many raters should there be? Should the same raters participate for each rating period? Should all raters react to the same competencies? Should all raters use the same form? These are questions without common answers. Decisions will have to be made on the basis of the information at hand.

Who should do the rating? Not only those who are capable of making valid judgments, but the student-trainees as well. In the final analysis, the most important opinion about the learner's capability is the learner himself. Only he or she will be able to do much about improving the competency during the ensuing period. When ratings of competent others are compared with their own ratings, they can see whether their judgments are realistic.

How many raters should there be? There is no limit. The answer is: enough to achieve the purposes of the rating. If co-workers are the focus of classroom instruction and occupational experience laboratory assignments, include them. If the objective of the evaluation requires the expertise of a personnel director, include one.

Should the same raters participate for each rating period? Not necessarily. There are some competencies that the teacher-coordinators believe to be basic, and they want to maintain a continuing record of them, so these criteria will be rated by the same parties throughout the school year, but other items to be rated are of interest only for a single

FARIBAULT SENIOR HIGH SCHOOL
CO-OPERATIVE VOCATIONAL EDUCATIONAL PROGRAM
Student's Monthly Rating and Progress Report

CLASS NO.					
NAME (Last, first, middle initial)		GRADE	EMPLOYMENT OBJECTIVE	TRAINING ESTABLISHMENT	TEL. NO.	REPORT FOR MONTH OF _____ 19__

Times Absent From Work	Times Absent From School	Wage Rate Beg ___ End ___ of Month	Your Job Instructor	Average Work Week Hrs.	Expected on-the-job schedule of hours:
			Your Employer	Total Wage This Month $	Monday ___ to ___ Friday ___ to ___ Tuesday ___ to ___ Saturday ___ to ___ Wednesday ___ to ___ Sunday ___ to ___ Thursday ___ to ___

NOTE:
This report is to provide information which will guide the school and the cooperating business agency to provide the most effective type of training for the student. Trainer is to check each unit where improvement is needed. Also check rating of student on back of this form.

REPORT OF TRAINING ON-THE-JOB

Unit No.	Units of Instruction	HOURS WORKED DAILY																														Total Hours	Improvement Needed
		1	2	3	4	5	6	7	8	9	10	11	12	13	14	15	16	17	18	19	20	21	22	23	24	25	26	27	28	29	30	31		
1																																			
2																																			
3																																			
4																																			
5																																			
6																																			
7																																			
8																																			
9																																			
10																																			
11																																			
12																																			
	Total hours worked each day																																		
	Total hours spent in school each day																																		

RELATED CLASSROOM INSTRUCTION

Related Training Topics Studied by Student	Source of Information	Unit or Job Related	Coordinator's Comments

ON-THE-JOB TRAINER'S RATING OF THE STUDENT

Complete the rating chart below.

Outstanding	Above Average	Average	Below Average	Fail	Traits or Characteristics
					1. Personal Appearance
					2. Interest
					3. Punctual
					4. Dependable
					5. Initiative
					6. Ability to work with others
					7. Progress—Quality of work
					8. Progress—Quantity of work
					9. Accuracy
					10. Ability to follow instructions
					11. Suitability of this occupation
					12. Courteous

COMMENTS BY TRAINER:

Signed _____ Date _____

COMMENTS BY STUDENT:

FIGURE 10-4

grading period. Technical competencies in particular tend to fall into the latter category.

Should all of the raters react to the same competencies? No. They could; much depends on the characteristics of the competency being rated. For example, an employer who does not maintain close contact with a student-trainee might not be competent to appraise the trainee's personal habits.

Should all of the raters use the same form? No. Not unless they have the same capabilities and are rating the same competencies. Sometimes the student-trainees themselves can prepare rating forms to be filled in by co-workers, for example.

Educating the Raters. In order to obtain valid, reliable ratings, the raters must be well motivated and carefully instructed in how to fill in the form. They should clearly understand its purpose, know the mechanics of responding to the directions, and have very definite knowledge of the standards to use when rating a student-trainee.

The best way to do this is to sit down with the rater and assist him with filling in the form for the first time. Discuss the ratings with him and solicit constructive suggestions as well as accept criticisms. When collecting the forms for the second rating period, provide him with his earlier rating form, preferably after the second form has been completed. Established teacher-coordinators make it a point to collect the ratings personally. This is one of their best opportunities to communicate with many employers.

Concluding Statement

The main purposes of coordination follow-up calls are to improve instruction and learning at the training agency, to assist the student-trainee in adjusting to work, and to obtain information from the training agency for instructional purposes. These are complex, professional, time-consuming responsibilities which can only be fulfilled with the aid of a carefully planned coordination schedule and pre-planned follow-up calls. The secret to productive coordination follow-up calls is organization and planning of a high order with a functional filing system to supply needed information about students and the program and a coordinator's notebook that contains information to preclude needless trips back to the school. Progress on the training plan, weekly work-record reports, and training profiles alert established teacher-coordinators to the need for special follow-up calls.

Evaluation of occupational experience laboratory experiences draws on many sources of information about the achievement level of student-trainees. Though very important, the rating form is but one of them. Planning a system of occupational experience laboratory achievement is not a unilateral task. No teacher-coordinator has the occupational experience and professional education background to build an equitable system alone. No matter how good a rating scale may be, it is of little value unless those who do the rating are capable and educated in the proper use of the form.

REFERENCES

1. Patterson, Edith. "Organize Yourself for Coordination." A NADET Mini-Project. Not dated. Austin: The University of Texas Division of Extension, Distributive Education Instructional Materials.
2. Sullivan, Janie. "Organize Yourself with a Filing System." A NADET Mini-Project. Not dated. Austin: The University of Texas Division of Extension, Distributive Education Instructional Materials.

ADDITIONAL REFERENCES

Crawford, Lucy, and Warren G. Meyer. *Organization and Administration of Distributive Education.* Columbus: Charles E. Merrill, 1972, 356 pp.

Denton, William T. *Student Evaluation in Vocational and Technical Education,* Information Series No. 97. Columbus: ERIC Clearinghouse on Vocational and Technical Education, The Center for Vocational and Technical Education, The Ohio State University, 1973, 30 pp.

Drawbaugh, Charles C., and William L. Hull. *Agricultural Education: Approaches to Learning and Teaching.* Columbus: Charles E. Merrill, 1971, 324 pp.

Harms, Harm, B. W. Stehr, and E. Edward Harris. *Methods of Teaching Business and Distributive Education.* Cincinnati: South-Western, 1972, pp. 453-67.

Hanson, Doris, E., Project director. *Career Ladders and Lattices in Home Economics and Related Areas.* Washington, D.C.: American Home Economics Assn., 1971, 225 pp.

Lombard, George F. F. *Behavior in a Selling Group.* Boston: Harvard University, Division of Graduate School of Business Administration, 1955.

Morgan, Vesta C. "Home Economics Occupations in Vocational Education Today." *Illinois Teacher for Contemporary Roles* 14, No. 4 (March-April 1971): 151-63.

Nichols, Daryl E. *Selection, Placement, and Evaluation in Distributive Education.* Columbus: The Ohio State University, Distributive Education Materials Laboratory, 1885 Neil Avenue; revised, 1971.

Uthe, Elaine F. *The Cooperative Vocational Program,* Multi-Media and Simulated Cases for Pre-service and In-service Development of Teacher-Coordinators. Athens: University of Georgia, Division of Vocational Education, 1972.

SUGGESTED ACTIVITIES

1. Develop your own coordination schedule of duties and responsibilities for a one-year period. Many tasks, duties, and responsibilities appear in appendix C. Content may also be gleamed from class discussions.

Your assignment is to assemble a "Coordinator's Schedule of Duties and Responsibilities" that includes the kinds of activities that would be performed during specific months. The outline for the project would be as follows:

   I.   Title Page
   II. Table of Contents
   III. Introduction (section describing the project in relation to a specific job assignment in the school of your choice)
   IV. Month-by-month listing of activities (performed only in the respective months listed from August through July)

Activities should be grouped within each month, using the major headings listed below. Keep in mind that these lists are not exhaustive and that you are to add other duties of your own choosing which would be appropriate for the job in the school you have selected as a model. Interviews with in-service personnel are also encouraged.

The categories into which you are to assign activities are listed as follows:

  1. Student Vocational Organization
  2. Professional Role and Development
  3. Coordination
     a. Select Student-Trainees
     b. Select Training Stations
     c. Develop Training Plan and Agreement
     d. Supervise Student-Trainees On-the-Job Experiences
     e. Evaluate On-the-Job Performance of Student-Trainees

2. Prepare a list of the ways in which teacher-coordinators can apply their knowledge of career development when planning and executing coordination follow-up calls.

3. Prepare a list of the ways in which teacher-coordinators can apply the theory of work adjustment when planning and executing coordination follow-up calls.

Chapter 11 EVALUATING THE PROGRAM

Whether a teacher-coordinator aspires to promotion to a higher position or prefers to continue receiving the satisfactions inherent in the one he holds, achievement of his career goal will be enhanced by a thorough knowledge of cooperative vocational education program evaluation. In order to fulfill the role of a leader or a good team member, he must be able to view the program in perspective—to see the total program in relation to its functions and parts. Program evaluation is the key to this capability.

In order to determine the quality of a program and to make enlightened decisions that will result in positive changes, it is necessary to assess the program's strengths and weaknesses using systematic evaluation procedures. Traditionally, this has been accomplished through a process evaluation or an appraisal of the program's characteristics such as program administration, program organization, nature of instruction, and physical facilities. In recent years the trend has been toward an evaluation of the products or outcomes of the program, namely the graduates and extent to which they measure up to program goals and objectives. Both types of evaluation serve a useful purpose, but the authors have chosen to emphasize the evaluation of outcomes. Usually assistance and good literature on the evaluation of program characteristics (1, 5) is readily available whereas that on evaluation of outcomes is more difficult to obtain.

This chapter has been divided into three parts: (1) systematic evaluation of outcomes, (2) cost-benefit analysis, and (3) evaluation of program characteristics.

As you are studying this chapter, you should gain competency which will help you to:

1. Accept the need for evaluation and describe the ways in which evaluation information is used;
2. Develop a plan for systematic evaluation of outcomes and describe the steps in conducting it;
3. Explain the relationship between program purposes and evaluation of program outcomes;
4. Determine what kinds of data should be gathered and the appropriate means for obtaining the data;
5. Identify the types of information that should be included in a report to the administration;
6. Develop questionnaires for use in follow-up studies of students and employers who have participated in the program to determine program outcomes;
7. Identify the types of data that may be used in a cost-benefit evaluation;
8. Identify program characteristics that should be evaluated;
9. Plan a procedure for evaluation of program characteristics and processes;
10. Describe several ways of evaluating student performance, classroom instruction, and on-the-job training.

Systematic Evaluation of Outcomes

There is really no choice in the matter of whether or not to have an evaluation of a cooperative program. Students, parents, school personnel, and employers will form judgments about the quality of a cooperative vocational education program based on their individual observations and experiences. The local school administration and the state funding agencies will want some information on the effectiveness of the program. Finally, a professional teacher-coordinator will want to know for himself what the outcomes were. Sometimes evaluation of a program is an afterthought at the end of the school year, and even though the outcomes seem good, they may bear little relationship to what the program was intended to accomplish. A systematic program evaluation provides the teacher-coordinator and the other program decision-makers, with the answer to the question: How effective

Evaluating The Program

was the program in achieving the goals and objectives for which it was intended? A systematic plan for program evaluation (4) consists of the following steps:

>Stating Program Purposes
>>Writing Performance Objectives
>>>Planning and Implementing the Program
>>>>Stating Criterion Questions
>>>>>Collecting the Data
>>>>>>Analyzing the Data
>>>>>>>Formulating Recommendations
>>>>>>>>Making Decisions

The teacher-coordinator profits most from a systematic program evaluation because he is responsible for all the actions taken between the time a program is initiated and the time people want to know the results. A systematic plan for evaluation provides a guide from which to operate during the course of the program and gives the teacher-coordinator the information needed to make appropriate changes and improvements in the program the following year.

STATING PROGRAM PURPOSES

It is essential that evaluation be considered in conjunction with formulating program purposes and goals. In chapter 1 the reader was advised to have realistic and clearly stated program purposes that would provide a basis for making decisions about how the program should be planned, implemented, and evaluated. The statement of program purposes provides the framework from which more specific objectives are delineated and program practices are selected. A statement of purposes should include:

1. A description of students the program will serve—numbers, characteristics, needs;
2. A description of the occupations or the occupational field in which they will be placed following completion of the program;
3. Satisfactory performance as determined by employers;
4. Satisfaction of student needs and expectations;
5. Other statements which indicate exactly what the program is intended to accomplish (see chapter 1).

If the evaluation is going to include a cost-benefit analysis, as may be the case at a time when there is great concern with accountability, then it may be necessary to state an acceptable estimated cost for training a student (2). Schools usually have an average annual cost per student, to which an additional cost for vocational preparation may be added (e.g., one-third to one-half of the coordinator's salary divided by the number of students enrolled). The purpose for having a cost goal is to demonstrate that the program was efficient relative to projected costs or to alternative programs and other ways the school may use its resources.

A clear statement of program purposes sheds some light on what is to be evaluated and how the outcomes will be measured. It also provides a teacher-coordinator with a basis for making decisions along the way.

WRITING PERFORMANCE OBJECTIVES

The next step in preparing for an evaluation is writing terminal performance objectives which state what competencies—knowledges, skills and attitudes—students will have upon completion of the program. The performance objectives are related to the program purposes and are derived from an analysis of student needs and the occupations for which they are preparing while enrolled in the program. All prospective teachers, and particularly vocational education teachers, should develop the ability to write good performance objectives.

In chapter 3 it was suggested that students need a combination of technical competencies, occupational adjustment competencies, and career development competencies, and that individual students should have some objectives or competencies that are specific to their individual needs and career goals. A good terminal performance objective is stated in terms that indicate (1) what the students will be able to do (e.g., operate cash registers); (2) under what conditions (e.g., in their places of employment or in the laboratory); and (3) at a specified level of performance (e.g., with one hundred percent accuracy or judged satisfactory by their supervisors). A properly stated objective tells the teacher-coordinator what competency needs to be taught and learned and how it will be evaluated.

PLANNING AND IMPLEMENTING THE PROGRAM

Planning and implementing the program are closely related to evaluation because the classroom instruction, the training plans, the youth organization activities, and all of the other program inputs should focus on the purposes and objectives that will be evaluated later. The teacher-coordinator is faced with many daily decisions while implementing the program. If the goals and objectives and the evaluation are kept in mind continually, there always will be a logical basis for making sound decisions.

The teacher-coordinator, or program manager as the job was referred to in chapter 3, controls a large number of inputs that impact on the program. When the purposes and objectives are clear and the evaluation is

Evaluating The Program

well planned, the decisions about students, training agencies, instruction, learning materials, and the teacher-coordinator's daily program of work are easier to make. For example, if a goal is to have students placed in jobs that enable them to be self-supporting upon completion of the program, the teacher-coordinator takes this into account when selecting training agencies and preparing the students for full-time employment. If the goal is to have students become active participants in the life of the community, the teacher-coordinator provides experiences whereby student-trainees participate in community activities and civic projects while they are enrolled in the program.

The teacher-coordinator will need to plan special learning experiences to facilitate the career development competencies that were discussed in chapter 4. The "theory of work adjustment" and the four aspects of adjustment that were explained in chapter 5 are given attention during placement, follow-up calls to the training agency, and other processes in the implementation of the program.

STATING CRITERION QUESTIONS

After the program purposes and objectives are specified, the teacher-coordinator must develop a meaningful list of criterion questions. The criterion questions are attempts to determine whether the program is achieving the purposes and objectives it was designed to serve. The teacher-coordinator would be prudent to enlist the help of the program advisory committee and selected members of the school administrative staff in formulating the criterion questions which would give them an input into the formulation of the evaluation process. They usually are interested in the program, and they are likely to have questions they would like to have included in the evaluation.

The criterion questions will largely control the kinds of data to be gathered and the sources used. The following questions are examples of what a teacher-coordinator, or others who are interested in the program, may want to know about program outcomes:

1. How many students are employed

    ... 3 months, 1 year, and/or 3 years after completion of the program?
    ... in the same occupation, in a related occupation, or in an unrelated job?
    ... at what level of responsibility or salary?

2. How do employers rate the performance of program graduates

    ... compared to other employees?
    ... relative to the time they began?
    ... on specific knowledges, skills, and attitudes?
    ... on their potential for promotion?

3. How do those who complete the program feel about
   ... the satisfaction they receive from their jobs?
   ... the usefulness of competencies acquired during the program?
   ... competencies they need which were not learned?
   ... progress they have made toward their career goals?
   ... the values or benefits derived from specific aspects of the program (e.g., youth organization activities, individual learning packages, on-the-job training)?
4. Are parents satisfied with the program?
5. Do those who complete the program
   ... participate in community activities?
   ... continue their education in post-secondary schools or adult classes?
   ... belong to employee and trade association groups?
   ... receive promotions and salary increases?
   ... become managers or owners of small businesses?
6. What is the average annual cost per student for the program?
   ... total cost including outside funding?
   ... net cost to the local school district?
   ... compared to planned cost per student?
   ... compared to cost per student in other vocational programs or similar programs in other schools?

COLLECTING THE DATA

The data for evaluation of program outcomes is obtained from a number of sources—students currently enrolled, follow-up surveys of graduates and/or dropouts, their employers, parents and other school personnel who are aware of outcomes. In addition to surveys by mailed questionnaires, the teacher-coordinator may wish to conduct personal interviews with students or employers.

Students Currently Enrolled. One method of assessing outcomes is to administer tests and inventories to measure student-trainees' knowledge, skills, and attitudes. When tests are used to obtain information about program outcomes, it is necessary to administer them just before the student-trainees complete the program. Even then it is difficult to establish that there is a cause-and-effect relationship between the program and the test results. Also, after they have graduated it is impracticable to conduct the testing. Standardized tests can be used to compare student-trainees with other groups and make some inferences about the effectiveness of the program.

In chapter 5 the *Minnesota Satisfaction Questionnaire* was suggested as a method of assessing job satisfaction. Measures of vocational maturity, work values, career awareness, self-concept and others that assess career development behaviors and attitudes are available now and can be useful in assessing these kinds of outcomes. Standardized tests for the various trades and for different occupational skills and technical knowledge may be used. The teacher-coordinator should refer to *The Mental Measurements Yearbook* (2) or consult with the counselor in his school to find out what tests are available and to determine which ones are appropriate for his purposes.

Follow-up Surveys of Graduates and/or Dropouts. Students who have graduated or left the program may supply the most useful data about the value of the program because it was designed to meet their needs. The data gathered from former student-trainees can include both objective and subjective kinds of information. Their willingness to participate and the reliability of their answers to questionnaires depends a great deal on the kind of relationship the teacher-coordinator established with them while they were enrolled. Before completion of the program the teacher-coordinator should inform the students that they will be contacted for information at various times to assist the school in providing relevant and stimulating instructional programs. The students should be asked to give the teacher-coordinator a permanent address where they may be reached at future times; also the address of their parents and grandparents. Experience has shown the latter to be the easiest to locate.

One follow-up survey of student-trainees is usually done three months to a year after completion of a program. If the objective is to make inferences about the effects of specific aspects of the program, a short span of time between completion of the program and the follow-up is necessary, due to the possibility of intervening variables and the ability of students to recall details of the program. Three to six months is usually a long enough period for students to have located a full-time job or to have experienced some increased responsibility in the jobs they held at the time of leaving the program.

Another follow-up at the end of three years may be useful in determining whether or not students have advanced in the occupational field for which they received training, whether they were employed steadily during that period of time, what further education and training they received, and their attitudes toward their occupational preparation after a three-year period.

The kinds of data that may be gathered from student follow-up studies are:

1. Jobs they have held;
2. Salaries of employed graduates;
3. Attitudes toward the program;
4. Areas of weakness;
5. Recommended program changes;

6. Future educational and vocational plans;
7. Job satisfaction.

In seeking information about attitudes and sincere opinions about the program, it may be necessary to protect the anonymity of the respondents. The phrasing of the questions and the ease of completing the form also increase the likelihood of quick and reliable responses. A sample form for a student follow-up survey is shown in figure 11-1.

FIGURE 11-1

STUDENT FOLLOW-UP SURVEY*

Your answers to the following questions are to be used by the school in the improvement of the Cooperative _____ Program. Please be frank in your response to the questions.

Name _____ Graduation date _____

Present employer _____ Address _____

Job title _____ Present weekly salary _____

JOBS HELD SINCE GRADUATION

Job Title	Employer	Dates From	To

ADDITIONAL EDUCATION OBTAINED

Name of School	Course or Major	Dates Attended From	To

Which of the following competencies are used in your present job?

	Frequently	Sometimes	Rarely	None
1. (example: Salesmanship)	___	___	___	___
2.	___	___	___	___
3.	___	___	___	___
4.	___	___	___	___

Evaluating The Program

(Note to teacher-coordinator: List all competency areas covered in the program.)

What additional competency areas would you like to have had instruction for while you were enrolled in the cooperative program? _____

How would you rate each of the following cooperative program elements?

	Excellent	Good	Average	Fair	Poor
Classroom learning activities	____	____	____	____	____
Reading materials	____	____	____	____	____
Individual study materials	____	____	____	____	____
Club activities	____	____	____	____	____
On-the-job instruction	____	____	____	____	____
Individual help from teacher-coordinator	____	____	____	____	____

What were the most beneficial experiences you had while enrolled in the program? _____

What suggestions do you have for improving the cooperative _____ program?

*Adapted from forms used in ths Illinois Occupation Curriculum Project (2)

Employer Follow-up Surveys. Teacher-coordinators conduct follow-up surveys with employers to get their evaluations of the performance of student-trainees and their attitudes toward the program. The employers' evaluations can be very valuable in program planning because they usually can tell where student-trainees are strong or weak and what skills, knowledge, and attitudes are most important on the jobs.

The kinds of data and information that might be sought through employer follow-up surveys are:

1. Importance of skills, knowledge and attitudes (unnecessary, desirable, essential);
2. Employee's performance of skills (very adequate, adequate, inadequate);
3. Comparison with other employees approximately the same age who had other training (does less well, as well, or better);
4. Need for further instruction and training;
5. Progress in competencies and traits since becoming an employee;
6. Estimated potential for promotion and increased responsibility.

A questionnaire which is easy to complete (accompanied by a cover letter explaining the purpose of the survey and assurance of confidentiality) should produce information that will be valuable in revising the program, in modifying its objectives, in improving the selection of students, or in continuing the program as it has operated if employers are satisfied.

Employers may be asked to complete a rating scale much as the *Minnesota Satisfactoriness Scales*, chapter 5, figure 5-4, or a form prepared by the teacher-coordinator such as the sample form shown in figure 11-2.

Other Follow-up Surveys. In some instances it may be wise to obtain evaluations from other groups such as the members of the advisory committee, parents of student-trainees and other faculty members of the school. If these groups feel that their opinions and suggestions regarding the program are valued and utilized in program planning, they probably will be supportive of the program.

The advisory committee may be asked to evaluate the extent to which the program has met the training needs of the community, the relevancy and adequacy of the facilities and equipment, and the content of the instructional program. They may make recommendations or assist the teacher-coordinator in effecting desirable changes.

An evaluation by parents is partly a matter of maintaining good public relations, but it also provides assurance that the program is successful or that there are weaknesses to be overcome. Casual negative comments by one or two dissatisfied parents can be outweighed by evidence that the majority of the parents are pleased with the outcomes of their children's participation.

For similar reasons, teachers may also be asked for evaluations to make certain that they are supportive of the program. Did students who were enrolled in the program complete their other studies satisfactorily? Did their teachers see any improvement in their performance, attendance, and work habits? What suggestions might they have for improving the program or making it a more attractive alternative to students?

ANALYZING THE DATA

In most evaluations the teacher-coordinator prepares an analysis of the data collected. This may consist of a tally of the responses to the questions in the survey, classification of information, and interpretation of the data. The comments or answers to open-ended questions may call for further investigation by personal interviews and provide the teacher-coordinator with very specific kinds of suggestions for making changes.

It is unlikely that the analysis of the data will require a sophisticated statistical treatment, unless the teacher-coordinator gathers data from a sampling of the total possible respondents or if different groups of respondents are to be compared on some characteristic. Whenever one uses a sample group to make inferences about the population from which the sample is drawn, a statistical analysis is warranted. If

FIGURE 11-2

Employer Follow-up Survey

Your answers to the following questions can be helpful to the school in improving the Cooperative _____ Program.

1. Is _____ employed by your firm? _____ Yes _____ No

    If No— When was employment terminated? _____

    Reason for leaving _____

    Name and address of current employer _____

    _____

    If Yes, complete the following questions.

2. What is this person's current job title? _____
3. How does this person compare with other employees at the same job level on the following traits:

	Above Average	Average	Below Average
Essential skills and knowledges	____	____	____
Attitude toward work and the job	____	____	____
Productivity	____	____	____
Ability to solve problems	____	____	____
Amount of supervision needed	____	____	____
Cooperation with fellow-employees	____	____	____

4. How would you evaluate this person generally as an employee?

    _____ _____ _____ _____ _____
    Outstanding   Above Average   Average   Below Average   Poor

5. Please rate the importance of each of the following competency areas, and then rate the person on his performance in each area.

Competency Areas in Coop Program Curriculum	IMPORTANCE			PERFORMANCE		
	Very Imp.	Imp.	Not Imp.	Good	Fair	Poor
1. Filing correspondence (Example)						
2.						
3.						
Etc.						

6. What suggestions do you have for improving the occupational preparation of students who are enrolled in Cooperative _____ Education?

277

a teacher-coordinator needs to use a statistical analysis and lacks expertise, he can seek assistance or refer to one of the many good books on methods of statistical analysis.

The same suggestion is made with regard to the use of computers for analyzing the data. They are not essential for the amount of data to be analyzed, or the type of analysis to be made, particularly if one wants to capture comments and responses that are not quantifiable and consistent in form. Usually a school that has computer service has programmers to assist in the analysis of data when the use of the computer seems appropriate.

The evaluation report should be written in a brief, easy to understand manner in order that an administrator, members of the advisory committee, and state supervisory personnel can get a clear picture of: (1) the purpose of the evaluation, (2) the method of obtaining the data, and (3) the results. A summary report should precede the more detailed report that is used primarily by the teacher-coordinator to make decisions about modifying objectives and practices.

FORMULATING RECOMMENDATIONS

The recommendations for methods of improving the program should be based on the findings of the evaluation. One needs to be somewhat cautious in making assumptions that are not supported by the evaluation data. For example, if the student follow-up study indicates that students feel that they have not benefited from youth organization activities, the teacher-coordinator recommends that the activities be examined for possible revision, rather than recommending that they be dropped altogether. If the evaluation shows that very few of the program objectives are met, the recommendation may be to reconsider the objectives or to reassess the needs of those the program was designed to serve.

The recommendations would appear in the summary of the evaluation report and in the detailed report that the teacher-coordinator prepares for his or her own use.

MAKING DECISIONS

Most of the decisions for program changes will be made by the teacher-coordinator based on what is learned from the evaluation. Major decisions such as deciding to extend the length of the program or any change which would require an increase in expenditures for the program should be approved by the administration and should be supported by the advisory committee. There is always a political dimension to the decision-making process, but a systematic evaluation with documented evidence of needs can gain support for the changes being recommended.

Making decisions about purposes, objectives, and improvements in the implementation is the start of the next evaluation cycle—systematically planned and followed to the next decision-making point.

Cost-Benefit Analysis

A relatively new concept and practice in program evaluation is a cost-benefit analysis. This method of evaluation compares program costs to quantitative program outcomes and benefits. Although this is a complicated procedure for program evaluation, it is an excellent way of demonstrating that money expended is justified by the benefits received. In an era of accountability, many administrators are vitally concerned with being able to show that the pay-off is commensurate with the costs of operating the program.

PROCEDURE FOR A COST-BENEFIT ANALYSIS

Step 1: Review program goals which should reflect the desired benefits and should be stated in measurable outcomes such as the number of students to be placed, types of jobs, their anticipated average weekly salary, and possibly employer, student, and parental satisfaction.

Step 2: In cooperation with the school administration and the advisory committee, determine what data and records are to be maintained for the cost-benefit analysis. These may include:

- a. Placement information;
- b. Employer follow-up forms;
- c. Student follow-up forms;
- d. Parental follow-up forms;
- e. Vocational and academic achievement records;
- f. Program costs (see Step 3).

Step 3: Develop a form for computing program costs which may include:

- a. Instructional salaries;
- b. Administrative salaries;
- c. Ancillary services;
- d. Depreciation of equipment;
- e. Instructional materials and supplies;
- f. Other assignable items;
- g. Outside funding.

Step 4: Collect the data and synthesize the benefits in accordance with what was specified in the goals and objectives. Prepare quantitative statements about the ou comes—number of students placed in full-time jobs, salary levels, number of students who were promoted, number of employers who rates students above average, and so on.

Step 5: Compute program costs in terms of:
   a. Total annual program costs;
   b. Net program costs (total cost less outside funding);
   c. Net cost per student enrolled (net program cost divided by number enrolled);
   d. Net cost per student placed (net program cost divided by number placed).

Step 6: Prepare a written report or program profile for the administration, the advisory committee and other interested parties, indicating the benefits derived from the amount expended per student. A sample form for reporting cost-benefit information is shown in figure 11-3.

Step 7: Comparisons may be made with cost-benefit analyses of similar programs in the same school or other schools, or with the desired cost levels which were specified in program objectives. If program costs exceed projected costs or costs of similar programs, the teacher-coordinator and the administration may want to identify cost-saving measures which would not alter the benefits substantially. It would certainly be a signal to the teacher-coordinator that certain aspects of the program should be modified.

As the demand for vocational education increases, and particularly for cooperative vocational programs, administrators are likely to be much more cost-conscious in deciding which programs to provide and look to those which yield the best return for the amount invested.

Evaluation of Program Characteristics

The evaluation of program outcomes also furnishes a general evaluation of program characteristics and procedures because it can be inferred that the inputs were effective if the follow-up surveys show that students were placed in satisfying jobs and have the necessary skills, knowledges, and attitudes. If the follow-up studies yield unfavorable results, it may be inferred that something was wrong with the inputs. Then it becomes necessary to examine program characteristics and procedures. Then too, a teacher-coordinator cannot wait until several months after the students have completed a program to find out whether or not the study materials, the content, and other elements of the program are relevant to the students' needs. Program characteristics and processes can be evaluated by assessing student performance periodically in the classroom and on the job and by having students participate

FIGURE 11-3

Cost-benefit Analysis

Title of Program _____
Time Period from _____ to _____

COST FACTORS	PROJECTED COST	ACTUAL COST
Total Program Cost		
Total Outside Funding		
Net Program Cost (Local Funds)		
Net Cost Per Student Enrolled		
Net Cost Per Student Placed		
Average Annual Cost Per Student Enrolled in Other Programs in the School		

OUTCOME FACTORS	PROJECTED GOALS (Numbers)	ACTUAL OUTCOMES (Numbers)
Student Enrollment		
Students Placed in Jobs (6 Mos. after Completion)		
Students Earning Over $500 per Month		
Students Rated Above Average by Employers		
Students Who Rated the Program "Highly Beneficial"		
Students Who Are "Very Satisfied" in Present Job		
Parents Who Rated the Program as "Very Beneficial"		
(Other Factors Taken from Program Goals)		

in the evaluation of instruction and on-the-job training while they are enrolled. Another method of evaluating program characteristics and procedures is to have external evaluators—experts from outside of the school—observe and rate the program on some accepted criteria and standards.

EVALUATION OF STUDENT PERFORMANCE

Student performance and progress are evaluated frequently through coordination calls to the training agency. If the teacher-coordinator has created the right relationships with training sponsors they are quick to point up the ways in which student-trainees excel and where they need further instruction.

In addition to the informal feedback given on coordination calls, the teacher-coordinator has the training sponsor complete a rating sheet, such as shown in chapter 10, figure 10-4, or the *Minnesota Satisfactoriness Scales* shown in chapter 5, figure 5-4 at regular intervals which may coincide with grading periods at the school. The rating sheet would reflect the knowledge and skills being taught in school and attempt to measure the student's ability to apply new learning on the job. The teacher-coordinator may also want some continuous appraisal of progress in general work habits and attitudes, but the rating sheet for each marking period should contain new skills and knowledges for which instruction was given during that period of time.

Employers and training sponsors may find it difficult to use a rating sheet for the first few times, and teacher-coordinators usually assist the employer in completing the rating sheet. Students should be evaluated on the same standards as other employees and the teacher-coordinator must assist the employer in arriving at the standards to be used. Without help, employers or training sponsors tend to overrate student-trainees in the beginning and create a false sense of achievement on the part of the student. The teacher-coordinator can also elicit additional information that is helpful in giving the student-trainees the proper guidance and instruction following the evaluation.

The teacher-coordinator also evaluates student performance when he observes the student on the job—when it is convenient and with the approval of the employer. The teacher-coordinator may observe how a trainee maintains his work station or how he handles a patient, customer, or client. He may want to examine a product the student has made or the records kept on his productivity. Care must be exercised not to interfere with performance of the work or service to customers and clients.

Instruction and students' performance are also evaluated in the classroom through written and oral tests and by having the students demonstrate that they can perform the tasks being learned. The acquisition of technical information can be measured with paper and pencil tests. Problem-solving abilities are measured through case problems and simulations. There are many inherent problems in selecting or developing proper assesment instruments. The first step in attempting to evaluate by testing is to have a clear statement of the performance objectives. The objectives should dictate what is to be tested and, to some extent, how it should be done.

In vocational education many of the objectives lend themselves to the use of performance tests in which the student is expected to demonstrate performance of an occupational skill in which some criterion situation is simulated. This could be anything from preparation of a meal to operating a piece of equipment. Prospective teacher-coordinators should have a good background in tests and measurement because they will need to develop many of their own tests.

STUDENT EVALUATION OF INSTRUCTION

Another method of evaluating instruction and program characteristics is to obtain student reactions. A good teacher does not feel threatened by student reactions to the content or the methods of teaching and learning presented in the classroom. Students can be very helpful to the teacher in planning appropriate instruction.

Rating sheets for student evaluation of instruction may call for students to rate or rank the following aspects of their program in terms of their relevance to perceived needs or their learning value:

1. Specific concepts, skills and attitudes presented in classroom instruction;
2. Textbooks, films, individualized self-study materials, trade journals, and other sources of information;
3. Learning activities such as field trips, resource speakers, and special projects;
4. Youth organization activities such as conferences, sales projects, social and civic activities, and chapter meetings.

A teacher-coordinator may want other kinds of feedback on the students' attitudes toward classroom management, grading, amount of individual help given, and assigned homework. The intent of these appraisals is to improve instruction and student motivation to learn. Student participation in the evaluation of instruction and the teacher-coordinator's behavior is based on an assumption that students can make an objective assessment and that their reactions would be gathered anonymously. The teacher-coordinator must create a climate in which this kind of interaction can occur. A sample form for student evaluation of instruction is shown in figure 11-4.

FIGURE 11-4

STUDENT EVALUATION FORM

Instructor's Name   Course or Program Title   Date

Please underline the one best alternative for each statement.

1. The objectives of the course (program) are (1) absolutely clear, (2) somewhat clear, (3) not clear.
2. The technical information and the skills taught are (1) very relevant to my needs, (2) sometimes relevant to my needs, (3) usually not relevant.
3. The classroom instruction is (1) very stimulating most of the time, (2) sometimes stimulating, (3) dull and unstimulating.
4. The reading assignments are (1) very interesting, (2) somewhat interesting, (3) dull and uninteresting.
5. The instructor seems to know the subject matter (1) very well, (2) adequately, (3) somewhat inadequately.
6. The quizzes and tests given in class are (1) closely related, (2) somewhat related, (3) not related to the objectives and instruction.
7. The instructor seems sensitive and interested in students (1) at all times, (2) some of the time, (3) rarely.
8. The instructor is fair and impartial in dealing with students (1) all of the time, (2) some of the time, (3) rarely.
9. The grading system for this course seems (1) very fair, (2) usually fair, (3) somewhat fair.
10. The classroom atmosphere and student behavior is (1) conducive to learning, (2) reasonably well managed, (3) not conducive to learning.

Which learning activities and assignments have been most interesting and helpful?

What suggestions do you have for improvement of instruction? instructor effectiveness? skills to be learned?

STUDENT EVALUATION OF ON-THE-JOB TRAINING

In chapter 10 a Training Profile (figure 10-3) was explained as a method of determining how to improve on-the-job training. The profile may also be a means of determining whether or not the training agencies are providing adequate training.

Another method of assessing the training agency input into training is to have the students submit a record of the new things they have learned on the job each week. This may include a list of the different tasks they have performed or areas to which they were assigned. The weekly report was explained in chapter 10 and an example of a form is shown in figure 10-2.

PROGRAM EVALUATION BY EXTERNAL TEAMS

Most schools have some type of evaluation periodically to maintain accreditation and will have a team of evaluators from outside of the school review the entire system, analyze its strengths and weaknesses, and make recommendations for improvements. The *National Study of Secondary School Evaluation* (5) is one of the accrediting agencies which provides this service and has criteria which cover the characteristics of sound vocational education programs. A team of two to three persons who are considered to have expertise in a vocational education field evaluates the following characteristics of the program in that field:

  I. Organization
  II. Nature of Offerings
  III. Physical Facilities
  IV. Direction of Learning
  V. Outcomes
  VI. Special Characteristics
  VII. General Evaluation

Before the external team makes its analysis, the teacher-coordinator makes his own assessment of how the program rates and what needs to be done to improve the operation. In conducting the evaluation, the external evaluators review written statements of program goals and objectives, and content outlines; they examine the facilities, equipment and instructional materials; they observe classroom instruction and teacher performance; and they interview students, parents, employers, advisory committee members, and other faculty members in the school about the program.

In the absence of an external evaluation for accreditation purposes or one required by the school administration, a conscientious teacher-coordinator who wants to improve the cooperative vocational education program may enlist the help of state department personnel, teacher-educators, advisory committee members, or some of his professional colleagues to appraise the program. Members of the profession are usually eager to participate in such evaluations and they can provide valuable assistance in developing a strong program. Some of the professional associations have developed criteria for a teacher-coordinator to rate his own program or to be used when a team of colleagues are engaged to conduct the evaluation (1).

Concluding Statement

Many studies have indicated that one of the most important factors in job satisfaction for most individuals is the sense of achievement they get from their work. A systematic plan for program evaluation should provide the teacher-coordinator with evidence that the efforts expended in good teaching and coordination yield high returns. Careful attention to the evaluation function is essential if one wishes to improve the effectiveness and efficiency of a program. The evaluation process guides the teacher-coordinator in making decisions and program changes and makes his job less difficult in the long run. Knowledge of program outcomes is the most important data for continuation or expansion of a program, but most coordinators will want to maintain a continuous evaluation of day-to-day operations and program characteristics so that changes can be made as the program evolves. Time spent in continuous and carefully planned evaluation is very worthwhile—the program gets better and the teacher-coordinator gets more satisfaction from his job. The most important benefit from a systematic plan for program evaluation is that student-trainees receive better instruction and training which facilitates their career development and work adjustment, two of the basic concepts underlying the philosophy and practices recommended in this book.

REFERENCES

1. Ash, Lane. *National Study for Accreditation of Vocational-Technical Education.* Washington, D. C.: American Vocational Association, 1972.
2. Borgen, Joseph A., and Davis, Dwight E. *Planning, Implementing and Evaluating Career Preparation Programs.* Bloomington, Illinois: McKnight, 1974, 472pp.
3. Buros, O. K., ed. *The Mental Measurements Yearbook.* Highland Park, N. J.: Gryphon Press, 1972. (Revised Periodically)
4. Denton, William T. *Program Evaluation in Vocational and Technical Education.* Information Series No. 98, ERIC Clearinghouse on Vocational and Technical Education. Columbus: Ohio State University, Center for Vocational and Technical Education, 1973, 30pp.

5. National Study of Secondary School Evaluation. *Evaluative Criteria.* 4th ed. Washington, D. C.: 1969.

ADDITIONAL REFERENCES

Crawford, Lucy C., and Meyer, Warren G. *Organization and Administration of Distributive Education.* Columbus: Charles E. Merrill, 1972, 356pp.

Cross, Aleene. *Home Economics Evaluation.* Columbus: Charles E. Merrill, 1973, 303 pp.

Denton, William T. *Student Evaluation in Vocational and Technical Education.* Information Series No. 97, ERIC Clearinghouse on Vocational and Technical Education. Columbus: Ohio State University, Center for Vocational and Technical Education, 1973, 30pp.

Moss, Jerome, Jr. "The Evaluation of Occupational Education Programs," Technical Report No. 3. Minneapolis: University of Minnesota, Research Coordination Unit in Occupational Education, 1968.

Robertson, J. Marvin. *Facilities Evaluation in Vocational and Technical Education.* Information Series No. 100, ERIC Clearinghouse on Vocational and Technical Education. Columbus: Ohio State University, Center for Vocational and Technical Education, 1973, 22pp.

Stufflebeam, Daniel L. *Education Evaluation and Decision Making.* Itasca, Illinois: F. E. Peacock, 1971.

SUGGESTED ACTIVITIES

1. Prepare a list of the outcomes that you feel should be evaluated for a cooperative program in your vocational field (e.g., job titles of student-trainees who completed the program).

2. Locate and study a list of criteria which could be used to evaluate the characteristics of a cooperative education program in your vocational field. Check with your state department for vocational education, *The National Study for Secondary School Evaluation*, and evaluation research literature for your field.

3. Prepare a list of the standardized tests that are available from commercial publishers and that seem to be appropriate for evaluation of achievement and/or performance of student-trainees in a program for your vocational field.

4. Locate and review a follow-up study of student-trainees for a cooperative vocational education program in your field. Prepare a brief report of the conclu-

sions and recommendations. (Master's papers or doctoral dissertations may be the best source for such studies.)

5. Prepare a list of criterion questions that should be answered for a cooperative program in your vocational field.

6. Outline a program of evaluation activities that you feel are necessary for the effective operation of a cooperative program in your field. Identify what forms must be prepared and from what sources the data could be obtained.

7. Prepare a list of ways in which teacher-coordinators can apply their knowledge of career development when planning and engaging in program evaluation.

8. Prepare a list of ways in which the theory of work adjustment can be applied when planning and engaging in program evaluation.

Appendix A

VOCATIONAL EDUCATION AMENDMENTS OF 1968

Comparative Analysis of Cooperative Education Programs and Work-Study Program

Part B	Part G	Part H
State Vocational Education Programs	*Cooperative Vocational Education Programs*	*Work-Study Programs for Vocational Education Students*
1. Money appropriated under Part B and allotted to the states may be expended for cooperative education programs	1. Money appropriated under Part G and allotted to the States shall be expended for developing new programs of cooperative education	1. Money appropriated under Part H and allotted to the States shall be expended for work-study programs
2. Purpose * To provide on-the-job work experience related to the student's course of study and chosen occupation	2. Purpose * To provide on-the-job work experience related to the student's course of study and chosen occupation	2. Purpose * To provide financial assistance to students who are in need of earnings from employment to commence or continue their vocational education program
3. Students Served * Individuals who desire and need such education and training in all communities of the State	3. Students Served * Individuals who desire and need such education and training in all communities of the State * *Priority is given to areas of high rates of school dropouts and youth unemployment*	3. Students Served * Economically disadvantaged full-time vocational education students

Part B

State Vocational Education Programs

4. Uses of Funds
   * Program operation and ancillary services

5. Federal Portion of Support
   * Based upon Statewide matching (50/50) for all basic grant vocational education programs. Application of State criteria for allocation of funds determines level of assistance

6. Instruction
   * In-school vocational instruction related to occupational field and training job

7. Work Periods
   * Alternate half days, full days, weeks, or other periods of time. (Number of hours of work generally equal the number of hours spent in school)

Part G

Cooperative Vocational Education Programs

4. Uses of Funds
   * Programs operation and ancillary services
   * *Reimbursement of added training cost to employers, when necessary*
   * *Payment for certain services or unusual costs to students while in cooperative training*

5. Federal Portion of Support
   * *All or part (100%)*

6. Instruction
   * In-school vocational instruction related to occupational field and training job

7. Work Periods
   * Alternate half days, full days, weeks, or other periods of time. (*Number of hours of work need not equal the number of hours spent in school*)

Part H

Work-Study Programs for Vocational Education Students

4. Uses of Funds
   * Compensation of students employed
   * Development and administration of program

5. Federal Portion of Support
   * *80%*

6. Instruction
   * In-school vocational instruction not necessarily related to the job

7. Work Periods
   * Maximum of 15 hours per week while attending school

8. Wage Payments
   * Regular wages established for the occupational field
   * Usually at least minimum wage or student-learner rate established by Department of Labor
   * Wages paid by employer

9. Age Limitations
   * Minimum age 14 as per Child Labor Laws

10. Eligible Employers
    * Public or private

11. Administration
    * Administered by the State or local educational agencies under supervision of the State Board for Vocational Education in accordance with State Plan provisions

---

8. Wage Payments
   * Regular wages established for the occupational field
   * Usually at least minimum wage or student-learner rate established by Department of Labor
   * Wages paid by employer

9. Age Limitations
   * Minimum age 14 as per Child Labor Laws

10. Eligible Employers
    * Public or private

11. Administration
    * Administered by the State or local educational agencies under supervision of the State Board for Vocational Education in accordance with State Plan provisions

---

8. Wage Payments
   * $45 per month, $350 per academic year or in certain cases $60 per month, $500 per academic year
   * Public funds are used for compensation

9. Age Limitations
   * 15 through 20 years of age

10. Eligible Employers
    * Limited to public, non-profit employers

11. Administration
    * Administered by the State or local educational agencies under supervision of the State Board for Vocational Education in accordance with State Plan provisions

Work Experience Education
Development Branch
DVTE/BAVLP/USOE
6/69

Appendix B TEACHING CAREER ANALYSIS

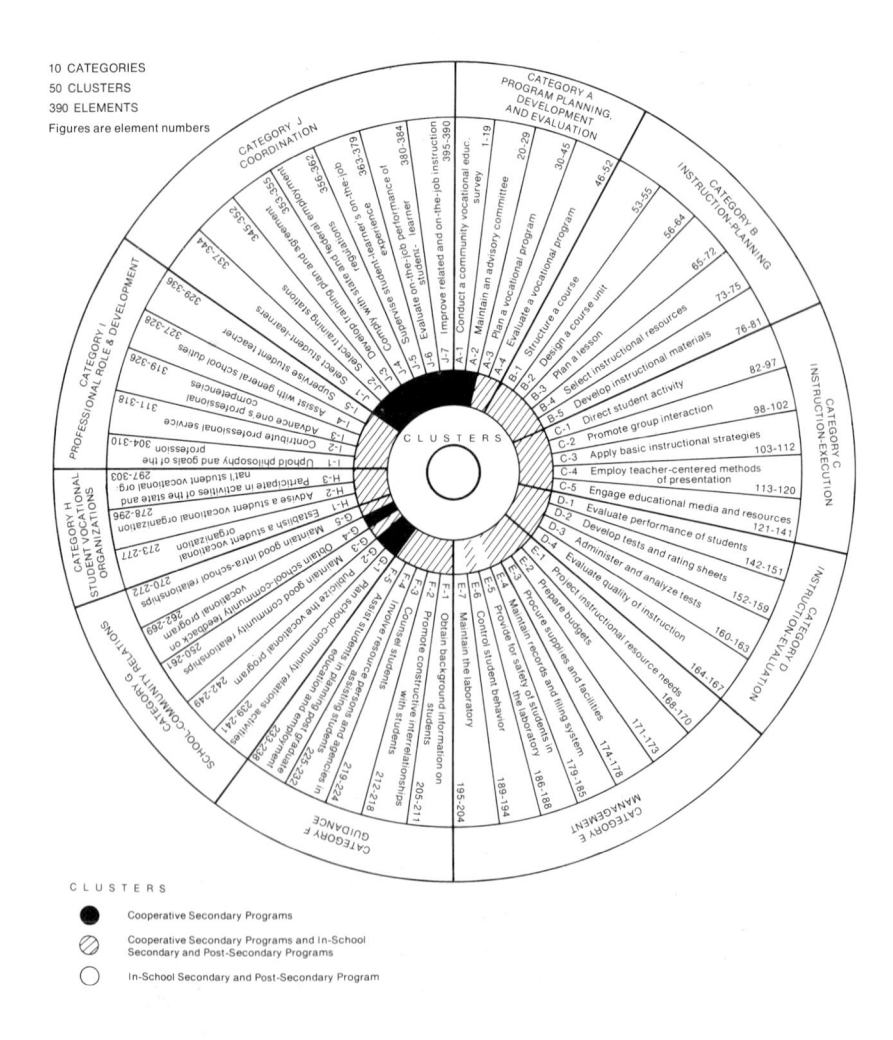

10 CATEGORIES
50 CLUSTERS
390 ELEMENTS
Figures are element numbers

CATEGORY A PROGRAM PLANNING, DEVELOPMENT AND EVALUATION
- A-1 Conduct a community vocational educ. survey 1-19
- A-2 Maintain an advisory committee 20-29
- A-3 Plan a vocational program 30-45
- A-4 Evaluate a vocational program 46-52

CATEGORY B INSTRUCTION-PLANNING
- B-1 Structure a course 53-55
- B-2 Design a course unit 56-64
- B-3 Plan a lesson 65-72
- B-4 Select instructional resources 73-75
- B-5 Develop instructional materials 76-81

CATEGORY C INSTRUCTION-EXECUTION
- C-1 Direct student activity 82-97
- C-2 Promote group interaction 98-102
- C-3 Apply basic instructional strategies 103-112
- C-4 Employ teacher-centered methods of presentation 113-120
- C-5 Engage educational media and resources 121-141

CATEGORY D INSTRUCTION-EVALUATION
- D-1 Evaluate performance of students 142-151
- D-2 Develop tests and rating sheets 152-159
- D-3 Administer and analyze tests 160-163
- D-4 Evaluate quality of instruction 164-167

CATEGORY E MANAGEMENT
- E-1 Project instructional resource needs 168-170
- E-2 Prepare budgets 171-173
- E-3 Procure supplies and facilities 174-178
- E-4 Maintain records and filing system 179-185
- E-5 Provide for safety of students in the laboratory 186-188
- E-6 Maintain the laboratory 189-194
- E-7 Control student behavior 195-204
- E-8 Obtain background information on students 205-211

CATEGORY F GUIDANCE
- F-1 Promote constructive interrelationships with students 212-218
- F-2 Counsel students 219-224
- F-3 Assist students in planning and securing post-graduate employment 225-232
- F-4 Involve resource persons to assist vocational educator in guidance activities 233-241

CATEGORY G SCHOOL-COMMUNITY RELATIONS
- G-1 Promote the vocational education program 242-249
- G-2 Publicize school-community relationships 250-261
- G-3 Assist in vocational-community relationships 262-269
- G-4 Maintain good intra-school relationships 270-272
- G-5 Establish a student vocational organization 273-277

CATEGORY H STUDENT VOCATIONAL ORGANIZATIONS
- H-1 Advise a student vocational organization 278-296
- H-2 Participate in activities of the state and nat'l student vocational org. 297-303

CATEGORY I PROFESSIONAL ROLE & DEVELOPMENT
- I-1 Uphold philosophy and goals of the profession 304-310
- I-2 Contribute professional service 311-318
- I-3 Advance one's professional competencies 319-326
- I-4 Assist with general school duties 327-328
- I-5 Supervise student teacher 329-336
- I-6 Select student-learners 337-344

CATEGORY J COORDINATION
- J-1 Develop training stations 345-352
- J-2 Conduct on-the-job supervision 353-355
- J-3 Prepare student and agreement schedules 356-361
- J-4 Coordinate off-the-job instruction and student's on-the-job experience 362-378
- J-5 Evaluate job performance of student-learners 379-384
- J-6 Improve related and on-the-job instruction 385-390

CLUSTERS
● Cooperative Secondary Programs
⊘ Cooperative Secondary Programs and In-School Secondary and Post-Secondary Programs
○ In-School Secondary and Post-Secondary Program

Source: The Center for Vocational and Technical Education, The Ohio State University, 1970.

Appendix C   PERFORMANCE REQUIREMENTS FOR TEACHER-COORDINATORS*

I. PROGRAM PLANNING, DEVELOPMENT AND EVALUATION
   (10 Clusters)

Clusters	Performance Elements
1. Vocational Survey (11 elements)	a. Solicit assistance of vocational education personnel from the state department and/or university in conducting a vocational education survey. b. Obtain administrative approval for conducting a vocational education survey. c. Organize a steering committee to assist in pre-planning activities of the vocational education survey. d. Publicize the purposes and objectives of the vocational education survey. e. Involve advisory committee in conducting a vocational education survey. f. Identify the geographical area in which a vocational education survey will be conducted. g. Devise a plan of activities for the survey staff to follow in conducting vocational education survey. h. Establish communication with employer representatives who will be involved in vocational education survey. i. Orient the survey staff to their duties and responsibilities in collecting vocational education data.

*Center for Vocational and Technical Education Model Curricula Study, Report No. III, March 1972, The Ohio State University.

		j. Suggest a vocational education program based on analysis of community survey. k. Disseminate the findings of the vocational education survey.
	2. Survey Preparation (3 elements)	a. Adapt an existing vocational education survey form to local needs. b. Recruit teachers and guidance counselors to participate in conducting a vocational education survey. c. Direct students in the collection of data for a vocational education survey.
	3. Consultation for Survey (3 elements)	a. Consult the local office of the U.S. Employment Service to obtain information on manpower trends and needs. b. Consult Chamber of Commerce to identify area employers to be contacted in vocational education survey. c. Persuade labor representatives to participate in vocational education survey.
	4. Administrative Approval of Advisory Committee (2 elements)	a. Obtain school board authorization for organizing an advisory committee. b. Obtain administrative approval of the selected advisory committee members.
	5. Advisory Committee (9 elements)	a. Identify the role and function of the advisory committee. b. Establish the criteria for selection of advisory committee members. c. Publicize the establishment of the advisory committee, its members, and its function to the school and community. d. Orient advisory committee members to their role and function. e. Plan the annual agenda to be considered by the advisory committee. f. Serve as secretary to the advisory committee. g. Communicate the date, place, and agenda for advisory committee meetings to all persons concerned. h. Invite resource persons who can provide consultation service to attend advisory committee meetings. i. Serve as liaison for the advisory committee and the school administration.
	6. Occupational Selection (4 elements)	a. Determine the occupations for which training is to be offered in the vocational education program. b. Collect student occupational interest data to identify vocational education needs. c. Identify the competencies needed for entry into an occupation. d. Describe the occupational standards of performance for each task in an occupation.

Appendix C

7.	Utilization of Advisory Committee and Labor for Occupational Analysis (2 elements)	a. Consult advisory committee in regard to planning an analysis of an occupation. b. Analyze occupations with assistance of employers and labor representatives.
8.	Follow-up of Graduates (2 elements)	a. Maintain continual follow-up information on placement, employment and training status of each graduate of the vocational program. b. Obtain follow-up data from employers of vocational program graduates.
9.	Planning and Evaluation of Vocational Education Programs (10 elements)	a. Assist in the identification of the vocational education purposes and objectives for the school. b. Determine the reasons students drop out of the vocational program. c. Identify knowledge and attitudes required for the performance of each occupational task included in a course. d. Develop vocational courses by clustering and sequencing related tasks. e. Assist in writing general objectives for courses offered in the vocational education program. f. Write student performance goals for vocational education courses. g. Review supervisory evaluation reports for assessing the vocational program. h. Assess the relevancy of the vocational program. i. Assess the adequacy of the vocational education facilities and equipment relative to technological change. j. Disseminate a summary of the vocational education evaluation to administrators, advisory committee members, and the board of education.
10.	Long-Range Planning (6 elements)	a. Assist in preparing the long-range program plan for vocational education in the school. b. Consult advisory committee in developing a long-range program plan for vocational education. c. Analyze long-range course needs for the vocational education program. d. Identify long-range needs for employing faculty for the vocational program. e. Specify long-range facility, equipment and supply needs for the vocational education program. f. Prepare a long-range budget which identifies the financial needs of the vocational education program.

II. INSTRUCTION—PLANNING
 (7 Clusters)

11.	Objectives and Performance Goals	a. Review general objectives for the program. b. Review student performance goals developed for the program plan.

　　　　　　　　　　c. Sequence performance goals (objectives) for a course.

12. Unit Planning
    (5 elements)
    a. Determine objectives for a unit.
    b. Identify the unit topics for a course.
    c. Write content outline for a unit.
    d. Identify lesson topics for a unit.
    e. Select methods of evaluating students' performance throughout a unit.

13. Student Involvement in Unit Planning
    (1 element)
    a. Involve the students in the planning of a unit.

14. Unit Plans for Individualized Instruction
    (2 elements)
    a. Correlate unit content with on-the-job and/or laboratory experiences.
    b. Determine group and individual learning experiences for the unit based on individual differences of students.

15. Preparation of Instructional Materials
    (3 elements)
    a. Prepare instructional materials with a spirit duplicator.
    b. Prepare instructional materials with a mimeograph machine.
    c. Prepare instructional (hard copy and transparency) materials with a photocopier.

16. Instructional Materials, Equipment and Supplies
    (5 elements)
    a. Develop original instructional materials such as individualized related assignment sheets, transparencies, charts.
    b. Write programmed instruction.
    c. Obtain textbook, reference and other instructional material.
    d. Assemble consumable supplies for instructional purposes.
    e. Select tools and equipment for a lesson.

17. Lesson Planning
    (8 elements)
    a. Identify the specific objectives for a lesson.
    b. Plan the content of a lesson.
    c. Plan the introduction of a lesson.
    d. Plan the summary of a lesson.
    e. Plan student learning experiences for a lesson.
    f. Select teaching techniques for a lesson.
    g. Write a lesson plan.
    h. Select methods of evaluating students' attainment of lesson objectives

III. INSTRUCTION—EXECUTION (13 Clusters)

18. Introduction and Closure of Lesson
    (2 elements)
    a. Introduce a lesson.
    b. Obtain summary for a lesson.

Appendix C

19. Teacher Centered Techniques (5 elements)	a. b. c. d. e.	Give an assignment. Present information with aid of chalkboard. Employ oral questioning techniques. Give a lecture. Give an illustrated talk.
20. Teaching Techniques (7 elements)	a. b. c. d. e. f. g.	Apply non-verbal techniques such as gestures, facial expressions and silence. Establish frames of reference to enable the student to understand a situation from several points of view. Acknowledge student verbal and non-verbal cues. Employ reward techniques. Present information with analogies. Present information through case study problems. Direct students in applying problem-solving techniques.
21. Traditional Educational Technology (2 elements)	a. b.	Present information with silent motion pictures. Present information with radio.
22. Educational Technology (8 elements)	a. b. c. d. e. f. g. h.	Present information with phonograph records. Present information with audio tape recorder. Present information with the overhead projector. Present information with slides. Present information with an opaque projector. Present information with filmstrips. Present information with sound motion pictures. Present information with single concept films.
23. Visual Aids (5 elements)	a. b. c. d. e.	Present information with bulletin boards. Present information with exhibits. Present information with aid of flip chart. Present information with aid of flannel board. Illustrate with models and real objects.
24. Directed Study (2 elements)	a. b.	Direct study of textbooks, bulletins and pamphlets. Direct student study of information and assignment sheets.
25. Individualized Instruction (3 elements)	a. b. c.	Present information by the use of individualized instruction. Enrich instruction to challenge the abilities of the abler student. Provide remedial work for slower students.
26. Laboratory Instruction (6 elements)	a. b.	Demonstrate a manipulative skill. Present a concept or principle through a demonstration.

	c. Direct student laboratory experience. d. Guide student progress through use of operation and/or job sheets. e. Direct student in preparing laboratory work or job plans. f. Present information by the project method.
27. Interaction Techniques (11 elements)	a. Lead group discussions. b. Conduct group supervised study. c. Present information used in a prepared skit. d. Employ question box technique. e. Conduct panel discussions. f. Conduct symposiums. g. Conduct debates. h. Conduct buzz groups. i. Conduct brainstorming sessions. j. Employ role-playing techniques. k. Direct the use of simulation material.
28. Instruction by Students (2 elements)	a. Direct student presentations. b. Direct students in instructing other students.
29. Outside Resources (3 elements)	a. Present information with the assistance of a resource person. b. Conduct field trips. c. Direct students in gathering information from sources in the community.
30. Educational Innovations (6 elements)	a. Direct written programmed instruction. b. Direct teaching machine programmed instruction. c. Present information by computer-assisted instruction. d. Present information with educational television programs e. Present information with videotape recorder or closed circuit television. f. Present information through team teaching.

IV. INSTRUCTION—EVALUATION (8 Clusters)

31. Student Performance Criteria and Evaluation (7 elements)	a. Formulate a system of grading consistent with school policy. b. Establish criteria for student performance. c. Consider cumulative data on students' ability and achievement in establishing performance standards. d. Administer subject matter standardized tests. e. Appraise students' performance in relation to instructional goals. f. Appraise students' products according to performance standards of the occupation. g. Determine grade for performance for on-the-job and related instruction.

Appendix C

32.	Student Involvement in Evaluation (5 elements)	a. Devise self-evaluation techniques for use by students. b. Arrange for students to evaluate their own progress. c. Formulate, cooperatively with students, procedures which provide for their participation in the evaluation of instruction. d. Engage in cooperative evaluation of achievement with students. e. Interpret students' evaluation of instruction.
33.	Evaluation of On-the-Job Experiences (3 elements)	a. Evaluate student learner's personal traits and characteristics on the job. b. Evaluate student learner's work qualities and habits on the job. c. Check student learner's progress in acquiring skills on the job.
34.	Laboratory Tests and Rating Sheets (2 elements)	a. Devise laboratory performance rating sheets. b. Devise laboratory performance rating tests.
35.	Formulation of Test Items (6 elements)	a. Formulate true-false items. b. Formulate multiple-choice test items. c. Formulate matching test items. d. Formulate completion test items. e. Formulate essay test items. f. Formulate test items for an oral examination.
36.	Administration and Analysis of Tests (4 elements)	a. Administer teacher-made tests. b. Analyze tests for validity. c. Analyze tests for reliability. d. Devise case study problems.
37.	Evaluating Instruction (3 elements)	a. Review student progress and/or achievement records to assess effectiveness of instruction. b. Evaluate quality of on-the-job training received by the student-learner. c. Evaluate individualized related assignments completed under directed study.
38.	Teacher Self-Evaluation (2 elements)	a. Seek opportunities for self-evaluation of instruction through self-rating devices and instructional media such as video or audio recording. b. Obtain information from fellow teachers and supervisory personnel regarding the quality of his instruction.
V.	MANAGEMENT (7 Clusters)	
39.	Budgeting and Supplies (7 elements)	a. Plan an operating budget proposal for consumable supplies, services and materials needed in a vocational course.

		b. Design a procedure for acquiring the consumable supplies and materials needed in a vocational course. c. Prepare purchase requests for approved vocational supplies and equipment. d. Arrange for the storage and security of vocational supplies and equipment. e. Prepare a budget for estimated travel expenses incurred in vocational activities. f. Prepare a capital outlay budget proposal for new equipment needed in a vocational course. g. Arrange for additional vocational facilities to accommodate expanded enrollments and technological advancements in a course.
	40. Fees and Gratuities (2 elements)	a. Devise a system for determining and collecting student fees for consumable supplies. b. Accept gifts or donations of supplies and equipment for the vocational program in accordance with school policy.
	41. Reference Books and Supplies (3 elements)	a. Identify new tools and equipment needed in a vocational course for the academic year. b. Compile a list of supplies needed for the academic year. c. Recommend reference books and periodicals related to vocational education that should be added to the library.
	42. Data and Records (8 elements)	a. Structure a filing system for records and report forms used in a vocational course. b. Record vocational student attendance according to school policy. c. Record vocational students' grades according to school policy. d. Assemble student file documenting personal habits, attitudes and grades. e. Maintain a record of individual work hours, wages, and work progression of on-the-job training. f. Devise a system for maintaining occupational information and opportunity data for use by vocational students. g. Devise a filing system for instructional materials. h. Supply administrators with data for vocational reports required by the state department of education.
	43. Laboratory Management (9 elements)	a. Arrange layout of vocational laboratory to simulate occupational environment. b. Arrange laboratory work areas and storage space to facilitate student work performance. c. Maintain an inventory of vocational tools, supplies, and equipment assigned to the laboratory. d. Implement student "check out" procedures for tools, supplies, and equipment used in vocational laboratory.

Appendix C

	e. Schedule laboratory equipment for maximum utilization by students. f. Direct students in a system for cleaning and maintaining the vocational laboratory. g. Establish a system for repairing and servicing tools and equipment in a vocational laboratory. h. Control heat, light, and ventilation in vocational laboratories and classrooms. i. Establish a policy for use of the physical facilities by outside groups and other school personnel.
44. Safety Measures (3 elements)	a. Provide approved safety apparel and devices for vocational students assigned to hazardous equipment. b. Establish a procedure for attending first aid needs of vocational students. c. Maintain a record of safety instruction presented in compliance with safety laws and regulations.
45. Student Behavior (6 elements)	a. Uphold school standards of expected student behavior. b. Uphold acceptable standards of student behavior in vocational classrooms and laboratories. c. Formulate with students acceptable standards of behavior in vocational classrooms and laboratories. d. Encourage students to exercise self-discipline. e. Carry out approved disciplinary action when warranted. f. Control outbursts of fighting and aggressive behavior.

VI. GUIDANCE (7 Clusters)

46. Teacher-Student Rapport (3 elements)	a. Maintain an open-door policy for student consultation. b. Demonstrate a regard for and an interest in the students as individuals. c. Encourage students to discuss career aspirations.
47. Personal Concern for Student (4 elements)	a. Demonstrate personal concern for the student and his family. b. Conduct home visits. c. Communicate with prospective and continuing students during the summer. d. Assist students with their problems by working cooperatively with agencies such as the health and welfare services.
48. Student Records (5 elements)	a. Determine students' background and environment. b. Review students' autobiographies for information to aid in understanding the students. c. Analyze students' cumulative records. d. Determine relationships among students through sociometric techniques (e.g., sociogram).

	e. Maintain anecdotal records on students.
49. Administering Standardized Tests (4 elements)	a. Administer subject matter diagnostic tests. b. Arrange with the guidance counselor for administration and interpretation of personality, aptitude and intelligence tests for specific students. c. Arrange for local office of the U.S. Employment Service to administer and to interpret the General Aptitude Test Battery. d. Interpret occupational tests and inventories to students.
50. Student Counseling (6 elements)	a. Conduct group counseling sessions. b. Recognize potential problems of students. c. Conduct a conference for counseling a student. d. Encourage two-way communication during a conference with a student. e. Assist students in developing good study habits. f. Confer with student and his parents regarding the student's educational development.
51. Occupational Counseling (7 elements)	a. Present information to students on occupational opportunities. b. Assist students in determining ways to best describe their salable skills. c. Assist students in securing and in filling out applications for jobs, scholarships, educational loans or college admission. d. Write letters of recommendation for students. e. Assist graduates or seniors in preparing for interviews with potential employers. f. Present information to students on post-high school training and educational opportunities available to them. g. Develop constructive working relationships among students.
52. Student Referral (5 elements)	a. Establish communication patterns for exchanging information and for cooperating with the guidance counselor. b. Supply guidance counselor with performance data about students. c. Refer students to guidance counselor and other specialists. d. Work with other teachers to help students with individual problems. e. Refer students to qualified personnel agencies for occupational and educational information.

VII. SCHOOL-COMMUNITY RELATIONS (7 Clusters)

53. Planning School-Community Relations (3 elements)	a. Assist in the development of policies regarding school-community relationships. b. Plan the school-community relations activities for the vocational program.

Appendix C

	c. Procure clearance from the school administration to conduct school-community relations activities related to the vocational program.
54. Feedback on Vocational Programs (8 elements)	a. Obtain informal feedback on the vocational program through contacts with individuals in the school and community. b. Consult advisory committee to obtain information concerning their expectations of the vocational program. c. Acquire information from members of the community power structure (e.g., political, social, economic pressure groups) regarding their expectations of the vocational program. d. Obtain information from parents relative to their expectations of the vocational program. e. Analyze enrollment trends to determine student and parent acceptance of the vocational program. f. Study in-school election results (student council, class officers) to determine the image of the vocational students in the school. g. Study community voting results on financial issues affecting the vocational program to determine community support of the program. h. Conduct opinion surveys in the school and community concerning the vocational program.
55. School and Community Service (6 elements)	a. Assist in planning the overall objectives of the total school program. b. Provide consultant services to local business and industry. c. Assist with community business and industry sponsored activities. d. Serve in a community civic, service or social organization to improve the image of the vocational program. e. Serve in professional nonvocational organizations to improve the image of the vocational program. f. Assist with special community social events.
56. Student-School-Community Activities (3 elements)	a. Conduct an open house to familiarize members of the school and community with activities of the vocational program. b. Sponsor student-parent activities for the vocational program. c. Sponsor employer-student banquet for the vocational program.
57. Unions (Labor and Management) (1 element)	a. Maintain liaison with union officials and employers.
58. Staff Relationships (3 elements)	a. Express a philosophy consistent with that of the vocational staff. b. Maintain working relationships with the faculty and administration.

	c. Maintain working relationships with the school supporting staff through cooperation and mutual effort.
59. Program Publicity (7 elements)	a. Provide brochures to inform the school and community of the vocational program. b. Provide displays in the school and in the community on the vocational program. c. Speak to school and community groups on the vocational program. d. Direct student presentations describing activities of the vocational program. e. Prepare news releases on activities of the vocational program for newspapers and other periodicals. f. Present activities of the vocational program on radio. g. Present activities of the vocational program on television.

VIII. STUDENT VOCATIONAL ORGANIZATION (5 Clusters)

60. Establishing Student Vocational Organization (4 elements)	a. Obtain approval from school administration for establishing a student vocational organization. b. Contact state leadership regarding the steps to be followed in organizing a student vocational organization. c. Organize a student committee to assess the interest of students in joining a vocational organization. d. Acquaint prospective members and their parents with the purposes, activities, and values of the student vocational organization.
61. Management of Student Vocational Organization (15 elements)	a. Conduct an organizational meeting for a student vocational organization. b. Orient students to the student vocational organization. c. Assist in the election and installation of officers of the student vocational organization. d. Conduct leadership training session for the officers of the student vocational organization. e. Assist students in developing a yearly program of activities for the student vocational organization. f. Design a procedure for acquiring consumable supplies and materials needed in a vocational organization. g. Assist students with the financial management of the student vocational organization. h. Assist in planning and organizing fund raising activities for the student vocational organization. i. Coordinate student vocational organization activities with instructional activities. j. Supervise social and educational activities for the student vocational organization.

Appendix C

                                                      k. Maintain student vocational organization as integral part of the instructional vocational education program.
                                                     l. Assist students with the publicizing of the student vocational organization activities.
                                                     m. Direct initiation activities of the student vocational organization.
                                                     n. Assist students in advancing within the available degrees in the student vocational organization.
                                                     o. Involve students in the evaluation of the student vocational organization.

62. Cooperation with State and National Organizations (7 elements)
    a. Affiliate the student vocational organization with the state and national vocational organizations.
    b. Send student representatives to district, state, regional and national student vocational organization activities.
    c. Provide advice and training for student entries in state and national student vocational organization contests.
    d. Participate in district, state, regional and national activities of the student vocational organization.
    e. Assist in the development of rules and procedures for conducting state, regional and national student vocational organization contests.
    f. Serve as an advisor or judge for district, state, regional or national student vocational organization contests.
    g. Assist in the preparation of state and national reports for the student vocational organization.

63. Books and Publications (3 elements)
    a. Maintain a file of publications available for the student vocational organization.
    b. Supervise the development of a chapter scrapbook for the student vocational organization.
    c. Supervise the development of an annual handbook for the student vocational organization.

64. Chapter Parents (1 element)
    a. Involve elected chapter parents in the activities of the student vocational organization.

IX. PROFESSIONAL ROLE AND DEVELOPMENT (7 Clusters)

65. Philosophy and Goals (6 elements)
    a. Express a professional philosophy relevant to the basic goals of teaching.
    b. Promote the attainment of the goals and objectives of the teaching profession.
    c. Maintain ethical standards expected of a professional educator.
    d. Identify current trends of the teaching profession.

	e. Exchange observational visits, innovations, and ideas with other teachers. f. Evaluate periodically his educational philosophy in relation to that held by a majority of other members of the teaching profession.
66. General School Duties (2 elements)	a. Participate in noninstructional school duties, i.e., cafeteria, homeroom, bus duty, chaperoning, PTA. b. Assist with nonvocational student organization activities.
67. Professional Service (6 elements)	a. Support professional organizations through membership and attendance at meetings. b. Serve professional organizations as an officer and/or chairman or member of a committee. c. Represent the teaching profession as a committee member or delegate to meetings and activities of other professions. d. Write an article or book for publication which contributes to the literature of the profession. e. Participate in experimental and other data collecting research activities. f. Serve community needs by contributing professional expertise to civic projects.
68. School Problems (2 elements)	a. Work with a team of professionals from school and/or community on pertinent school problems. b. Assist teachers who are new in the system to understand the policies and regulations of the school.
69. Student Teaching (8 elements)	a. Plan activities for the student teacher which draw upon and enrich college course work. b. Interpret the policies and regulations of the local school district to the student teacher. c. Provide opportunities for potential teachers to observe and participate in the public school program. d. Assign responsibilities to the student teacher commensurate with his or her background of knowledge and experience. e. Demonstrate pedagogical skills to student teachers. f. Consult regularly with the student teacher regarding planning, execution, and evaluation of teaching. g. Confer with college supervisor and student teacher regarding performance in the student teaching situation. h. Confer with college supervisor and student teacher regarding plans for and evaluation of the total student teaching experience.

Appendix C 307

70. Self-Evaluation (3 elements)	a.	Select the position which is in keeping with personal and professional abilities and limitations.
	b.	Use a self-analysis form to evaluate personal and professional abilities and limitations.
	c.	Consult supervisory and administrative evaluations to determine attitudes of others toward personal and professional abilities and limitations.
71. Updating Competencies (4 elements)	a.	Acquire new occupational skills needed to keep pace with technological advancement in teaching.
	b.	Maintain professional certification through enrolling in graduate, extension and inservice education programs.
	c.	Expand educational background and leadership potential by achieving advanced degrees.
	d.	Upgrade professional personnel file regularly.

X. COORDINATION (11 Clusters)

72. Resource Material (1 element)	a.	Provide prospective student-learners with resource materials on occupational opportunities to aid them in selecting a vocation.
73. Student-Learner Selection (7 elements)	a.	Establish criteria for selection of student-learner.
	b.	Gather student-learner selection data (e.g., test results, records, grades).
	c.	Administer occupational tests relative to student learner selection and placement.
	d.	Interview students and parents to obtain student-learner interest and aptitude information.
	e.	Identify a prospective student-learner on basis of selection criteria and data.
	f.	Match a student-learner's unique characteristics with an appropriate training station.
	g.	Approve on-the-job training hours and wages for student-learner.
74. Training Station (3 elements)	a.	Establish criteria for evaluating training station potential of an employer.
	b.	Identify prospective cooperating employers to provide on-the-job training stations.
	c.	Assess educational adequacy of a prospective training station's facilities and equipment.
75. Union (1 element)	a.	Arrange with a union to make contract provision for student-learner.
76. Employment Regulations (Federal and State) (5 elements)	a.	Determine federal and state wage and hour classification of a prospective cooperating employer.

	b. Assist cooperating employer in acquiring federal permit to pay a training wage. c. Establish a cooperating employer's qualifications for reimbursement for training a student-learner. d. Obtain reimbursement for cooperating employer providing on-the-job training. e. Obtain reimbursement for student-learners for allowable training costs such as clothing and tools.
77. Safety (3 elements)	a. Develop a procedure to insure students' safety and protection in the training station. b. Assess safety provisions of facilities and equipment of the prospective training station. c. Assist cooperating employer in verifying the legality of employing a student-learner in a hazardous occupation.
78. Persuasion (1 element)	a. Convince an employer to provide a training station for cooperative education.
79. Training Agreement (4 elements)	a. Develop a cooperative training agreement between student-learner, parents, school and cooperating employer. b. Arrange school and work schedules with student-learners, faculty, and training station personnel. c. Develop a plan for teacher-coordinator supervision of on-the-job training. d. Develop systematic training plan with the on-the-job instructor.
80. Coordination of On-the-Job Training (13 elements)	a. Prepare student-learner for interview with cooperating employer and training station personnel. b. Aid student-learner in procuring work permit. c. Assist student-learner in on-the-job training orientation. d. Encourage on-the-job instructor to follow the progression of experiences for the student-learner outlined in the training plan. e. Assess occupational experience daily reports with student-learners to plan future instruction. f. Check student-learner progress with the on-the-job instructor and other training station personnel. g. Maintain student-learner progress record forms for on-the-job training and related instruction. h. Examine student-learner progress records to determine future on-the-job training experiences and related classroom assignments. i. Assess student-learner's performance with assistance of the on-the-job instructor. j. Obtain suggestions from on-the-job instructor to guide the selection of related class instruction lessons.

Appendix C

                                          k. Assist students in the solution of problems related to on-the-job training.
                                          l. Assist the cooperating employer's personnel in accepting the training status and role of the student-learners.
                                          m. Inform administration of daily coordination itinerary.

81. Student Control On the Job (3 elements)
    a. Control student-learner absenteeism from related class and on-the-job training.
    b. Control the transfer of student-learners within the cooperative program and to other school programs.
    c. Conduct termination procedures for on-the-job training for a student-learner when conditions demand it and at the close of a training program.

82. Related On-the-Job Instruction (6 elements)
    a. Establish criteria to evaluate qualifications of prospective on-the-job instructors.
    b. Assess training capability of the on-the-job instructors.
    c. Assist on-the-job instructor with development of teaching techniques during visits to the training stations.
    d. Obtain from advisory committee information on ways to improve related instruction and on-the-job training.
    e. Expand related instruction for student-learners on the basis of information obtained from employers on new technology.
    f. Provide teacher-training workshop to assist on-the-job instructor in techniques for teaching student-learners.

Appendix D

Form Approved:
Budget Bureau No. 44-R0308

U.S. DEPARTMENT OF LABOR
WAGE AND HOUR AND PUBLIC CONTRACTS DIVISIONS

LEAVE THIS SPACE BLANK

APPLICATION FOR A CERTIFICATE TO EMPLOY A STUDENT-LEARNER

The certification of the appropriate school official on the reverse side of this application shall constitute a temporary authorization for the employment of the named student-learner at less than the statutory minimum wage applicable under section 6 of the Fair Labor Standards Act or at wages below the applicable Walsh-Healey Public Contracts Act or McNamara-O'Hara Service Contract Act wage determination, effective from the date this application is forwarded to the Divisions until a student-learner certificate is issued or denied by the Administrator or his authorized representative, provided the conditions specified in section 520.6(c)(2) of the Student-Learner Regulation (29 CFR 520) are satisfied.

PRINT OR TYPE ALL ANSWERS. PLEASE READ CAREFULLY THE INSTRUCTIONS FOR COMPLETING THIS FORM

1. NAME AND ADDRESS, INCLUDING ZIP CODE, OF ESTABLISHMENT MAKING APPLICATION:

3A. NAME AND ADDRESS OF STUDENT-LEARNER:

B: DATE OF BIRTH:
(Month, day, year)

2. TYPE OF BUSINESS AND PRODUCTS MANUFACTURED, SOLD, OR SERVICES RENDERED:

4. NAME AND ADDRESS, INCLUDING ZIP CODE, OF SCHOOL IN WHICH STUDENT-LEARNER IS ENROLLED:

5. PROPOSED BEGINNING DATE OF EMPLOYMENT (Month, day, year)
6. PROPOSED ENDING DATE OF EMPLOYMENT (Month, day, year)
7. PROPOSED GRADUATION DATE (Month, day, year)
8. NUMBER OF WEEKS IN SCHOOL YEAR
9. TOTAL HOURS OF SCHOOL INSTRUCTION PER WEEK
10. NUMBER OF SCHOOL HOURS DIRECTLY RELATED TO EMPLOYMENT TRAINING
11. HOW IS EMPLOYMENT TRAINING SCHEDULED (Weekly, alternate weeks, etc.)?
12. NUMBER OF WEEKS OF EMPLOYMENT TRAINING AT SPECIAL MINIMUM WAGES
13. NUMBER OF HOURS OF EMPLOYMENT TRAINING A WEEK
14. ARE FEDERAL VOCATIONAL EDUCATION FUNDS BEING USED FOR THIS PROGRAM?
15. WAS THIS PROGRAM AUTHORIZED BY THE STATE BOARD OF VOCATIONAL EDUCATION?
16. IF THE ANSWER TO ITEM 15 IS "NO", GIVE THE NAME OF THE RECOGNIZED EDUCATIONAL BODY WHICH APPROVED THIS PROGRAM:

17. TITLE OF STUDENT-LEARNER OCCUPATION:
18. NUMBER OF EMPLOYEES IN THIS ESTABLISHMENT
19. NUMBER OF EXPERIENCED EMPLOYEES IN STUDENT-LEARNER'S OCCUPATION
20. MINIMUM HOURLY WAGE RATE OF EXPERIENCED WORKERS IN ITEM 19
21. SPECIAL MINIMUM WAGE(s) TO BE PAID STUDENT-LEARNER (if a progressive wage schedule is proposed, enter each rate and specify the period during which it will be paid):
22. IS AN AGE OR EMPLOYMENT CERTIFICATE ON FILE IN THIS ESTABLISHMENT FOR THIS STUDENT-LEARNER? (If not, see instructions)
23. IS IT ANTICIPATED THAT THE STUDENT-LEARNER WILL BE EMPLOYED IN THE PERFORMANCE OF A GOVERNMENT CONTRACT SUBJECT TO THE WALSH-HEALEY PUBLIC CONTRACTS ACT OR THE MC NAMARA-O'HARA SERVICE CONTRACT ACT?

ATTACH SEPARATE PAGES IF NECESSARY   Form WH-205 (Rev. 4/68)

24. OUTLINE THE SCHOOL INSTRUCTION *directly* RELATED TO THE EMPLOYMENT TRAINING *(list courses, etc.).*

25. OUTLINE TRAINING ON-THE-JOB *(describe briefly the work process in which the student-learner will be trained and list the types of any machines used).*

26. SIGNATURE OF STUDENT-LEARNER:

I have read the statements made above and ask that the requested certificate, authorizing my employment training at special minimum wages and under the conditions stated, be granted by the Administrator or his authorized representative.

| (Print or type name of student) | Signature of Student | Date |

27. CERTIFICATION BY SCHOOL OFFICIAL:	28. CERTIFICATION BY EMPLOYER OR AUTHORIZED REPRESENTATIVE:
I certify that the student named herein will be receiving instruction in an accredited school and will be employed pursuant to a bona fide vocational training program, as defined in section 520.2 of Student-Learner Regulations.	I certify, in applying for this certificate, that all of the foregoing statements are, to the best of my knowledge and belief, true and correct
(Print or type name of official)	(Print or type name of employer or representative)
Signature of School Official Date	Signature of employer or representative Date
Title	Title

ATTACH SEPARATE SHEETS IF NECESSARY

INDEX

Acceptance, 119, 120
Accountability, 45, 50, 51, 267, 279
Achievement, 23, 39, 86, 105, 110, 111, 114, 118, 130, 141, 157, 193, 253, 256-60, 279, 282, 286
Adaptability, 12
Adjustment, 19, 20, 29, 33, 38, 41, 42, 43, 67, 81, 98-122, 126, 150, 161-2, 169, 178, 179, 207, 214, 216-8, 222, 226, 235-7, 259
Advancement, 86, 93, 106, 111, 118, 126, 164, 197, 226
Advantages, 2, 17-24, 163
Alternatives, 19, 93
Aspirations, 83, 129, 134, 160, 161
Assessment, 108-15, 179, 283, 285
Attitudes, 2, 14, 15, 16, 28, 42, 47, 61, 80, 87, 98, 101, 103, 114, 115, 120, 132, 134, 139, 151, 160, 161, 162, 164-5, 168, 195, 197, 248
Availability, 6, 15, 44, 64, 92, 131, 163, 165
Awareness, 82, 86, 91, 101, 102, 108, 115, 153, 273

Background, 16, 168
Behavior, 32, 42, 70, 82, 87, 91, 115, 141, 152, 170, 214, 221, 226, 235, 249, 273
Benefits, 132, 257-8, 272
  cost, 279-80
Center for Vocational and Technical Education, 68, 69, 89
Change, 11-2, 13, 82, 84, 98, 120, 267, 273, 286
Challenges, 29, 37-9
Choice, 61, 77, 81, 84, 95, 126, 133, 170, 215
Clarification, 93, 104, 256
Classification, 76, 276
Communication, 42, 43, 157, 227, 258
Community, 21-3, 35-6, 40, 53, 103, 184, 211-2, 221, 222, 223, 251, 271
Compensation, 106, 111, 114, 118
Conflict, 119, 237
Content, 20, 52, 59, 60, 73, 75-6, 77, 207-8, 221-2, 236, 237-8, 280, 285

313

Index

Control, 16, 21-2, 71
Counseling, 39, 41-3, 70, 84, 94-5, 112, 186, 227, 228, 258
Criticism, 93, 260
Curriculum, 18, 37-41, 48, 52, 75, 85, 87, 92, 101, 130, 184, 197, 218-20

Decision making, 17, 61, 65, 89, 95, 131, 157, 183, 220, 278-9
Demands, 119, 280
Discipline, 140
Discussion, 19, 74, 89, 94, 222, 253, 258
Diversity, 15, 162-3
Dropout, 4, 10, 16, 213, 273-4

Efficiency, 106, 164, 286
Employability, 3, 4, 102, 146, 153-4, 226
Entry, 81, 87, 114, 126, 130, 132, 163
Environment, 18, 19, 20, 47, 66, 72, 73, 74, 76, 80, 82, 87, 91, 105, 111, 115, 120, 153, 160-2, 184, 235
Equipment, 29, 94, 156, 165, 183, 223-30, 235, 279, 285
Evaluation, 39, 51, 52, 61, 65, 67, 69, 70, 72, 85, 89, 93, 104, 112, 115, 168, 186, 193, 197, 198, 234-5, 256-60, 267-88
Expectations, 2, 11-6, 66, 106, 108 119, 121, 132, 269
Experience, 15, 19, 21, 23, 27, 54, 64, 74, 125, 132, 168
Expertise, 67, 225, 236, 285
Exploration, 85, 86, 92, 93-5, 126, 129, 130

Facilities, 20, 29, 64, 125, 165, 223-30, 235, 267
Feedback, 20, 27, 37, 38, 41, 71, 74, 89, 93, 115, 120, 121, 209, 282, 283
Flexibility, 12, 39, 85, 220, 227, 228
Funding, 7-8, 10, 11, 279

General Aptitude Test Battery, 35, 110, 141
Growth, 81, 85, 100, 106

Guidance, 20, 23-4, 61, 73, 81, 82, 85, 92, 100, 104, 108, 115, 121, 124-47, 165, 206, 227, 228, 282

Habits, 15, 87, 151, 162, 165, 184, 264, 282
Handicaps, 16, 134

Implementation, 39, 63
Improvement, 31, 93, 233-5, 251
Incentive, 98, 108
Income, 84, 132
Initiative, 66, 134, 147, 192, 250
Inputs, 36, 38, 63, 74, 208, 221, 230, 234, 258, 280
Intent, 61, 127
Interaction, 70, 89, 99, 209, 221, 222, 283
Interview, 64, 92, 130, 137-40, 145, 169, 173-7, 197, 222

Judgments, 140, 153, 168, 183

Life style, 73, 93, 100, 101, 104, 131-2, 134, 237, 260
Limitations, 24, 36, 43, 125

Materials, 64, 94, 183, 197, 242, 280, 285
Maturity, 14, 15, 38, 39, 45, 49, 91, 103, 272
Media, 36, 48, 49, 223
Methods, 52, 72, 73, 207, 221-3, 278
Minnesota Importance Questionnaire, 111-2, 179, 248
Minnesota Satisfactoriness Scales, 115, 116-7, 282
Mobility, 39, 99
Models, 94, 95, 129, 165
Motivation, 52, 82, 87, 114, 129, 169, 220, 222, 228, 230, 256, 258

Occupational Reinforcer Patterns, 112, 179
Opinion, 53, 141, 145, 248, 253, 259, 260, 261, 274, 276
Opportunity, 17, 52, 84, 91, 92, 93, 94, 95, 111, 125, 126, 130, 131, 151, 153, 163, 164, 173, 192, 237, 256

Index

Orientation, 81, 86, 101, 134
Outcomes, 77, 80, 89-91, 105, 161, 183, 193-7, 208, 226, 259, 260, 267, 268, 272, 273, 276, 279, 286

Participation, 104, 167, 220, 237, 251, 276
Performance, 28, 64, 65, 78, 83, 94, 99, 101-2, 103, 105, 106, 108, 111, 115, 120, 121, 146, 171, 233, 237, 256, 259-64, 269, 270, 271, 282-3, 285
Personality, 73, 74, 83, 141, 168, 169, 218, 221
Perspective, 75, 82, 95, 129, 234, 267
Placement, 6, 40, 43-5, 61, 93, 99, 100, 108, 110, 115, 121, 134, 150-79, 235, 279
Planning, 10-11, 14, 69, 74, 85, 89, 93, 94, 95, 102, 121, 127, 131, 159-63, 206, 208-13, 218-20, 225, 229, 234, 239-45, 269, 270-1, 283
Potential, 36, 160, 216
Preparation, 39, 84, 89, 101, 102, 104, 126, 154-5, 187, 260
Problem solving, 19, 30, 183, 282-3
Productivity, 45, 77, 86, 100, 106, 177, 209, 289
Progress, 64, 81, 84, 85, 93, 95, 115, 234, 248, 256, 272, 282
Promotion, 72, 98, 164, 271, 275
Publicity, 35, 36, 48, 49, 63-4, 65, 71, 127, 129, 226

Qualifications, 52, 156

Recognition, 51, 93, 106, 108, 111, 114, 118, 120, 121, 130, 165

Reimbursement, 11, 63, 67
Reinforcement, 94, 106, 108, 111, 112, 121, 178
Reputation, 152, 164
Research, 51-3, 59, 175, 257
Resources, 15, 19, 70, 74-5, 124, 154, 212, 225
Rewards, 98, 100, 106, 108, 111, 114
Role playing, 29, 197, 222, 226

Salary, 132, 253, 270, 271, 273, 279
Security, 86, 111, 118
Selection, 59, 64, 69, 71, 73, 77, 125, 144, 150, 163-8, 170, 187, 207
Self-assessment, 126
Self-concept, 86, 87, 91, 102, 153, 273
Self-confidence, 177
Self-direction, 31, 95, 134
Self-fulfillment, 80, 81, 83, 86, 87, 95
Self-image, 125, 153
Stability, 6, 22, 134, 164, 168
Standards, 1, 152, 163, 164, 168
Success, 93, 114, 130, 133, 141
Supervision, 110, 151
Survey, 12, 131, 155-9

Tenure, 19, 45, 151, 235
Termination, 98, 119

Understanding, 19, 24, 43, 75, 160, 161, 197
Unemployment, 4, 10, 13

Values, 18, 19, 58, 85, 89, 91, 94, 100, 101, 104, 105, 111, 115, 118, 120, 132, 133, 134, 272, 273
Variables, 108, 131

Work ethic, 91, 101, 102, 105, 153-4, 178

DISCHARGED

DISCHARGED

SEP 2 6 1977

OCT 21 1977

JUN 26 1978

JUL 7 1978
JUL 15 1978
JUL 28 1978

AUG 4 1978

JUN 16 1979